Global Imbalances, Exchange Rates and Stabilization Policy

Also by Anthony J. Makin

GLOBAL FINANCE AND THE MACROECONOMY

INTERNATIONAL CAPITAL MOBILITY AND EXTERNAL ACCOUNT DETERMINATION

INTERNATIONAL MACROECONOMICS

OPEN ECONOMY MACROECONOMICS

Global Imbalances, Exchange Rates and Stabilization Policy

Anthony J. Makin

palgrave
macmillan

First published 2009 by
PALGRAVE MACMILLAN

Palgrave Macmillan in the UK is an imprint of Macmillan Publishers Limited, registered in England, company number 785998, of Houndmills, Basingstoke, Hampshire RG21 6XS.

Palgrave Macmillan in the US is a division of St Martin's Press LLC, 175 Fifth Avenue, New York, NY 10010.

Palgrave Macmillan is the global academic imprint of the above companies and has companies and representatives throughout the world.

Palgrave® and Macmillan® are registered trademarks in the United States, the United Kingdom, Europe and other countries.

ISBN-13: 978-0-230-57685-8 hardback
ISBN-10: 0-230-57685-0 hardback

This book is printed on paper suitable for recycling and made from fully managed and sustained forest sources. Logging, pulping and manufacturing processes are expected to conform to the environmental regulations of the country of origin.

A catalogue record for this book is available from the British Library.

A catalogue record for this book is available from the Library of Congress.

10 9 8 7 6 5 4 3 2 1
18 17 16 15 14 13 12 11 10 09

Printed and bound in Great Britain by
CPI Antony Rowe, Chippenham and Eastbourne

Contents

Charts, Figures and Tables

Charts

Figures

Tables

Preface and Acknowledgements

As economies become more integrated with the rest of the world, the need to better understand international real, monetary and financial linkages becomes ever more important. In particular, more needs to be known about the key determinants of trade and current account imbalances, exchange rates, international capital flows and interest rate differentials, as well as the implications of financial globalization for economic growth and for the operation and effectiveness of domestic fiscal and monetary policies.

The main aim of this book is to advance new conceptual frameworks for interpreting international macroeconomic and financial linkages for globally integrated economies. To achieve this, the work proposes a suite of compatible theoretical approaches, mainly diagrammatic, that provide alternative ways of analysing key issues in the field. As such, it is primarily theory oriented, though on occasion includes illustrative macroeconomic data.

The book addresses perennially important international macroeconomic questions that include the following: What are the macroeconomic causes and consequences of global imbalances? How do exchange rates influence trade and current account imbalances? How does international borrowing and lending behaviour affect domestic and world interest rates? How do international capital flows affect national income? How are monetary and fiscal policy changes transmitted in modern open economies? Are traditional propositions about the effectiveness of monetary and fiscal policies under alternative exchange rate regimes still relevant? What exchange rate regime best suits an economy in light of its macroeconomic characteristics? What is the optimal way to stabilize and/or reduce unsustainable public debt levels? What constitutes best practice for monetary policy? What are the benefits and risks of transnational capital flows? What are the costs of capital controls? Is freer international trade in saving a global economic policy problem or not?

In addressing these questions, this book extends the analysis of my previous Palgrave volume *Global Finance and the Macroeconomy* and can be viewed as a natural and complementary sequel to that work that further develops the implications of financial globalization and international capital movements for macroeconomic policy. It draws on material published in *Agenda, Asean Economic Bulletin, Australian Economic Papers, Business Economics, China and World Economy, Contemporary Economic Policy, Economic Modelling, Economic Issues, Economic Record* and *Global Economy Journal.*

The author thanks anonymous reviewers for constructive comments, Michael Howard and Sharalyn Rozanski for excellent research assistance, as well as Taiba Batool, Gemma Papageorgiou, staff of Macmillan Publishing Solutions, India and the editorial and production team at Palgrave Macmillan for so adeptly bringing this work to fruition.

1
Introduction

Macroeconomic policy debates inevitably revolve around discussion of fluctuations in aggregate measures, such as national income, interest rates, inflation, unemployment, trade imbalances, exchange rates, and various wealth series, such as house price and stock-market indices. Sharp swings in these aggregates most keenly interest economists engaged in analysing their implications for the real sector, the financial sector and macroeconomic policy.

Yet most contemporary theoretical research, particularly in the field of international macroeconomics and finance, appears removed from this reality. Invariably based on microeconomic foundations that assume optimizing representative agents, it underemphasizes standard national accounting aggregates that form the basis of macroeconomic policy analysis.

A major theme of this book is that the dominant prevailing paradigm, known as the representative agent, general equilibrium approach, overemphasizes the importance of micro precepts as a necessary prerequisite for macro model building. As a result, the international macroeconomics and finance field has become overly complex and its lessons for policymakers obscure.

Problems with the prevailing paradigm

The prevailing paradigm (sometimes referred to as the 'new open economy macroeconomics') contrasts sharply with the use of aggregative methods and tools that have been long used to great effect in mainstream macroeconomics and international economics textbooks where microeconomic foundations are simply not deemed necessary to convey key linkages between the important variables in the field.

A sharp divide has therefore emerged between the prevailing research template of international macroeconomics and finance, as characterized in Obstfeld and Rogoff's (1996) monumental text, and the aggregative and behavioural methods used in standard undergraduate pedagogy of the field.

Basing international macroeconomic theory exclusively on microfoundations to the neglect of aggregative and behavioural approaches is unsatisfactory for several reasons. First, proponents of the ruling paradigm assert its superiority over other approaches on the grounds that traditional methods are too *ad hoc* without microfoundations.

Yet, as has been persuasively argued by Gandolfo (2001) and Van Hoose (2004), standard macroeconomic tools, such as the consumption function, are just as empirically verifiable, more realistic, and in principle involve no more *ad hocery*, than the selection of a particular utility function form. Moreover, conventional aggregative methods used in macroeconomics-related areas remain strongly defensible on pedagogical grounds (Romer 2000).

Colander (2007) has also criticized the utility of microfounded macroeconomics as taught at graduate level on the basis that it fails to explain how economies actually function and neglects to equip graduates with the necessary skills for future employment as applied economists.

Due to excessive reliance on microeconomic underpinnings, fiscal and monetary policy prescriptions arising from representative agent, stochastic general equilibrium models are highly sensitive to underlying assumptions, such as utility function choice, which makes them ambiguous and hence impractical for policy purposes.

Second, as a related point, models founded on microeconomic precepts and optimizing representative agents have become overly complex compared to earlier generation models, such as the Mundell-Fleming (MF) model, with its clear policy prescriptions. Models in the spirit of the MF approach continue to be the mainstay of textbook international macroeconomics and remain the most widely used means of analysing the impact of fiscal and monetary policy on exchange rates, the balance of payments and national income.

For instance, the MF model predicts that, if capital mobility is perfect, fiscal consolidation should either have no impact under floating rates or have a contractionary effect on national income under fixed exchange rates.

Yet unfortunately, the MF paradigm yields numerous results at odds with a growing body of empirical evidence. This is because aggregate models of the short run invariably start from the assumption of aggregate demand side dominance. In contrast, consistent with the precepts of standard long-run analysis, many models in this book start from the alternative assumption of aggregate supply side dominance.

In this way the book presents an alternative approach both to the representative agent-stochastic general equilibrium models of the ruling open economy macroeconomics paradigm with its overly elaborate microeconomic foundations, as well as to the older aggregative approaches. It also relies heavily on much-neglected economy-wide precepts, especially the distinction between aggregate output and expenditure in the absorption sense and the principles of traditional flow-of-funds analysis, to derive a range of new analytical frameworks and results.

Apart from emphasizing aggregates over microeconomic foundations, a subtle assumption underlying numerous models of this book concerns the relationship between aggregate supply and demand. Often, domestic goods and services are treated as originating on the production side via a macroeconomic production function. Within the period, these goods are then made available for sale along with imported foreign goods and services which, in use, are treated as either consumption or investment expenditure.

Hence, the sequencing of macroeconomic activity can be perceived as running from aggregate supply to aggregate demand in the first instance, rather than the other way around, although production by firms is obviously undertaken with prospects of aggregate demand in mind. This has important implications for macroeconomic policy, especially for the effectiveness of fiscal policy.

In sum, by addressing deficiencies in extant models, the aggregate supply-side-oriented frameworks developed in the book provide new perspectives on the determination of global imbalances, the role of capital flows in the growth process, as well as new results about the effectiveness of macroeconomic policy under both fixed and floating exchange rate regimes.

These new results are contrasted throughout with those of extant approaches. Hence, by departing on methodological grounds from the prevailing research paradigm, the book's innovative frameworks respond to Krugman's (1995) call for practicable guides to address unresolved questions in international macroeconomics and finance.

Chapter preview

This chapter has introduced the key methodological points of difference between the approaches outlined in this book and those of the prevailing research paradigm. Chapter 2 discusses key developments in the world economy since 1980, emphasizing international macroeconomic developments from the Asian financial crisis of 1997–8 to the global financial crisis of 2007–9 with a focus on the growth and significance of 'global imbalances'. The term global imbalances has become synonymous with the simultaneous widening of the current account deficit (CAD) of the United States and counterpart rise in the current account surpluses (CASs) of East Asian (most notably China's) and the oil-exporting economies.

Chapter 3 develops straightforward two-region frameworks for interpreting the effect of exchange rate policy on an economy's trade balance and that of its trading partners in the context of limited capital mobility and discrepant economic growth rates. Recognizing that external imbalances reflect divergent national production and expenditure growth, it reveals that exchange rates remain central to any explanation of global imbalances.

Using the case of China and its trading partners, it reveals how exchange rate misalignment can artificially assist China's output growth and limit its household consumption, thereby slowing the rise in China's living standards. Meanwhile, due to currency misalignment, China's Western trading partners, most notably the United States and the European Union, simultaneously experience larger external deficits, lower output, lower saving and higher investment than otherwise.

Chapter 4 presents an alternative short- to medium-term framework for analysing the simultaneous determination of current account imbalances and the path of national income. Using standard macroeconomic behavioral relationships, it first examines how and why CADs matter by investigating links between domestic consumption, government spending, output, saving, investment, interest rates and capital flows. This rendered Keynesian cross-framework yields results relevant to the 'twin deficits' hypothesis that are contrary to those of standard models. In particular, it shows that increased public expenditure lowers not raises potential national income over the medium term.

Next it proposes methods for assessing the proximity of CADs and the associated foreign debt to their upper bounds based on the principle that productive investment fundamentally sets the feasible limit for CADs, whereas the capital-to-output ratio ultimately sets the foreign debt to GDP limit.

Chapter 5 centres on the contribution of foreign saving to national income, both in the long and short runs. Using extended loanable funds analysis, it demonstrates how perfect capital mobility contributes to economic development, contrary to a prevalent view that international borrowing is inimical to the welfare of developing economies. As a corollary, the analysis shows that capital controls, irrespective of form, generally reduce development potential and economic welfare by widening real cross-border interest differentials. Using growth accounting precepts and treating Australia as a case study, the chapter also demonstrates how foreign borrowing can contribute significantly to raising an economy's national income.

Chapter 6 introduces new frameworks for analysing the relationship between exchange rates, domestic saving, investment, international borrowing and lending, and domestic and foreign interest rates. It establishes how a range of domestic and international shocks simultaneously determine these key international macroeconomic variables over any given time and derives some general propositions. It then suggests that foreign factors, most notably the rise in net saving in East Asia, have mainly been responsible for the rise in the large CADs of the United States and other borrower economies, such as Australia and New Zealand.

Chapter 7 proposes an alternative monetary model for examining the effects of domestic monetary shocks on the exchange rate and the balance of payments that is consistent with the macroeconomic framework introduced in Chapter 3. Contrary to previous monetary approaches, the approach suggests a new chain of causality that runs from domestic money to the exchange rate to the price level, rather than from money to the price level to the exchange rate. It also shows that under fixed rates, external adjustment is consistent with money market equilibrium and price level stability, and that under floating exchange rates monetary policy in open economies works in the short to medium runs via its impact on exchange rates and aggregate expenditure.

Chapter 8 presents an alternative international macroeconomic model for evaluating the effectiveness of fiscal and monetary policy in stabilizing national income under fixed and floating exchange rates. It encompasses national output and income, money and capital flows and linkages between the exchange rate, price levels and real interest rates consistent with international parity conditions.

This output-oriented approach, compatible with the modelling of Chapter 4, demonstrates that the nature of government spending is pivotal to the effectiveness of fiscal policy. It reveals that, *ceteris paribus*, higher public consumption expenditure contracts national income and depreciates the exchange rate, whereas higher productive public investment spending has opposite effects. The framework also shows that the effectiveness of fiscal and monetary policy as macroeconomic policy instruments is not ultimately dependent on the exchange rate regime in the long run due to passthrough effects.

Chapter 9 presents an alternative international macroeconomic framework for analysing the impact of domestic and foreign monetary and real shocks on nominal and real exchange rates, the current account balance and price levels in financially globalized economies. Combining standard macroeconomic relations with precepts from international finance, this distinct approach provides further insights on a range of international monetary issues.

These include an alternative perspective on the monetary transmission mechanism under floating exchange rates, whether restrictive monetary policy can narrow trade deficits, the importance of ensuring low inflation expectations, the domestic repercussions of changes in monetary conditions abroad and the impact of productivity and investment surges on competitiveness, external imbalances and national income.

It also reconsiders the issue of exchange rate choice revealing that in the short run pegged exchange rates facilitate real income growth for emerging economies, while lowering its variability when exports and productivity are improving and monetary shocks predominate. Meanwhile, floating exchange rates may best suit less open advanced economies with relatively stable monetary sectors that frequently experience negative real shocks.

Chapter 10 canvasses two issues of importance to stabilization policy. The first, of particular relevance to the conduct of monetary policy, examines how unexpected inflation or disinflation arbitrarily redistributes income between domestic savers and borrowers in the economy. Using a loanable funds framework, it reveals that, in theory, borrowers benefit at the expense of savers whenever inflation rises unexpectedly and how the opposite occurs during disinflation episodes.

The chapter also analyses the sustainability of public debt and its international macroeconomic significance by deriving key formulae and presenting new graphical techniques that indicate how central government fiscal authorities can reduce public debt levels over time by targeting primary budget imbalances. It also canvasses issues related to fiscal consolidation emphasizing the importance of the distinction between government consumption and investment.

An Epilogue concludes the book by critically evaluating the economic significance of 'global imbalances'. It canvasses the benefits of increased international trade in saving and addresses fallacies about external imbalances It then examines key factors that raise the risk of financial crises, including the role of public debt. The book concludes by highlighting lessons of the book for economic policymakers. Most notably, it suggests extra public spending intended to provide fiscal 'stimulus' is only effective in raising national income if in the form of productive public investment.

References

Colander, D. (2007) *The Making of an Economist, Redux*, Princeton University Press, Princeton, NJ.

Fleming, J. 'Domestic Financial Policies under Fixed and under Floating Exchange Rates', *IMF Staff Papers*, 12, 1962, 369–80.

Gandolfo, G. (2001) *International Finance and Open Economy Macroeconomics*, Springer-Verlag, Berlin.

Krugman, P. (1995) 'What Do We Need to Know about the International Monetary System?' in P. Kenen (ed.) *Understanding Interdependence: The Macroeconomics of the Open Economy*, Princeton University Press, Princeton.

Mundell, R. (1963), 'Capital Mobility and Stabilization Policy under Fixed and Flexible Exchange Rates', *Canadian Journal of Economics and Political Science*, 29, 475–85.

Obstfeld, M. and Rogoff, K. (1996) *Foundations of International Macroeconomics*, MIT Press, Cambridge.

Romer, D. (2000) 'Keynesian Macroeconomics without the LM Curve', *Journal of Economic Perspectives*, 14 (2), 149–69.

Van Hoose, D. (2004) 'The New Open Economy Macroeconomics: A Critical Appraisal', *Open Economies Review*, 15, 193–215.

2
The Global Economy and External Imbalances

Introduction

Since the breakdown of the Bretton Woods monetary system that prevailed from 1945 to the early 1970s, there has been greater exchange rate variability combined with phenomenal growth in the volume of international capital flows. This expansion of capital flows followed dismantling of the edifice of exchange controls that supposedly facilitated exchange rate management under the Bretton Woods system.

Over the past three decades, there has been major transformation of the world economy, mainly as a result of accelerated economic growth in Asia. This higher growth has changed national income relativities and the respective contributions of economic regions to global economic output, as shown in Chart 2.1. Most notably, the relative contributions of China and India to global production have risen, while the relative contributions of major advanced economy regions, the US, EU and Japan, have fallen.

The restructuring of the world economy over recent decades was primarily due to the mobilization of labour to produce cheap manufactures and policy initiatives that encouraged increased output in emerging Asian economies. This major supply-side boost had implications for price levels and inflation worldwide. Inflation fell through the 1980s from the historically high inflation rates of the 1970s. Indeed the worldwide fall in inflation to the relatively low levels experienced by the 1990s and early 2000s was one of the most remarkable global economic phenomena of the past half-century.

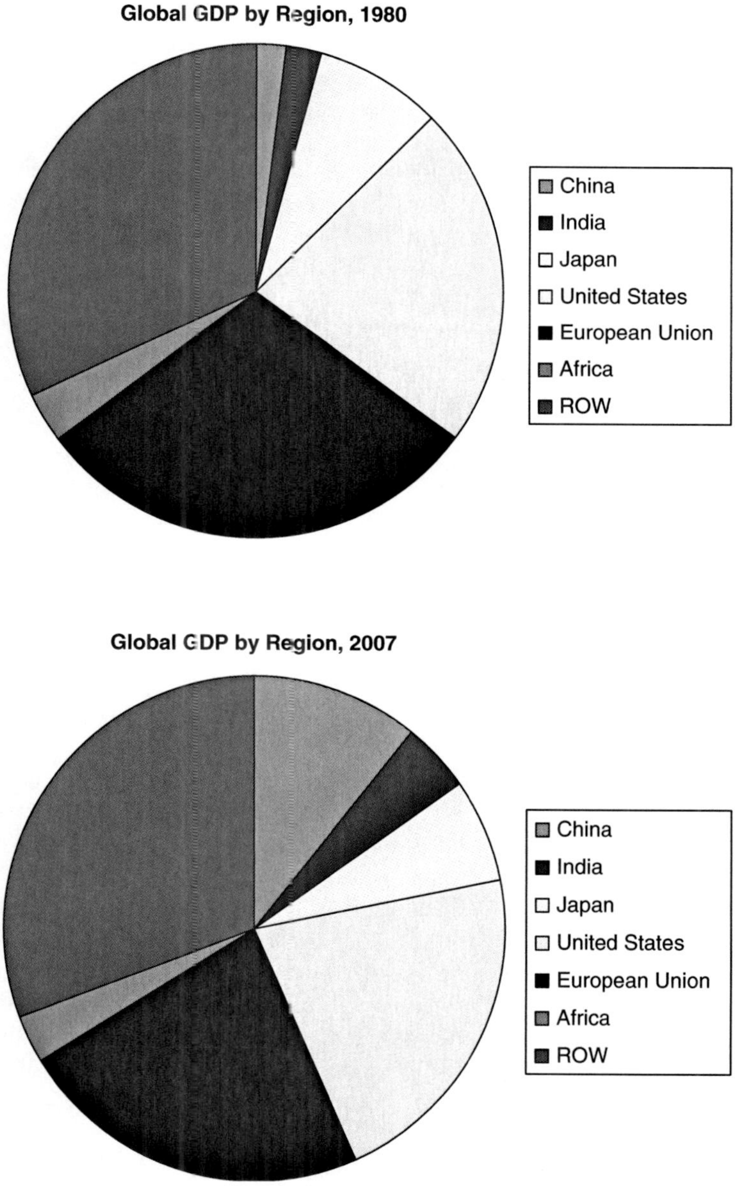

Chart 2.1 Global GDP by region, 1980 vs 2007
Source: Based on data from IMF *World Economic Outlook*.

Inflation in advanced economies fell from an average of around 6 per cent in the 1980s to around 2.5 per cent in the 1990s and fell from much higher levels in many developing countries of the world. On a decade average basis, inflation halved or more than halved, for instance, in the US, Canada, the United Kingdom, Australia and the EU. In short, economies everywhere witnessed a complete rewind of a global phenomenon that first surfaced two and a half decades previously. However, from the mid-2000s inflation again began to rise around the world, spurred by sharp rises in commodity prices, including oil prices.

Over recent decades, the current account imbalances of many advanced and emerging economies have also risen sharply as a proportion of GDP. Financial liberalization has enhanced international capital mobility and thereby facilitated the global delinking of domestic saving and investment rates. As a result, in financially open economies, national saving and investment are more independent. Matching the increased capital flows around the world, the counterpart to these imbalances has been marked changes in nations' external liability positions, with capital exporters increasing foreign asset holdings and capital importers increasing foreign indebtedness.

Asia-Pacific imbalances

Since the turn of the century, the most significant external account imbalances in the world have been between the major Asia-Pacific economies, as indicated in Chart 2.2 which depicts annual average values of global imbalances by region. China, Japan and other East Asian economies have experienced huge CASs, while the US had large long-running external deficits. Within the Asia-Pacific, Australia and New Zealand, though much smaller than the US in terms of GDP, have also run relatively large external deficits.

Outside the Asia-Pacific region, the oil-exporting economies have also run sizeable CASs, whereas select European economies, notably Spain, Greece and the United Kingdom, have run significant CADs.

Private and public capital inflows have tended to raise CADs, reduce domestic interest rates and raise aggregate investment rates in host economies. To the extent that the higher CADs that match increased private capital inflows reflect an excess of domestic investment over domestic saving, the external deficits themselves should

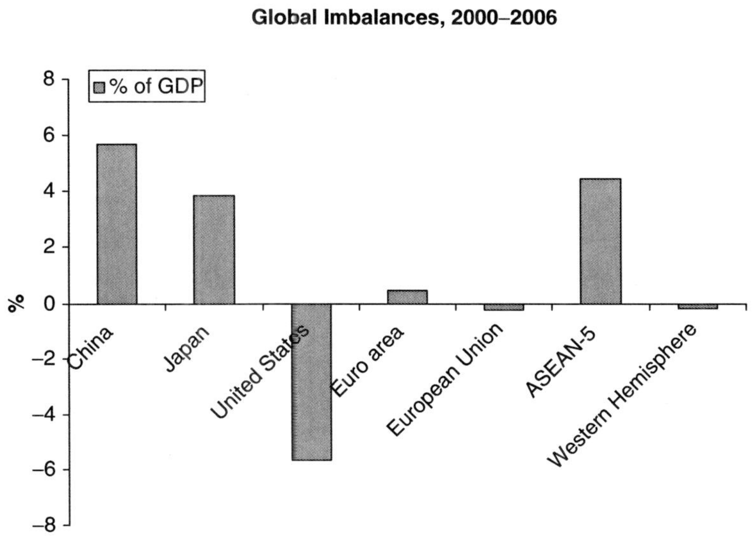

Chart 2.2 Global imbalances
Source: Based on data from IMF *World Economic Outlook*.

not be considered problematic, in and of themselves. Indeed, external imbalances can simply be interpreted as manifestations of increased international trade in private saving which can contribute to higher world income growth.

Private capital inflow that matches the CAD enables borrower countries to accumulate more real capital than if domestic saving alone funds domestic investment. Another way of thinking about the significance of the external imbalance is that it measures the volume of consumption spending that borrower countries would have to forego in order to lift domestic saving to the level required to fund the investment levels from which they benefit.

The servicing costs associated with external liabilities are widely perceived as a net income drain on debtor economies. Yet investment income paid abroad can alternatively be interpreted as the return to foreign investors for funding expansion of a nation's capital stock. Unfortunately, though income paid abroad is easily identified as a debit item in standard balance of payments accounts, additional domestic output and income attributable to capital inflow is nowhere discernible in either the national or external accounts of any economy.

Significant changes to saving and investment behaviour influenced Asia-Pacific imbalances between the Asian crisis of 1997–8 and the Global Financial Crisis of 2007–9. The external deficits of those East Asian economies worst affected by the first crisis episode (South Korea, Thailand, Malaysia, Indonesia) were greatly reduced or switched to surplus by the second. Meanwhile, the most prominent Asia-Pacific imbalance, that between China and the US, widened.

The Asian crisis of 1997–8

Capital flight from the emerging economies of East Asia in 1997–8 precipitated the most notable geofinancial crisis of the second half of the twentieth century with lasting international economic and political effects. Thailand, Malaysia and Indonesia were especially stressed by near-simultaneous exchange rate and asset price collapses that devastated banking and financial sectors, slashed real investment and induced recessions.

South Korea, an advanced economy, also suffered directly although it quickly recovered, while Hong Kong, Chinese Taipei and Singapore were affected indirectly through associated trade shocks that dampened or negated previously strong growth rates. (For further discussion of the causes and consequences of the Asian crisis, see Eichengreen 2002; Glick et al. 2001; Furman and Stiglitz 1998; Goldstein 1998; Makin 1999a, 1990b; and Radelet and Sachs 1998.)

Rises in the external deficits of select advanced economies in the Asia-Pacific (the US, Australia and New Zealand) coincided with a major shift in the pattern of saving and investment in East Asia following the Asian crisis. Since that time, saving in crisis-affected East Asian economies has risen significantly, accompanied by an especially rapid increase in China's saving. Meanwhile, East Asian investment rates have fallen over the period compared to pre-crisis rates (IMF 2005). This excess East Asian saving over investment has been invested abroad.

Although the Asian financial crisis affected all key macroeconomic variables in stricken economies, including interest rates, stock market prices, national income, employment and inflation rates, it was East Asian exchange rates that fell fastest and furthest. For this reason, the Asian crisis was essentially a currency crisis that caused serious macroeconomic problems and which began after foreign investors suddenly divested Asian financial assets, including deposits in and loans to Asian banks, on reassessing their risk exposure in the region.

From the early 1980s, many East Asian emerging economies had liberalized capital accounts and subsequently attracted relatively large capital inflows. However, with relatively fragile domestic financial systems, many of these economies experienced severe capital flow reversals, banking and currency crises and recession.

Before the Asian crisis struck, foreign funds were intermediated through a banking system that directed funds to unproductive investment activities encouraged by government interference. Substantial 'connected' and government- 'directed' lending was undertaken, and a lack of transparency delayed foreign investors' awareness of the extent of underlying structural problems. Once foreign investors realized the extent of these deficiencies, equities and debt instruments were quickly liquidated in favour of relatively more attractive, less risky investment opportunities elsewhere in the world.

Numerous factors triggered the international capital flow reversals that caused the Asian financial crisis. These included poor corporate governance, overvalued exchange rates and excessive foreign borrowing by domestic banks for unproductive projects. However, fiscal balances had generally been sound and inflation rates moderate.

In contrast, budget balances of the worst-affected economies, measured as a proportion of GDP, deteriorated markedly after the crisis, turning pre-crisis fiscal surpluses to deficits that were high by the standards of developed economies. Consolidated public debt to income ratios also rose above pre-crisis levels and exceeded the average public debt to income ratio of advanced economies.

Public debt grew strongly because governments actively deployed fiscal policy as a post-crisis countercyclical measure to boost domestic demand in the context of a global economic slowdown. Accelerated domestic financial liberalization also facilitated issuance of public debt instruments in home markets over this time.

In addition, when financial systems experienced balance sheet distress after currencies collapsed, there was substantial recapitalization of banks, the fiscal cost of which was either recorded explicitly in the budget accounts or recorded off-budget through the quasi-fiscal activities of central banks.

Moreover, the public sectors of stricken economies subsumed significant commercial bank liabilities (due to implicit guarantees to protect depositors and other creditors), as well as foreign exchange debt of some corporations. As a result, consolidated public debt (inclusive of the debt of all tiers of government and public enterprises) to GDP ratios rose to historically high levels across the region.

By the turn of the century East Asia's economies had recovered from the worst of the crisis, though Japan's output growth had stagnated throughout the 1990s and remained weak into the 2000s. Not directly affected by the crisis, China continued to record strong growth relative to the rest of the world, before, during and after it.

China's rise as a trading power

China's remarkable integration into the world economy has resulted from its international trade expanding at an annual average of 15 per cent, more than double the global rate over the past quarter century (IMF 2006). This phenomenal trade growth occurred in the context of astounding average annual real GDP growth rate near 10 per cent over this time, the legacy of economic reforms initiated by the leader Deng Xiaoping.

Since 2000 China's export growth has easily outpaced import growth, giving rise to escalating trade and CASs. At record levels relative to GDP, the CAS became a major economic point of contention between China and Western industrialized trading partners, especially the US and the EU, experiencing large bilateral trade deficits with China. Adding to international concerns about these global imbalances, the Bank for International Settlements (2006) suggested they pose a serious longer-term problem for the global economy.

Many East Asian economies, including Japan, South Korea, Hong Kong SAR, Chinese Taipei, Singapore, Malaysia and Thailand, ran sizeable trade surpluses with Western trading partners from 2000. However, China's trade surplus attracted most international policy attention because it rose so sharply against a backdrop of robust economic growth and a tightly managed exchange rate. The inflexibility of China's exchange rate contrasts with the prevalence of more flexible exchange rate regimes adopted by the majority of developing and emerging economies (Rogoff et al. 2004).

China's international trade has benefited capital and resource intensive trading partners providing inputs for a burgeoning manufacturing sector. Yet the dislocation of manufacturing industry in advanced economies that compete against low-priced Chinese imports invited direct trade policy 'solutions' such as higher tariffs on imports and export subsidies.

Hence, trade and current account imbalances between China and its Western trading partners are widely perceived as a trade competitiveness problem, especially at the manufacturing industry level, and in the US the large bilateral trade deficit with China has prompted proposed retaliatory action in the form of new tariffs against Chinese imports.

China's quarter century of economic growth, at an annual average of 9–10 per cent, has been some three times higher than the average growth rate of its trading partners (see Chart 2.3).

These amazing growth rates have resulted from the economic liberalization programme, including encouragement of foreign direct investment (FDI) which continued in phases throughout the 1980s and 1990s to the present. Greater labour mobility, higher saving due

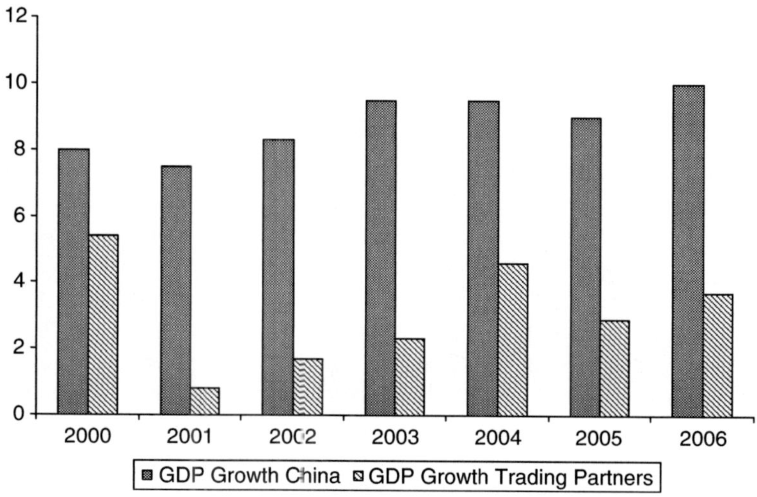

Chart 2.3 Economic growth in China and trading partners
Source: Based on data in IMF (2006a).

to contraction of social welfare entitlements previously extended by the state sector and an improved investment climate for the private sector with less corruption have been other key factors underpinning output expansion.

The broadened capital stock resulting from high domestic saving and investment has been combined with an urban workforce that surged after controls over internal migration from rural to urban areas were eased from the mid-1990s. A new managerial class also emerged to start up predominately manufacturing enterprises and restructure privatized and reformed state-owned enterprises. Meanwhile, the labour force is far better educated than previously.

China has a disproportionately high tradable sector and small non-tradable sector relative to the structure of advanced industrial economies. As a ratio to GDP, its total exports plus imports of goods and services at near three-quarters is well above comparable ratios for the US, Japan and Germany. The tradable sector is also large compared to other large emerging countries at similar stages of development, such as Brazil. In China, services industries, usually part of the non-tradable sector, have been officially discouraged relative to manufacturing.

China joined the World Trade Organization (WTO) in 2001 and has benefited from the global liberalization of trade over the past three decades. However, for China high export growth at rates comparable to those of Japan and South Korea during their post-war take-off phases was evident before it joined the WTO. Policies that have encouraged FDI have also substantially boosted exports by multinational firms (such as Motorola, Toshiba, Nokia and LG) operating in coastal China (Hale 2006).

China's CAS which grew markedly after it became a member of the WTO essentially reflects the trade surplus component. The difference between the trade and overall CAS mainly reflects foreign interest income earned on the vast stock of international reserves of the central bank, the People's Bank of China (PBC) (see Chart 2.4). As the trade account has essentially driven the current account balance, the two terms can be used interchangeably when analysing China's external imbalance.

Persistent trade surpluses and capital inflow (overwhelmingly in the form of FDI) enabled the PBC to amass foreign exchange reserves that exceeded $US two trillion by 2008, most of which are in the

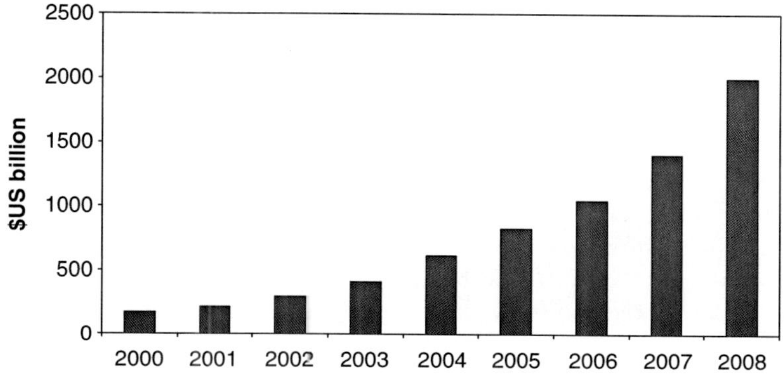

Chart 2.4 China's gross international reserves
Source: Based on data in IMF (2006a).

form of US government securities. Extensive capital controls still impede financial capital inflows and outflows such that recorded non-official capital outflows remain negligible.

With a large tradable sector centred mainly on producing manufactured goods, exchange rate management has minimized exchange rate uncertainty and thereby facilitated export growth. But that has not been the only way a tightly controlled exchange rate has facilitated China's exports and economic growth. Exchange rate management has also contributed to economic development by maintaining competitiveness.

From China's perspective, numerous economic benefits arise from retaining a pegged exchange rate. This policy allows export growth to be faster than otherwise because an undervalued exchange rate boosts the competitiveness of both its export- and import-competing industries, including the large and politically sensitive agricultural sector.

Yet it also implies that exporters abroad sell less than otherwise which may act to limit trading partners' growth. In this way, China's exchange rate policy may be interpreted as a form of industry protection, or 'exchange rate protectionism', to be discussed further in the next chapter.

Moreover, the PBC's high levels of international reserves provide a large stock of funds with which to defend the yuan in the event of another regional currency and financial crisis like that of 1997–8.

Relatedly, the peg of the yuan provides a measure of stability for China's underdeveloped banking and financial system and means Chinese enterprises can avoid managing their own currency risk. Dealing with currency risk would require a stronger banking system, broader and deeper financial markets and more instruments than presently exist.

Offsetting the benefits to China of pegging the currency, however, there are numerous macroeconomic risks. Although most foreign exchange market intervention undertaken to peg the yuan is sterilized, there are limits to the use of sterilization. Neutralizing the monetary impact of intervention by issuing debt instruments can put upward pressure on domestic interest rates which exacerbates the non-performing loans problem overhanging the domestic banking system.

Furthermore, interest earned on an ever-escalating stock of foreign reserves in the form of advanced economy securities could fall short of the interest the central bank has to pay residents on bills issued to sterilize its foreign exchange market intervention. A growing fiscal cost then arises from the sterilization process and the international interest differential, along with expectations of an inevitable yuan revaluation, would induce non-official capital inflow, notwithstanding the capital controls in place.

Higher money growth resulting from foreign exchange market intervention that is not sterilized and not matched by sufficient money demand growth eventually fuels inflation. Higher domestic inflation raises the relative price of domestic goods to foreign goods increasing imports and pushes up domestic costs of production curbing exports.

Increased imports and reduced exports then reduce trade imbalances. However, automatically restoring external balance via higher inflation would take some time and be disorderly since it would create investment uncertainty and strain on China's banking system.

Analytical frameworks introduced in the next chapter reveal that misalignment of the yuan against major currencies artificially assists China's output growth, contributes to global imbalances and limits household consumption, slowing the rise in living standards. Meanwhile, China's Western trading partners, most notably the US and the EU, simultaneously experience external deficits, lower output and lower saving due to exchange rate misalignment.

The US current account deficit

With record CADs over 5 per cent of GDP in the 2000s, the US has easily been the world's largest international borrower, at times drawing in over half of traded global saving (see Chart 2.5), a phenomenon that has concerned domestic and international financial markets and policymakers.

Candidate causes of the US deficit have been extensively analysed in recent literature (see, for example, Blanchard et al. 2005; Corden 2007; Obstfeld and Rogoff 2005; Truman 2005; and Xafa 2007). These include excessive US budget deficits; an overvalued US dollar, especially against the yuan; low US household saving; and foreign investors' expectations of higher US productivity growth relative to emerging economies experiencing low investment returns relative to risk. Most of the studies aimed at identifying the likely determinants of the external deficit and borrowing have focused primarily on domestic rather than foreign factors, and no consensus appears imminent.

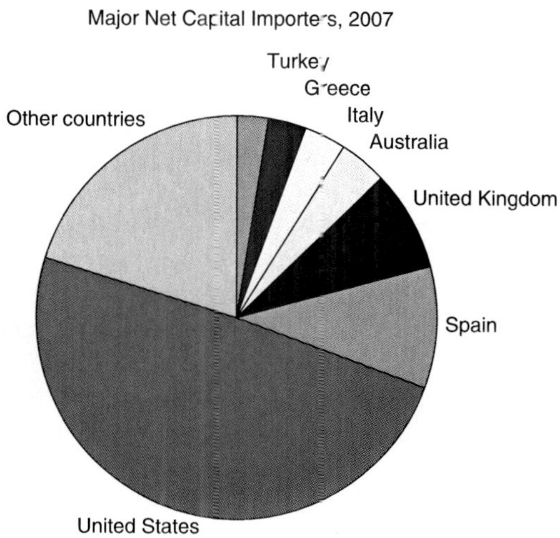

Countries that Import Capital	
Turkey	2.5
Greece	3
Italy	3.5
Australia	3.8
United Kingdom	8
Spain	9.8
United States	49.2
Other countries	20.2

Chart 2.5 Country shares of international capital inflows, 2007
Source: Based on data from IMF, *Global Financial Stability Report, 2009*.

Former Federal Reserve Chairman Mr Alan Greenspan, in discussing the implications of the record US CAD, has also suggested that 'There is no simple measure by which to judge the sustainability of ... current account deficits or external claims that need to be serviced.' Several authors have nonetheless argued that an economy's external deficit is 'excessive' if it approaches 5 per cent of its GDP (Milesi-Ferreti and Razin 1996; Freund 2005).

Freund (2005), for instance, has shown that, since 1980, the median high deficit recorded in the Organisation for Economic Co-operation and Development (OECD) economies before current account reversals was around 5 per cent of GDP. In some countries, double-digit deficits as a proportion of GDP were reached before turning around, mostly without attendant crises.

However, the 5 per cent sustainability limit, also popular with financial market participants, has never been justified analytically, and seems arbitrary in light of the scope for much larger differences between the domestic saving and investment rates of advanced and emerging economies. This issue will be examined in greater depth subsequently.

Meanwhile, long-run interest rates around the world have been well below historical averages. The fact that low long-term interest rates have coincided with the large US external deficit, sizeable fiscal deficits and high public debt levels has been termed a conundrum.

This apparent conundrum raises the following important questions. What factors, domestic and foreign, have been responsible for widening the US CAD? And why did global and US interest rates simultaneously reach their lowest level for a century? These questions are answerable with reference to international borrowing and lending behaviour, as later modelled in Chapter 6.

The US dollar depreciated between 2002 and 2008 by over 30 per cent in nominal effective terms, one of the largest dollar declines in the post-Bretton Woods era, with significant ramifications for US competitiveness, world commodity prices and global inflation. Over this period the US simultaneously experienced record high CADs that peaked at 7 per cent of GDP in 2005.

Indeed, by the end of the latest depreciation episode the US CAD, at over 5 per cent of GDP, remained wider than before the dollar began weakening. This failure of the US CAD to narrow despite massive dollar depreciation seems paradoxical and contrasts sharply with the shrinking US external deficit associated with a similar slide of the dollar from 1985–91.

The global financial crisis 2007–9

The US housing market-related banking crisis that began on Wall Street in 2007 crushed asset values and jolted financial institutions around the world. Yet the underlying causes of the US crisis were remarkably similar to the Asian and regional financial crises experienced elsewhere, proving that certain iron laws of finance cannot be broken. These laws are that credit should not be extended without regard to creditworthiness and that debt, both private and public, should primarily fund productive economic activity.

Banks have always been at the core of the global financial system, although the increasing role played by financial markets – the debt, equity, derivative and foreign exchange markets – means that financial disturbances can now be magnified through those markets. Moreover, with more internationally integrated financial markets, instability is quickly transmitted abroad.

Each banking crisis has a different trigger, but essentially all involve liquidity and solvency problems. In the first instance, banks suddenly experience cash shortages. The US financial crisis was first and foremost sparked by problems in the US housing market with its roots in public, not private, sector mismanagement that included extensive government interference and underwriting of the US sub-prime mortgage market.

Financial crises triggered by the failure of one or more banks routinely follow a boom in asset prices and then a bust. Typically, bank credit is advanced against temporarily inflated asset values, and many borrowers' credit risk has been ignored. What transforms a correction of asset prices into a collapse is the reinforcing panic behaviour of investors selling off financial assets and liquidating bank deposits. Contagion effects lead to runs on other banks and the emergence of full-scale financial crises.

Like the Asian financial crisis a decade before, the US-centred global financial crisis was characterized by widespread bank lending for unproductive real estate and deficient corporate governance standards in financial institutions. The latest global financial crisis has demonstrated once again how quickly domestic and international investors will respond to new economic information that raises perceived risk levels. The key ingredients of crises are persistent underestimation of default risk followed by a loss of investor confidence.

US policymakers concluded that the shortage of US dollars at the heart of the crisis could be remedied by injecting hundreds of billions of dollars into the financial system either as loans or cash injections, including budgetary commitments to purchase low-grade mortgage-related debt instruments held by financial institutions. However, the painful paradox is that despite the liquidity crisis there was no shortage of US dollars in the world as a whole. If anything, there were too many greenbacks held outside the US due to the exchange rate policies of external surplus economies, most notably in East Asia and the Middle East.

Since the turn of the century, trillions of dollars had been acquired by foreign central banks, notably China and Japan, and the oil exporters of the Middle East, through US dollar purchases in foreign exchange markets. As long as these dollars were used to buy US securities they registered as capital inflow to the US, without any net effect on liquidity in US financial markets and the US money supply.

Historically, this investment has mainly been in treasury bonds, generated in great abundance due to high US budget deficits. In addition to the overextension of credit for housing in the US and the associated securitization of non-performing loans, the large US budget deficits of the Bush administration also played a major role and reached a point where foreigners, including via sovereign wealth funds, became reluctant to fund it.

In this way, the current crisis has features in common with fiscal policy related crises experienced since the 1990s at national levels by emerging economies in Europe, including Bulgaria, the Czech Republic, Russia and Ukraine, and in Latin America in Argentina, Brazil, Ecuador and Mexico, where public sector excesses were at the heart of the crises.

Like the US, these countries had fiscal deficits and high public debt levels in the years immediately preceding the crises. The specific determinants of fiscal vulnerability were too much unproductive public spending, low tax ratios, widespread tax exemptions and bail outs of state banks.

Measured as a proportion of GDP, budgetary positions worldwide have deteriorated markedly so far this century. In the US, the consolidated budget balance turned from surplus in 2000 to a deficit a over 10 per cent of national income, very large by historical standards.

Normally, the US dollar should have depreciated sharply under such circumstances, but China and other Asia-Pacific currency peggers were unwilling to allow this. Hence, Asian central banks continued to accumulate US dollar reserves but then did not fully reinvest them in US securities. Thus began the US liquidity shortage which spiralled internationally with grave consequences.

Sovereign wealth funds

The unprecedented reserves of foreign central banks have also spawned sovereign wealth funds, created by reserve-rich governments to enable greater portfolio diversification to improve returns on foreign currency assets. The governments of numerous economies, including those of China, Australia, Norway, Kuwait, Russia, Saudi Arabia, Singapore and the United Arab Emirates, have for different reasons established sovereign wealth funds to manage public sector financial assets.

For instance, sovereign wealth funds of China and Singapore exist to increase financial returns on the foreign exchange reserves of central banks, while the oil exporters insulate their national budgets from oil price swings. In Australia's case, its sovereign wealth fund provides for unspecified future pension liabilities on the government's balance sheet from sources other than individual pension contributions.

Growth of such funds around the world has raised international concerns about the expanded role of governments in global financial markets and national industries, as well as a lack of transparency in their operations.

Conclusion

This chapter has briefly surveyed key international macroeconomic developments over recent decades, highlighting the significance of international capital flows, external imbalances, exchange rate behaviour and inflation, with particular attention to the Asia-Pacific region.

In the earlier gold standard era from the 1870s to World War I known as *la belle époque*, sizeable CADs were associated with high economic growth rates in New World economies. External imbalances this decade are presently large compared with imbalances of the Bretton Woods era or the 1920s and 1930s. Indeed, financial capital is arguably at least as mobile now as in the relatively frictionless international environment of the late nineteenth and early twentieth centuries. Then, for example, the flow of funds from the United Kingdom averaged 5 per cent of GNP between 1870 and 1913 and the inflow of capital to Canada averaged 13 per cent of GDP between 1910 and 1913 (Edelstein 1982).

This earlier era of high capital mobility was undoubtedly influenced by the *laissez faire* views of the classical economists, Adam Smith, David Hume, David Ricardo and John Stuart Mill who strongly advocated free trade in goods and services and, by implication, were untroubled by trade imbalances *per se* under the gold standard regime.

Subsequent chapters aim to improve understanding of the theoretical interrelationships between external imbalances, exchange rates and other macroeconomic variables, including money supplies, interest rates, price levels and national accounting aggregates that are directly or indirectly subject to control via domestic fiscal and monetary policies.

References

Bank for International Settlements (2006) *BIS Annual Report*, BIS.

Blanchard, O., Giavazzi, F. and Sa, F. (2005) 'The U.S. Current Account and the Dollar', NBER Working Paper No. 11137.

Corden, M. (2007) 'Those Current Account Imbalances: A Sceptical View', *The World Economy*, 30 (3), 363–82.

Edelstein, M. (1982) *Overseas Investment in the Age of High Imperialism*, Columbia University Press, New York.

Eichengreen, B. (2002) *Financial Crises and What to Do about Them*, Oxford University Press, Oxford, UK.

Freund, C. (2005) 'Current Account Adjustment in Industrial Countries', *Journal of International Money and Finance*, 24, 1278–98.

Furman, J. and Stiglitz, J. (1998) 'Economic Crises: Evidence and Insights from East Asia', *Brookings Papers on Economic Activity*, 2, 11–35.

Glick, R., Moreno, R. and Spiegel, M. (2001) *Financial Crises in Emerging Markets*, Cambridge University Press, Cambridge, UK.

Goldstein, M. (1998) *The Asian Crisis: Causes, Cures and Systemic Implications*, Institute for International Economics, 55, Washington, DC.

Greenspan, A. (2002) 'Saving for Retirement', Speech to National Summit on Retirement Savings, the Department of Labor, Washington, DC, 28 February.

Hale, D. (2006) *In the Balance: China's Unprecedented Growth and Implications for the Asia-Pacific*, Australian Strategic Policy Institute, Canberra.

International Monetary Fund (2005) 'People's Republic of China: 2005 Article IV Consultation', November, IMF, Washington, DC.

International Monetary Fund (2006) *International Financial Statistics*, IMF, Washington, DC.

Makin, A. (1999a) 'The Great East Asian Capital Flow Reversal: Reasons, Responses and Ramifications', *The World Economy*, 22 (3), 407–19.

Makin, A. (1999b) 'Preventing Financial Crises in East Asia', *Asian Survey*, 39 (4), 668–78.

Milesi-Ferreti, G. and Assaf, R. (1996) 'Current Account Sustainability', Princeton Studies in International Finance, 81, Princeton University, NJ.

Obstfeld, M. and Rogoff, K. (2005) 'The Unsustainable U.S. Current Account Position Revisited', NBER Working Paper No. 10869.

Radelet, S. and Sachs, J. (1998) 'The East Asian Financial Crisis: Diagnosis, Remedies, Prospects', *Brookings Papers on Economic Activity*, 1, 1–74.

Rogoff, K. Husain, A. Mody, A. Brooks, R. and Oomes, N. (2004) *Evolution and Performance of Exchange Rate Regimes*, IMF Occasional Paper 229, Washington, DC.

Truman, E. (2005) 'Postponing Global Adjustment: An Analysis of the Pending Adjustment of Global Imbalances', Institute for International Economics Working Paper No. 05–06.

Xafa, M. (2007) 'Global Imbalances and Financial Stability', IMF Working Paper 07/111, International Monetary Fund, Washington, DC.

3
Global Imbalances and Exchange Rates

Introduction

This chapter develops new frameworks for analysing the international monetary repercussions of trade imbalances and exchange rate policy in an economic growth context. It first develops an alternative two-region flow model of trade imbalances and the exchange rate that combines exports, imports and monetary flows. It then examines links between the exchange rate and output–expenditure relations to show how exchange rate misalignment simultaneously influences global imbalances and macroeconomic conditions in each region.

In preview, in the context of restricted capital flows and discrepant growth rates, this framework shows how pegging exchange rates can generate large trade surpluses for the faster-growing region with counterpart trade deficits in the other. An important corollary is that under these conditions persistently large external surpluses matched by deficits imply exchange rate misalignment.

A two-region balance of payments framework

This section interprets the interrelationship between economic growth, trade imbalances, exchange rates and the monetary sector. The starting premise is that in flow terms, the balance of payments records the supply and demand of an economy's currency, with the nominal exchange rate ensuring equality between the trade balance and monetary flows, both official and private.

An economy with a trade deficit (surplus) has an excess demand (supply) for foreign currency satisfied by an excess supply (demand) of foreign currency, provided through matching capital inflows (outflows). Hence, both trade and monetary flows need to be taken into account when modelling exchange rate management. Yet this is usually not acknowledged in many exchange rate models, such as standard asset market approaches based on stock adjustment of financial portfolios.

In what follows, the macroeconomic variables for trading partners that correspond to the key variables for the fast-growing economy or region, for the sake of presentation hereafter presumed to be China, are denoted with an asterisk. The effective exchange rate of China's currency, the yuan, is the inverse of trading partners' effective rate against the yuan, that is $E = {}^{1}/_{e}$, so that an appreciation of the yuan is a depreciation of trading partner currencies, in practice with a heavy weight given to the US dollar.

At this stage, we abstract from capital flows arising from foreign FDI and assume that China's existing and recently strengthened capital controls effectively limit other inflows and outflows from China. Hence, the initial focus is on the primary determinants of trade flows.

Exchange rates and inter-regional trade flows

The export functions of China and its main trading partners can be specified as

$$X = f(\overset{+}{e}; \overset{+}{\ell}, \overset{+}{K}, \overset{+}{A}) \tag{3.1a}$$

$$X^{*} = g(\overset{+}{E}; \overset{+}{\ell^{*}}, \overset{+}{K^{*}}, \overset{+}{A^{*}}) \tag{3.1b}$$

Where ℓ and K are respectively the size of the labour force and capital stock and A is multifactor productivity. Nominal exchange rate depreciation, for given cost levels and factor inputs, improves competitiveness, increases foreign demand and encourages greater short-run production and exports.

Hence, an upward sloping export schedule for China can be drawn in exchange rate-foreign currency space as shown in the left panel of Figure 3.1. Given the inverse relationship between movements

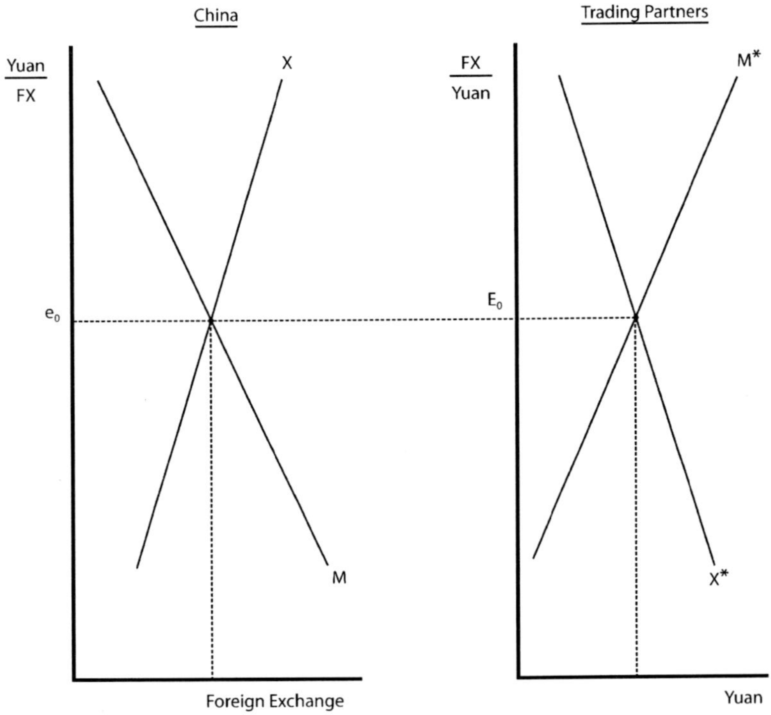

Figure 3.1 Exchange rates and trade flows for China and its trading partners

in these exchange rates, the downward sloping export schedule of China's main trading partners is drawn in the right panel.

Variables in this panel can alternatively be read as the upside down, reverse image of corresponding left panel variables, with the value of trading partners' exchange rate read from top to bottom. Increases in the labour force, capital stock and multifactor productivity, shift respective export schedules rightwards.

The Chinese and trading partners' import functions are

$$M = f(\overset{-}{e};\ \overset{-}{P^{*}/P},\ j(\overset{-}{i},\ \overset{+}{\varphi},\ \overset{+}{G})) \tag{3.2a}$$

$$M^{*} = g(\overset{-}{E};\ \overset{+}{P^{*}/P},\ j^{*}(\overset{-}{i},\ \overset{+}{\varphi},\ \overset{+}{G})) \tag{3.2b}$$

Other things the same, a stronger exchange rate lowers the domestic currency price of imports, increasing import demand. Hence, a downward sloping import schedule M for China can be drawn in exchange rate-foreign currency space as shown in the left panel of Figure 3.1.

Given the inverse relationship between movements in the two exchange rates, the import schedule for trading partners is drawn sloping upwards in exchange rate-foreign currency space in the right panel of Figure 3.1. A negative sign above any shift variable implies a leftward movement of the schedule following an increase in that variable, whereas a positive sign implies a rightward shift.

Changes in the ratio of an index of the prices of Chinese tradable goods relative to a counterpart tradable goods price index for trading partners, as well as in aggregate expenditure, j, j* (itself a function of domestic interest rates, i, wealth, ϕ, and government spending, G) also shift the import schedules.

The weaker the exchange rate, the higher the excess supply of goods and services and hence the greater each economy's net supply of foreign currency from international trade. In the absence of capital flows, trade accounts are balanced, and the nominal exchange rate is in equilibrium where exports equal imports at e_0, E_0.

Trade surpluses, deficits and exchange rate management

Having established these foundations, it is possible to show how higher export-oriented growth determines the trade imbalance between China and its trading partners. First, in view of stronger output growth in China relative to expenditure, exports increase relatively faster than imports, as reflected in a rightward shift of the X schedule in the left panel of Figure 3.2.

The growth in production in China due to utilization of high saving and the mobilization of relatively cheap labour at a rate in excess of the expansion of domestic demand also implies that the prices of China's tradable goods fall relative to tradable goods prices abroad. The relative price fall shifts the M* schedule in the right panel of Figure 3.2 out.

Hence, excess production in China is absorbed through excess demand in its trading partners via a change in relative prices. Other things the same, the higher export volume from China that is equal to the higher import volume for its trading partners would appreciate

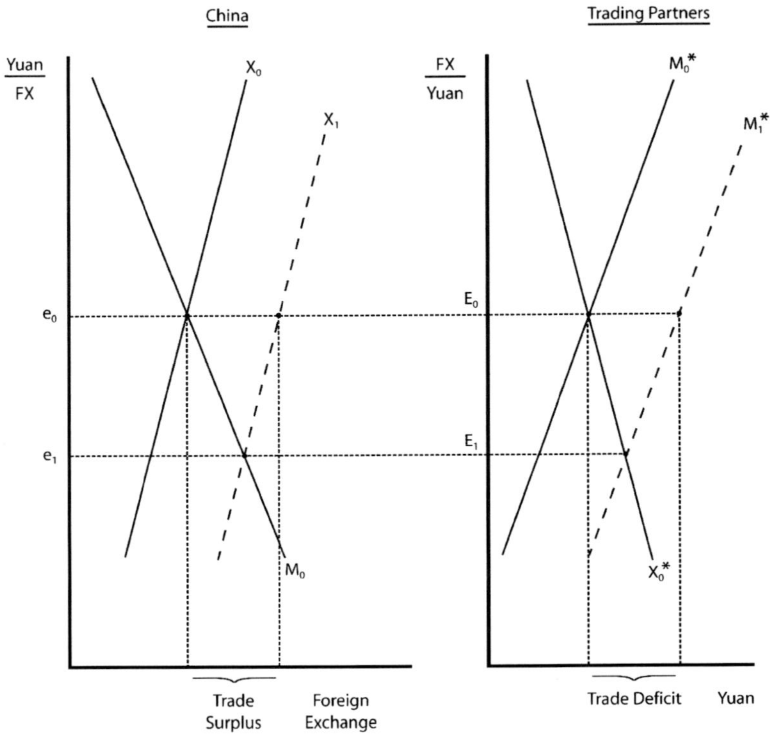

Figure 3.2 The trade balance effects of a pegged yuan

the nominal value of the yuan from e_0 to e_1 and depreciate the currencies of trading partners on an effective basis from E_0 to E_1.

The framework therefore shows how, if free to move, the nominal exchange rate would strengthen to ensure balanced trade accounts for China and its trading partners. Under the pegged arrangements, however, China's trade surplus expands and is matched by growth in the consolidated deficit of its trading partners.

Consequently, the trade deficits of individual trading partners are effectively determined exogenously because of the pegged exchange rate system administered by the PBC. In this way, the trade imbalance is indeed 'Made in China'. The corollary is that the larger is China's external surplus, the more undervalued is the yuan.

Additionally, Figure 3.2 can illustrate the effects of a fiscal expansion in the US and Europe or in other trading partners that increases aggregate spending and increases import demand. Bond-financed fiscal expansion from a point of initial trade balance increases expenditure relative to production and shifts out the M* schedule in the right panel of Figure 3.2, widening the trade deficit, other things equal.

With China's output growing faster than spending, the increased import demand from trading partners is satisfied by higher exports from China. Again, however, if the yuan was free to move against the exchange rates of trading partners, including against the US dollar, it would appreciate and they would depreciate in nominal terms. Such exchange rate adjustment would automatically ensure the trade accounts of the two regions remained in balance. Yet China's tightly managed exchange rate policy prevents this.

Pegging the yuan maximizes China's exports as it prevents any loss of competitiveness stemming from nominal appreciation. To achieve this, the central bank purchases foreign currency and invests it in foreign currency denominated securities, mainly G7 treasury bonds held as international reserves.

While the purchase of foreign currency reduces foreign money supplies, the acquisition of foreign currency denominated bonds leaves foreign money supplies unchanged. Consequently, capital inflow from China to purchase foreign securities satisfies the excess foreign demand for yuan arising from imports exceeding exports.

Meanwhile, by pegging the yuan to prevent losses in competitiveness, China's exports and short-run output are higher than if the PBC had allowed the nominal effective exchange rate to strengthen. Hence, exchange rate management becomes a crucial instrument for achieving higher short-run growth.

At the same time, with less imports of foreign consumer goods and services than otherwise, China's living standards, as measured by absolute consumption levels, are lower than they could be. Meanwhile the reverse is true in trading partners. Short-run output and presumably employment in the tradable sector is lower and household consumption higher.

Monetary implications

To prevent yuan appreciation in the face of a growing trade surplus and capital inflow, the PBC has intervened massively in foreign exchange markets, buying foreign currency and selling yuan. This intervention has sustained higher exports, lower imports and higher trade surpluses than otherwise. Foreign exchange market intervention of course has direct monetary consequences, and the PBC has also had to neutralize the monetary effects of capital inflows, mainly in the form of FDI given the restrictive nature of China's capital controls.

Specifically, central bank purchases of US dollars to fix the value of the yuan will increase China's money supply in the first instance, other things equal. The expansion of the domestic money supply and credit raises expenditure and imports. In theory, if the intervention is not sterilized this should bring about an automatic correction of the excess of exports over imports and eventually restore external balance.

In practice however, the following factors explain why this automatic adjustment mechanism becomes inoperative. First, the PBC sterilizes foreign exchange rate intervention by issuing local currency denominated debt instruments to offset the liquidity effects of its intervention.

This dampens inflationary pressures and domestic expenditure growth and puts upward pressure on domestic interest rates. The extensive exchange controls that restrict financial inflows also has been critical to the success of sterilization because, without a highly regulated capital account, additional financial inflows would require that much extra sterilized intervention.

Second, money supply growth stemming from intervention that remains unsterilized is less inflationary under conditions of very rapid output growth. This is because strong economic growth raises real domestic money demand and, as standard monetary theory suggests, an expanding money supply will not generate inflationary pressure if it simply accommodates real money demand that is rising at the same rate. By the same token, deflationary pressures build if money demand growth outstrips money supply growth.

China has therefore been able to accommodate high money and credit growth (see Chart 3.1) because real money demand has been expanding simultaneously with income. Indeed, the relatively low inflation rate in recent years largely reflects the difference between money growth and output growth.

Third, automatic monetary correction is less likely to operate the more the central bank directly controls credit made available by

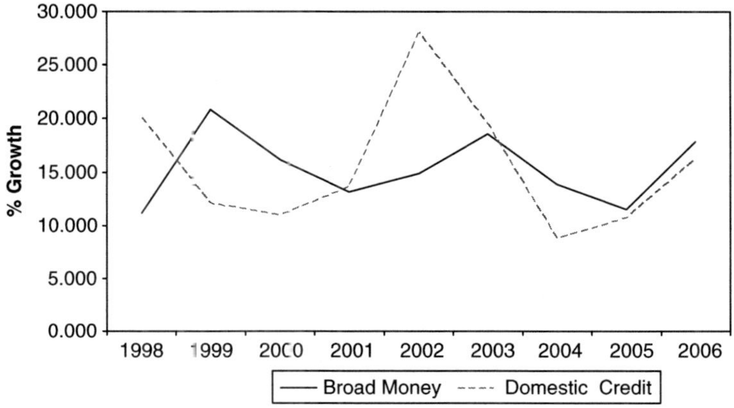

Chart 3.1 China's money and credit growth
Source: Based on data in IMF (2005a).

the banking sector and the less market oriented is the economy's financial system. China's banking system remains quite vulnerable despite ongoing reform and limited foreign investment in the sector, as many banks over a lengthy period were not lending on a commercial basis.

Although this left a legacy of non-performing loans, banking reform has progressed along with limited foreign investment in that sector. Taken together, these factors muted the inflationary impact of pegging the yuan, allowing China's output to outpace expenditure.

A two-region output-expenditure framework

In addition to viewing external imbalances as differences between exports and imports, international macroeconomic accounting dictates that trade and current account imbalances reflect regional output-expenditure gaps (Alexander 1952), strongly influenced over the short to medium run by overall competitiveness, as measured by real exchange rate movements. Since the exchange rate is a shared variable, China's external surplus reflecting excess production over expenditure has implications for the external deficits of Western trading partners which signify an excess of expenditure over production.

Yet there has been a paucity of macroeconomics-oriented analysis focusing explicitly on the nexus between exchange rate policy and relative output and expenditure flows. Hence, we develop a basic output-expenditure framework compatible with the trade approach to further explain current account imbalances between China and its Western trading partners.

The real exchange rate, spending and income

Again, in what follows, macroeconomic variables for trading partners that correspond to the same variables for China are denoted with an asterisk.

The emphasis in international monetary theory on asset markets and capital account transactions as primary influences on the nominal exchange rate (see Branson 1983; Dornbusch and Fischer 1980; Frenkel and Mussa 1985; Isard 1995; Sarno and Taylor 2002) contrasts with the traditional flow approach in which the exchange rate simultaneously equalizes net demand and supply of foreign currency arising from both current and capital account transactions.

The real exchange rate influences aggregate output and expenditure and hence the current account balance. For China, it is defined as

$$R = \frac{eP^*}{P} \tag{3.3a}$$

where e is the nominal effective exchange rate, P is China's domestic price level and P^* is the weighted price level of its trading partners. For its trading partners, it is defined as

$$R^* = \frac{EP}{P^*} \tag{3.3b}$$

where E is the weighted nominal effective exchange rate of China's trading partners.

It is assumed that the foreign and domestic price levels are stable in the short run, consistent with low worldwide inflation. Hence, movements in the nominal exchange rate account for short-term real exchange rate variation.

The aggregate output or supply functions are specified as

$$Y = Y(\overset{+}{R}(\overset{+}{e}); \overset{+}{A}, \overset{+}{K}, \overset{+}{\ell}) \tag{3.4a}$$

$$Y^* = Y^*(\overset{+}{R^*}(\overset{+}{E}); \overset{+}{A^*}, \overset{+}{K^*}, \overset{+}{\ell^*}) \tag{3.4b}$$

where A, A*, K, K* and ℓ, ℓ^* are the key drivers of production, multi-factor productivity, capital and labour.

Nominal exchange rate depreciations improve competitiveness and hence encourage higher short-run production in anticipation of increased exports of goods and services. Following substantial FDI in China over past decades that has directly augmented the capital stock, multinational corporations produce a sizeable part of annual output for export.

On the aggregate demand or expenditure side,

$$AE = C + I \tag{3.5a}$$

$$AE^* = C^* + I^* \tag{3.5b}$$

where AE, AE* is absorption or aggregate expenditure; C, C* is consumption; I, I* is investment.

The trade account balance (or current account balance absent income paid abroad) measures the divergence between national output and expenditure, such that

$$Y - AE = CAS \tag{3.6a}$$

$$AE^* - Y^* = CAD^* \tag{3.6b}$$

where Y, Y* is national output or income, CAS is the current account surplus and CAD* is the counterpart trading partner external deficit.

The aggregate expenditure functions can then be written as

$$AE = AE(\overset{+}{R}(\overset{+}{e}); \overset{-}{r}(\overset{+}{M^S}), \overset{+}{\Im}, \overset{+}{\varphi}) \tag{3.7a}$$

$$AE^* = \overset{+}{AE^*}(\overset{+}{R^*}(\overset{+}{E^*}); \overset{+}{r^*}(\overset{+}{M^{S*}}), \overset{+}{\Im^*}, \overset{+}{\phi^*}) \tag{3.7b}$$

Aggregate expenditure is influenced by domestic interest rates, r, the fiscal policy stance, $\Im$ (with a rise in $\Im$ implying fiscal expansion), and residents' wealth, ϕ. In turn, domestic interest rates are influenced by the money supply.

Total expenditure in an open economy includes spending on imported goods and services whose prices are initially set in foreign currency. A stronger exchange rate lowers the domestic currency price of imports, increasing import demand and total expenditure. Hence, a downward sloping aggregate expenditure schedule AE for China can be drawn in exchange rate-expenditure space as shown in the left panel of Figure 3.3.

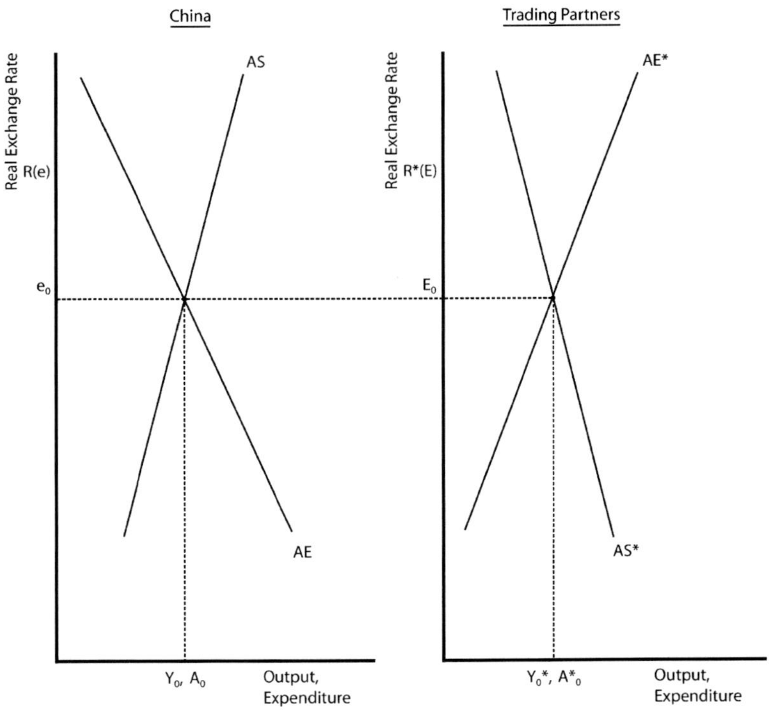

Figure 3.3 Exchange rates and output – expenditure imbalances

As China's national product includes that part of output sold abroad as exports, total output is positively related to competitiveness, which, given the assumption about short-run price level stability, reflects nominal exchange rate movements. Hence output is represented by an upward sloping AS schedule in exchange rate-output space, as also shown in the left panel of Figure 3.3.

Divergences between domestic expenditure and output manifest not only as external imbalances, but as excess demand or supply of foreign currency. In the absence of capital flows, the current account is balanced and the nominal exchange rate is at equilibrium at the point where national expenditure equals national output. The weaker is the exchange rate, the higher is the excess supply for goods and services, and hence the greater the economy's net supply of foreign currency due to CASs.

The effective exchange rate for China against the weighted exchange rate of its trading partners is the inverse of trading partners' exchange rate against the yuan, that is $E = {}^{1}/_{e}$, so that a depreciation of the yuan is an appreciation of trading partner currencies.

Hence, if the vertical axis in the right panel measures the same exchange rate as the left panel but is read from the top down, the aggregate expenditure and production schedules for trading partners in the right panel have the opposite slopes to those shown in the left panel. The trade accounts of China and its Western trading partners balance where aggregate supply and demand schedules intersect at nominal effective exchange rates e_0, E_0.

Global imbalances and exchange rate misalignment

Having established these foundations, it is possible to show how strictly macroeconomic factors simultaneously determine external account imbalances, inter-regional capital flows and shared exchange rates.

First, China's rapid manufacturing-driven development implies that in relative terms its domestic output growth outpaces its domestic expenditure growth, so that exports exceed imports and the trade surplus rises. This is conveyed by a rightward shift of the *AS* schedule in the left panel of Figure 3.4.

Other things equal, higher domestic output growth (inclusive of the output of multinational corporations producing for export only), relative to domestic expenditure growth, appreciates China's exchange rate and depreciates the currencies of its trading partners.

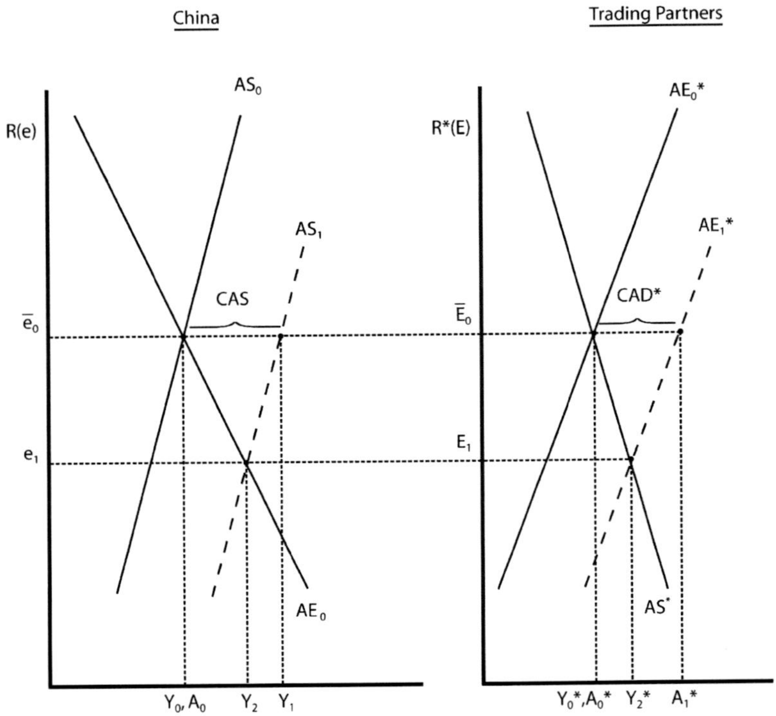

Figure 3.4 Exchange rate misalignment, imbalances and macroeconomic behaviour

However, to avoid the loss of competitiveness that a nominal appreciation entails, the PBC purchases foreign currency. This is invested in treasury bonds which are added to foreign reserves. While the exchange of yuan for foreign currency in the foreign exchange market reduces the money supply of its Western trading partners, other things equal, the subsequent purchase of foreign currency denominated bonds with the foreign currency acquired by the PBC leaves foreign money supplies unchanged.

The excess demand for bonds pushes up their price and lowers interest rates in trading partners. In turn, lower interest rates sustain higher expenditure than otherwise in trading partner economies. Consequently, capital outflow from China ensures its external surplus matches the capital inflow and external deficit of its trading partners.

Since China is accumulating foreign currency reserves by running a trade surplus at a pegged exchange rate, the external deficit of its trading partners is again 'Made in China', more specifically by the PBC's exchange rate policy. With China's output growing faster than spending, the increased import demand from trading partners is satisfied by higher exports from China.

Again however, if the yuan was free to move against the exchange rates of trading partners, including against the US dollar, it would appreciate and they would depreciate in nominal terms. Such exchange rate adjustment would automatically ensure the trade accounts of the two regions remained in balance. Yet China's tightly managed exchange rate policy prevents this.

Additionally, Figure 3.4 can illustrate the effects of a fiscal or monetary expansion in Western trading partners that increases aggregate spending relative to production. Suppose there is additional bond-financed fiscal expansion in trading partners. From a point of initial trade balance this increases expenditure, shifts out the AE* schedule in the right panel of Figure 3.4 and widens the trade deficit, other things equal. By investing in bonds issued by Western trading partner governments the PBC ensures lower foreign interest rates, thereby sustaining increased expenditure and external deficits abroad.

Exchange rate protection

Figure 3.4 also reveals important, though hitherto neglected, macroeconomic consequences of pegging the yuan. Specifically, by maintaining a misaligned exchange rate, China's exports, short run output (and hence employment levels), are higher than if the PBC had allowed foreign exchange market pressures to appreciate the yuan. Hence, exchange rate management becomes an instrument for stimulating higher short-run output growth as indicated at level Y_1 in Figure 3.4.

This exceeds the level of Y_2 that would obtain under a fully flexible exchange rate system. Accordingly, China's pegged exchange rate policy may be seen as conferring a form of trade protection to domestic manufacturing industry, including multinational enterprises, that can be termed 'exchange rate protection' (see also Schwartz 2005).

At the same time, despite China's very high domestic output growth, its exchange rate policy results in domestic consumption being lower than otherwise. In turn, this implies that China's living standards, as gauged by the level of consumption households could potentially enjoy, are suboptimal.

Meanwhile, in Western trading partner economies a pegged yuan implies that CADs arise. More importantly, however, an inflexible exchange rate results in short-run national output and employment, particularly in the manufacturing segment of the tradables sector, being lower than if the exchange rate was flexible.

In the right side panel of Figure 3.4, other things equal, in the face of China's relatively faster growth, trading partner GDP remains at Y_0^* while expenditure increases to A_1^*. Under a pegged exchange rate, the output-expenditure difference is the collective current account deficit, CAD*.

Yet with a fully flexible exchange rate regime, exchange rates would realign with real sector consequences for both China and its trading partners. For instance, trading partner GDP would rise to Y_2^* and both consumption and investment spending would fall compared with the pegged rate outcome such that, collectively, trading partner output would equal expenditure and current accounts with China would balance. With lower consumption and higher output in trading partner economies, domestic saving rates would also rise unambiguously and investment fall to ensure saving-investment equality consistent with current account balance.

Contrary to the dictates of standard macroeconomic theory, strong rises in US national expenditure may no longer be strongly associated with commensurate output and employment expansion (hence so-called jobless recoveries). This framework shows how this eventuates. Under a pegged exchange rate system increased domestic expenditure simply widens external imbalances in the first instance.

If trading partner bonds are subscribed at the prevailing domestic interest rates, their external deficit is fully funded by excess Chinese saving over investment. The capital inflow to trading partners (capital outflow from China) allows lower global interest rates. Capital inflow sustains higher expenditure in trading partners at the subsequent cost to national income of interest paid to China on outstanding public debt, whereas China's national output is augmented by interest income received on foreign currency bond holdings.

Should china's exchange rate be more flexible?

This chapter has proposed a simple framework for analysing trade balances and monetary flows. It has modelled the exchange rate implications of rapid output growth in China matched by strong import growth in its trading partners. These developments imply that the yuan exchange rate has been undervalued since China became a member of the WTO and has contributed directly to the size of trade deficits in its trading partners.

This exchange rate focus contrasts with the view that the external imbalance is best interpreted as a result of relative national saving and investment patterns (IMF 2005b) without reference to exchange rate management. It is also at odds with the standpoint of some economists, including Eichengreen and Masson (2004), that yuan undervaluation has not been significant.

Although it is difficult to empirically estimate an equilibrium exchange rate for an emerging economy undergoing great structural change, Chart 3.2 suggests that since joining the WTO in 2001, the

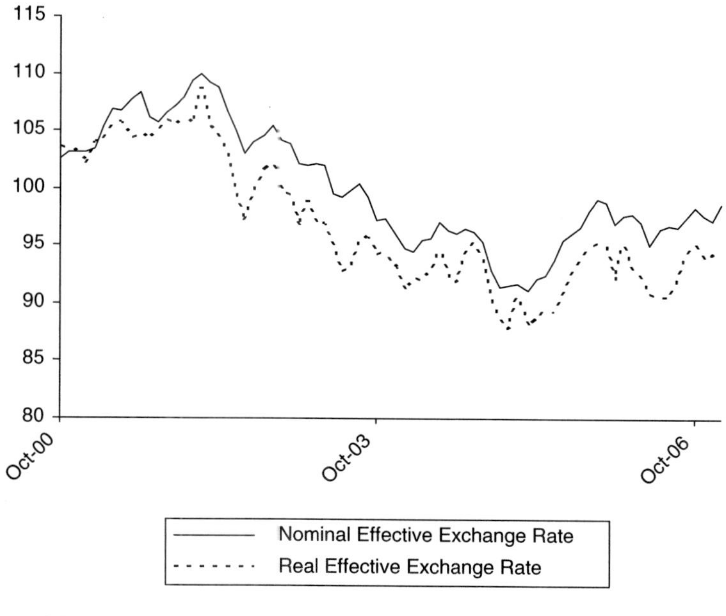

Chart 3.2 China's nominal and real effective exchange rates
Source: BIS (2008).

nominal and real effective exchange rates of the yuan have reached low levels.

The above conceptual framework clearly shows that with a more flexible exchange rate regime any tendency for China to record trade surpluses naturally leads to yuan appreciation against the currencies of its Western trading partners and that pegging the exchange rate determines the actual size of the surplus eventually recorded. This tendency obviously becomes more pronounced once capital inflows, including FDI, are taken into account. Accordingly, continued strengthening of the external surplus will amplify the degree of undervaluation of the yuan.

Conclusion

This chapter has proposed alternative international monetary frameworks for examining the trade balance and real sector consequences of exchange rate misalignment. Founded on the distinction between national output and expenditure, an important finding is that China's inflexible exchange rate bestows additional output gains on China at trading partners' expense and that exchange rate misalignment is central to understanding global imbalances.

Maintaining undervalued currencies through heavy foreign exchange market intervention also has monetary implications. Specifically, the purchase of foreign currency by the PBC increases China's money supply which should lower domestic interest rates in the first instance and shift the AE* right. In theory, this should bring about an automatic correction of the excess of production over expenditure and eventually restore external balance.

In practice, however, as argued, this automatic correction process may not occur because the PBC sterilizes foreign exchange rate intervention by issuing local currency denominated bills to offset the liquidity effects of intervention. This limits expenditure by maintaining a floor under domestic interest rates. At the same time China's highly regulated capital account facilitates sterilized intervention via controls restricting financial inflows.

Moreover, under conditions of very rapid output growth, money supply increases need not be fully sterilized because strong real money demand growth permits seigniorage without inflationary consequences. Third, the automatic monetary adjustment mechanism under pegged exchange rates is less likely to operate, the weaker and less developed is the economy's banking and financial system. Taken together, these factors appear to have negated the inflationary consequences of China's pegged exchange rate and allowed it to sustain huge external surpluses matched by deficits abroad.

Several authors (Hausmann et al. 2001; Calvo and Reinhart 2002) have argued that pegged exchange rates are essentially adopted by emerging economies due to a 'fear of floating' that stems from concerns about financial stability, policy credibility and currency mismatches.

However, this model shows that a pegged exchange rate regime may instead be favoured on the grounds that it provides a mechanism for maximizing output growth. Moreover, the impact on the financial sector of exchange rate appreciation is likely to be minimal in light of the limited foreign exchange exposure of the banking sector and a growing capacity to hedge against exchange rate risk.

References

Alexander, S. (1952) 'Effects of a Devaluation on a Trade Balance', *IMF Staff Papers*, 2, 263–78.

Branson, W. (1983) 'Macroeconomic Determinants of Real Exchange Rates', in R. Herring (ed.) *Managing Foreign Exchange Risk*, Cambridge University Press, Cambridge, UK.

Calvo, G. and Reinhart, C. (2002) 'Fear of Floating', *Quarterly Journal of Economics*, 117, 379–408.

Dornbusch, R. and Fischer, S. (1980) 'Exchange Rates and the Current Account', *American Economic Review*, 70 (5), 960–71.

Eichengreen, B. and Masson, P. (2004) 'Chinese Currency Controversies', Discussion Paper Series No. 4375, Centre for Economic Policy Research.

Frenkel, J. and Mussa, M. (1985) 'Asset Markets, Exchange Rates and the Balance of Payments', in R. W. Jones and P. B. Kenen (eds) *Handbook of International Economics*, vol. 2, North Holland, Amsterdam, Ch. 14, 679–747.

Hausmann, R., Panizza, U. and Stein, E. (2001) 'Why Do Countries Float the Way They Float?', *Journal of Development Economics*, 66 (4), 387–414.

International Monetary Fund (2005a) *People's Republic of China: 2005 Article IV Consultation*, November, IMF, Washington DC.

International Monetary Fund (2005b) *World Economic Outlook*, IMF, Washington DC.

Isard, P. (1995) *Exchange Rate Economics*, Cambridge University Press, Cambridge, UK.

Sarno, L. and Taylor, M. (2002) *The Economics of Exchange Rates*, Cambridge University Press, Cambridge, UK.

Schwartz, A. (2005) 'Dealing with Exchange Rate Protectionism', *Cato Journal*, 25 (1), 97–106.

4
External Imbalances and National Income

Introduction

The current account imbalances of many advanced and emerging economies have widened significantly as a proportion of GDP in the wake of the international capital market liberalization that began in the early 1980s. As a result, international borrower countries, especially the US, Australia and New Zealand, have experienced sharp rises in external indebtedness.

This has concerned policymakers and, at various times, been a major focus of macroeconomic policy. Misinterpretations of the causes of current account imbalances can lead to misplaced policy reactions that impose large economic and societal costs. Unfortunately, many mainstay macroeconomic models are ill equipped to interpret the significance of external imbalances because they fail to recognize explicitly that in financially open economies, domestic expenditure diverges from domestic production to the extent of foreign borrowing or lending.

Prevailing international macroeconomic policy frameworks generally neglect the role current account imbalances explicitly play in determining national income over the medium to longer term. Although the basic Keynesian cross and MF approaches to national income determination include net exports as part of an economy's aggregate demand, a major deficiency of these approaches is that national output simply adjusts endogenously to aggregate demand pressures. Implicitly, this presumes the economy has substantial underutilized capacity and high unemployment, rather than operating at levels of capacity consistent with normally high employment levels.

What is not adequately taken into account is the medium-term influence of supply side factors on aggregate output, including foreign capital inflows and an evolving capital stock. In sum, standard short-run models of national income determination (for example as exposited in introductory and advanced macroeconomics textbooks) underemphasize the role of the supply side over the short to medium runs and that, in the first instance, a production function generates national output by combining available factor inputs.

Meanwhile, neoclassical growth theory (Solow 1956; Swan 1956) is founded on the premise that economic growth is essentially a supply-side phenomenon driven by factor accumulation and productivity, where aggregate output is either consumed or invested, and whose path inevitably leads to a long run stationary or steady state.

Yet the continuous time analysis usually employed in growth theory does not explain how national income may fluctuate from period to period and in the medium term with reference to domestic and international factors, including consumption, investment, government spending, the current account balance, world interest rates and capital flows.

To address these deficiencies in orthodox analysis, this chapter introduces an alternative framework for examining how national output, spending and the current account interact to determine the path of national income over the medium term. Methodologically, it departs from recent practice in international macroeconomics founded on microeconomic principles and optimizing representative agents, instead relying on conventional macroeconomic tools such as consumption functions, 45^0 diagrams and investment opportunities frontiers.

Although large CADs and foreign debt levels remain a source of concern for international financial markets and policymakers, exactly what an 'excessive' external deficit or liability position for an advanced economy is at any time has never been adequately defined. This chapter also addresses the question by proposing new methods for assessing the proximity of CADs and the associated foreign debt to their upper bounds.

It proposes that productive investment fundamentally sets the feasible limit for CADs, whereas the capital to output ratio ultimately sets the foreign debt to GDP limit. Benchmark estimates for the US, Australia, New Zealand and the United Kingdom, advanced economies that have borrowed heavily since 1990, reveal external deficits have usually been well within limits, although recent US experience is an exception.

Rendering the Keynesian cross diagram

The following foundations underpin the analytics of a new framework that reinvents the textbook Keynesian cross diagram allowing explicit consideration to external imbalances and their role in determining national income. The economy is comprised of four sectors – households, firms, government and the rest of the world – and all macroeconomic variables are expressed in real terms. The initial stock of foreign debt is zero, such that national output and income are equivalent at the outset of the analysis.

Saving, investment and the current account

The horizontal axis of Figure 4.1 measures national product, the output of final goods and services, made available for sale at home and abroad, and national income, net of income paid abroad assumed to be in the form of interest only. Real output expands as the capital stock increases, assuming a given labour force or, alternatively, assuming national accounting aggregates are expressed in per worker terms.

The vertical axis of the figure measures household consumption, autonomous government purchases, private investment, national saving and the current account balance. Household consumption depends on after-tax income, and the proportion of income consumed within the period which determines the slope of the expenditure function through time. Government spending is assumed autonomous and in the nature of consumption.

National savings is also the sum of private savings and public savings:

$$S = S_p + S_g = (Y - T - C) + (T - G) = Y - C - G \tag{4.1}$$

where Y is domestic product, net of capital stock depreciation; S_p is private saving; S_g is public saving; T is income taxation; C is private consumption; and G is government spending.

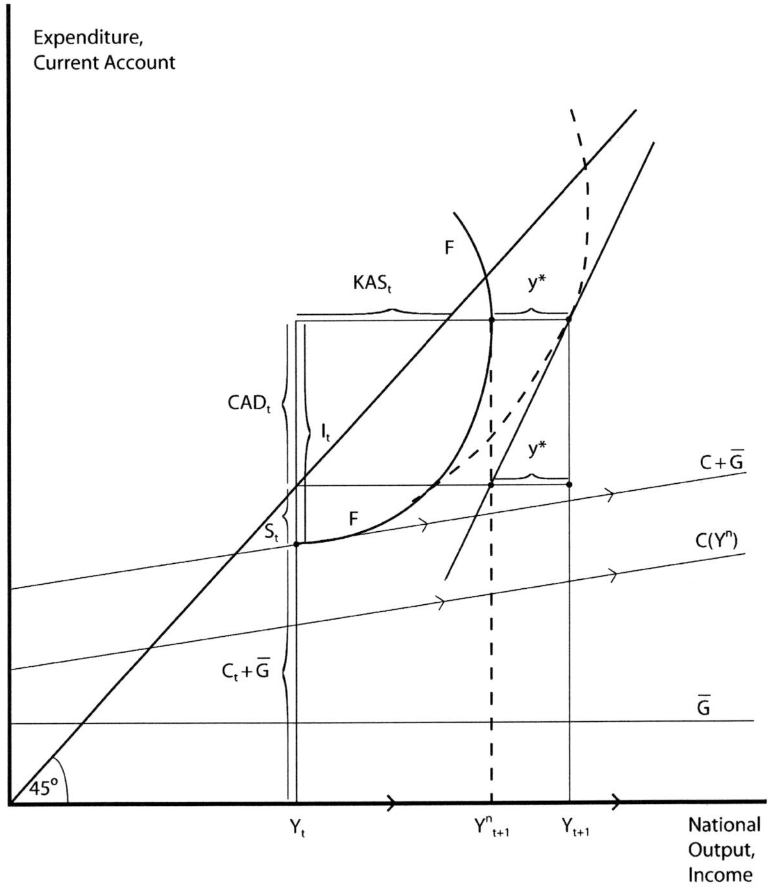

Figure 4.1 A rendered Keynesian cross diagram

As the following analysis is conducted in discrete time we now introduce time subscripts for the standard macroeconomic variables introduced previously. Hence, national output produced in initial time period *t* is Y_t, and assuming the pre-existing stock of foreign debt is zero, national saving in Figure 4.1 is S_t, the vertical distance between $C_t + \bar{G}$ and the 45° line. For a given value of output determined in period *t*, national saving varies as private and public consumption rise or fall.

Private investment, net of capital stock depreciation, I_t, in period *t* is governed by an investment opportunities frontier. First devised by Irving Fisher (1930) and later applied by authors, including Makin (1994), Frenkel and Razin (1996) and Sachs (1981) to convey how present income may be transformed into longer run future income via saving and investment, the investment opportunities frontier has traditionally specified two periods only, the present and the entire future.

Here, however, the device is used to convey how additional capital expenditure in one period enlarges national output and income in a sequence of discrete periods, such that

$$Y_{t+1} = Y_t + g(I_t),\quad Y_{t+2} = Y_{t+1} + h(I_{t+1}),\quad Y_{t+3} = Y_{t+2} + j(I_{t+2}) \text{ etc.} \qquad (4.2)$$

Throughout the analysis, the short run is therefore defined as the current period *t*, whereas the medium run spans the subsequent multi-period sequence.

In effect, Figure 4.1 proposes an output-expenditure analogue of the Keynesian-cross diagram that underpins textbook macroeconomic analysis. Note, however, that total expenditure or aggregate demand differs from the way it is specified in the textbook cross diagram and the MF model. There, aggregate demand means absorption plus net exports, whereas here, as in the previous chapter, domestic demand is simply defined as absorption of goods and services by resident entities, inclusive of imports following Alexander (1952).

That is, total spending in the short run (period *t*) is the vertical sum of $C_t + G_t + I_t$ representing all home spending on domestically produced and imported goods and services. At the same time, aggregate supply is defined as the total quantity of goods and services provided for sale at home and abroad, recognizing that part of output satisfies export demand. Accordingly, the current account balance and associated external borrowing requirement can be identified explicitly for any output level determined within the period through the production process.

The expenditure schedule intersects the 45^0 line directly above Y_t, the value of GDP produced in period *t*, in the special case of a fully closed economy. Alternatively, it intersects the 45^0 line directly above Y_t, when the current account happens to be balanced at Y_t, such that the portion of output produced for sale abroad and recorded as exports of goods and services exactly equals imports, the spending by resident entities on goods and services produced abroad. When domestic demand equals aggregate supply in this model, the economy neither incrementally borrows nor lends internationally.

Interest rates and capital flows

Figure 4.1 also shows how a CAD, CAD_t, may initially be determined by the excess of the economy's total expenditure over national output and income of Y_t. Equivalently, CAD_t is the excess of investment, I_t, over national saving, S_t, at that same income level, assuming the pre-existing stock of foreign debt is zero.

Domestic investment, inclusive of that part funded by foreign saving, rises to the point where the marginal product of capital, reflected in the slope of the dashed portion of the investment opportunities frontier in Figure 4.1, equals the prevailing world interest rate at the point of tangency. This effectively assumes real interest parity and perfect international capital mobility, as also assumed in the MF and intertemporal current account models. The perfect capital mobility assumption can be relaxed, but this would overly complicate the analysis without affecting the key results.

Assuming static exchange rate expectations and abstracting from other risk factors that limit capital mobility, the exogenous world interest rate then sets the equilibrium domestic interest rate, *i*, and level of investment, I_t, through the investment opportunities frontier. Presuming the net demand for foreign currency to fund CAD_t continually matches the net supply of foreign currency accompanying KAS_t also implies an invariant exchange rate throughout, thereby avoiding the complications of competitiveness effects.

Output in period t+1 exceeds output in period *t* due to additional investment which depends positively on the productivity of additional capital, reflected in the slope of the investment opportunities frontier, and negatively on the world interest rate. However, national income, Y^n_{t+1} is less than Y_{t+1} since the capital inflow in period *t* must be serviced at the world interest rate. In the figure, $Y_{t+1} - Y^n_{t+1} = i^*$ CAD_t is equivalent to distance y*, by geometry. The CAD is sustainable when the increased output in t + 1 that flows from excess investment over national saving exceeds the value of y*.

This relationship between national output and income suggests that the investment opportunities frontier can be modified to derive a new frontier showing how capital inflow in one period directly increases national income to its next period equilibrium value. Such a frontier, hereafter referred to as the *FF* frontier, is geometrically derived as a curve whose slope at any point represents the difference between the marginal product of foreign-financed investment, obtained from the dashed investment opportunities curve and given world interest rate.

In Figure 4.1 the tangency point on the investment opportunities frontier yields equilibrium national income of Y^n_{t+1}. Directly above Y^n_{t+1} the *FF* frontier must therefore be vertical. At this point, capital inflow to fund excess investment over national saving no longer contributes positively to national income. Beyond this point the *FF* frontier bends backwards as the exogenous interest rate would then exceed the marginal product of capital, reducing national income. Improvements in expected capital productivity would shift the investment opportunities and *FF* curves outwards, increasing the size of CAD_t and national income in subsequent periods, other things equal.

This alternative framework is useful for several reasons. It graphically illustrates how current account balances at any time are determined simultaneously by total spending-production *and* saving-investment imbalances. Additionally, as conveyed in Figure 4.2, it reveals how external deficits facilitate faster economic growth of national output and national income than otherwise, provided the return on foreign-funded capital exceeds the external debt servicing cost.

To highlight this result, Figure 4.2 shows the lower level of equilibrium national income, Y^c_{t+1}, that would result if capital controls prohibited external finance. As household consumption increases with income through time, it is also apparent that external deficits enable living standards to be higher compared to autarky.

Fiscal policy and the current account

This model may now be used to analyse the short to medium run impact of fiscal policy on national saving, the current account balance and national income. In Figure 4.3, reduced public consumption spending raises national saving which lowers the expenditure schedule, and equivalently diminishes CAD_t within the period the fiscal stance changes. This implies national income will be higher in successive intervals following the fiscal contraction because national saving is higher and, for given investment opportunities, less external debt requires servicing.

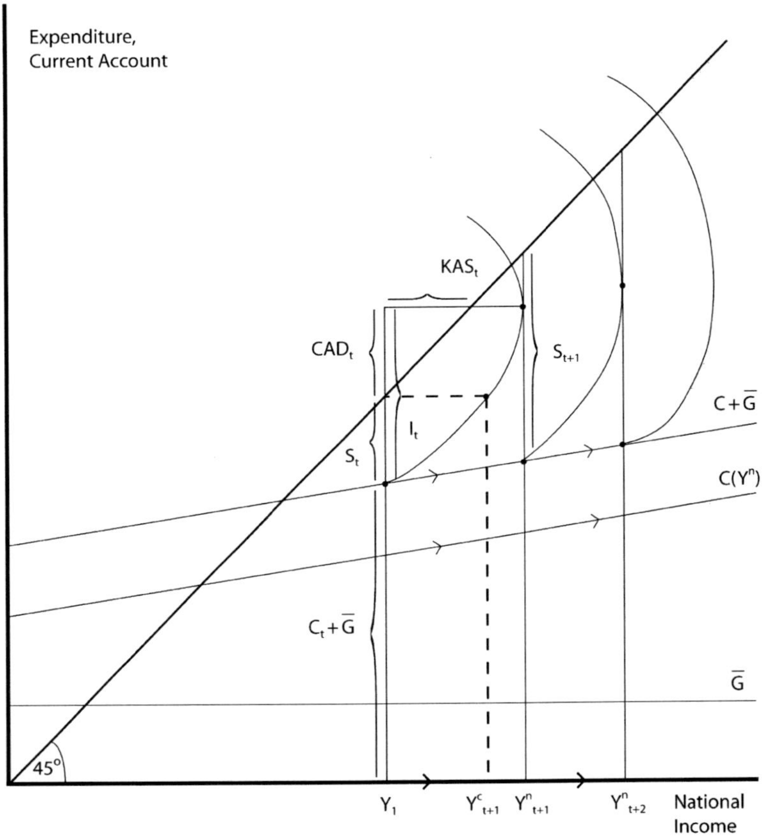

Figure 4.2 Fiscal deficits, external imbalances and national income

Moreover, the framework shows a direct theoretical link between the government's budget ($G_t - T_t$) and CAD_t, consistent with the 'twin deficits hypothesis' that implies budget and external deficits are linked. Usually, it is presumed that the deficits linkage is dollar for dollar, irrespective of whether spending or tax changes alter the budget deficit.

In sum, Figure 4.3 shows that fiscal contraction (expansion) can raise (lower) income in the medium term, contrary to standard closed economy Keynesian results about the impact of fiscal policy

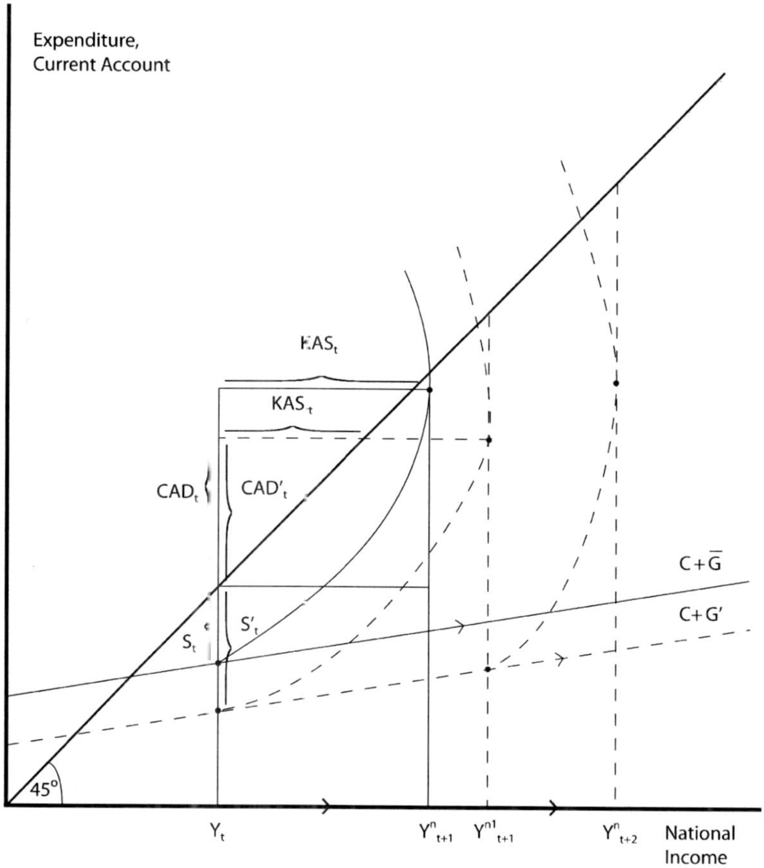

Figure 4.3 Reduced public consumption

on national income. This result also contradicts the predictions of MF analysis about the impact of fiscal policy under either fixed or floating exchange rates.

The analysis of the economywide impact of discretionary income tax changes is less straightforward than public spending changes, however. If household consumption is a simple linear function of current disposable income, defined as $Y^n_t - T_t$, then

$$C_t = a + c(Y^n_t - T_t) \tag{4.3}$$

Where a is autonomous consumption and c the propensity to consume.

National saving is the sum of private saving, S_p, the difference between national income and consumption, and public saving, S_g, the difference between government revenue and government spending, Hence using equation (4.3) in an expression for national saving, and ignoring t time subscripts for simplicity, national saving can be expressed as

$$S = S_p + S_g = \left[Y^n - T - a - c(Y^n - T)\right] + \left[T - G\right] \tag{4.4}$$

From this expression, dS/dT = c. Hence it follows that for each dollar rise in income taxes that reduces the budget deficit by a dollar, national saving rises by only c × 100 cents in the dollar, as $0 \leq c \leq 1$.

Accordingly, the CAD would also narrow by less than the total reduction in the budget deficit induced by a discretionary income tax rise, other things equal. This provides an important qualification to the twin deficits proposition as it breaks the dollar-for-dollar link between public account and external account deficits. Moreover, for subsequent national income gains would be less than those obtained from the spending cuts option.

The deficits link would be further complicated if residents perceive income tax changes as temporary rather than permanent influences on their disposable income. For instance, if an income tax rise that lowered the budget deficit was seen as temporary and households maintained pre tax rise consumption levels, lower private saving would fully offset higher public saving.

If households ignored the tax rise, national saving and hence CAD_t would remain unchanged in the presence of a budget deficit as the overall relationship between national saving and investment is unaffected. Additionally, there are supply-side complications associated with income tax changes. These stem from possible work incentive effects affecting production which may offset their impact on income through the national saving channel.

Moreover, Ricardian effects are possible in the wake of fiscal expansions of any kind. In the extreme, though empirically unsupported case, a one-for-one offset of private consumption by households mindful of future tax obligations would obviate any link arising between the budget and external deficits in the first instance. Fiscal consolidation involving reduced public investment in the nature of productive infrastructure rather than public consumption would also reduce the CAD, but to the extent that this reduced the output-generating capacity of the economy, such cuts could lower subsequent income below potential.

In brief, this analysis shows how fiscal consolidation can be expansionary if it contracts public consumption expenditure in open economies experiencing high CADs and significant levels of foreign debt. By lowering expenditure relative to output, reduced public consumption, easily the largest component of total public spending in most economies, raises domestic savings relative to domestic investment, lowers an economy's external borrowing requirement, and hence raises national income.

Figure 4.3 can also be used to demonstrate that, for given investment opportunities, a rise in national saving due to a fall in autonomous consumption, shifts the expenditure schedule down. An increased household saving rate thereby reduces the CAD and raises national income in the medium term, consistent with the predictions of orthodox growth theory. Contrariwise, if household consumption rises, national saving falls which implies national income is subsequently less than otherwise due to higher servicing costs on a larger stock of borrowed funds.

Importantly, however, the rise in the CAD still allows net investment and subsequent national income to be higher than it would be in autarky, provided national saving remains positive. This of course presumes there are no problems intermediating both domestic and international funds through the economy's banking and financial system, an assumption further discussed in the concluding section.

Effective interest rate movements

Thus far, an invariant world interest rate has been assumed. However, international monetary conditions may suddenly change, leading to a higher or lower world interest rate. With reference to Figure 4.4, if there was a rise in the world interest rate, this implies a higher borrowing cost and a rise in the slope of the *FF* frontier. As a result, I_t and CAD_t would presently fall, with intertemporal consequences.

Static exchange rate expectations have also been assumed on the part of foreign investors purchasing the domestic currency denominated debt instruments issued by the host country to fund additional

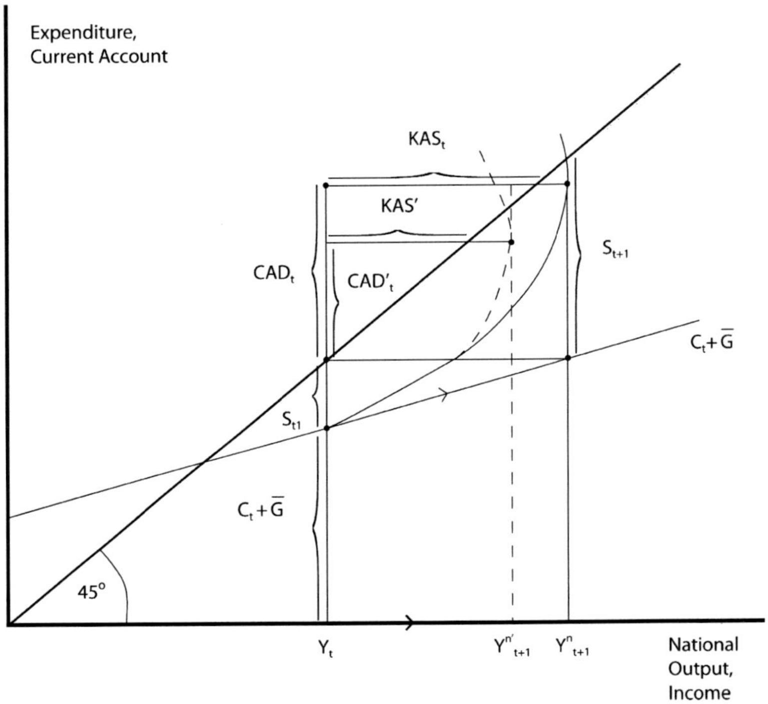

Figure 4.4 Increased effective borrowing rate

investment over domestic saving. Yet abstracting from other risk factors, these expectations may suddenly change if investors revise their exchange rate expectations.

For instance, if $e_t < e^e_{t+1}$, where the first term is the current exchange rate, defined as domestic currency units per foreign currency unit, and the second term is the spot exchange rate expected in the next period, then foreign investors would insist on a yield premium above the world interest rate equal to the expected depreciation, as suggested by uncovered interest parity:

$$i = i^* + \left(\frac{e^e_{t+1} - e_t}{e_t} \right) \tag{4.5}$$

Accordingly, the effective external borrowing rate would rise, steepening the slope of the *FF* frontier, as was the case with a rise in the exogenous foreign interest rate. Similarly, I_t and CAD_t would fall, as would Y^n_{t+1}. On the other hand, an expected currency appreciation would have the same effect as a fall in world interest rate, raising the CAD and national income in the short run.

The above analysis assumes that resident and foreign investors have identical expectations about the output-generating capacity of the additional investment suggested by the *FF* frontier. However, it is possible that foreign investors are less optimistic than resident investors, and perceive some degree of risk. Under these circumstances, the effective interest rate would be higher and the slope of the *FF* frontier steeper, such that the current account and growth in national income would be smaller.

Feasible limits for external deficits and debt

Financial markets and policymakers worry that sizeable external deficits and debt levels are unsustainable because due to inadequate domestic saving an economy may be incapable of servicing its external obligations when unsustainable limits have been reached. As economies approach such limits, they are exposed to sudden shifts in investor sentiment that may precipitate currency and financial crises and reduce economic growth (Adalet and Eichengreen 2005; Edwards 2005; Mann 2002).

Such developments have obvious macroeconomic implications as they affect financial stability, business conditions and industry competitiveness, although the form of the capital inflow may also be relevant in assessing external vulnerability. In particular, FDI, being long term by nature, is relatively more stable than indirect or portfolio capital inflows that may quickly reverse.

Sudden reversals of international portfolio investment experienced by East Asian economies in 1997–8, for instance, imposed short-term economic, social and political costs through large exchange rate depreciations, financial distress, higher domestic interest rates, lost output-increased unemployment and higher inflation.

For this reason, external imbalances and debt levels feature prominently in empirical studies of the primary causes of currency crises, although to date no consensus exists on their explanatory power. Some studies suggest that external imbalances significantly contribute to currency crises, whereas others conclude the opposite.

Numerous authors have interpreted the notion of external sustainability by invoking intertemporal precepts (see, for instance, Milesi-Ferreti and Razin 1996). This has involved testing current account movements to see if they meet a solvency requirement based on permanent income approaches to consumption and saving. However, no study to date has primarily focused on investment rather than consumption to define the upper limits that CADs and foreign debt levels may reach relative to GDP. Nor has any attempt been made to ascertain an economy's proximity to such bounds at any particular time.

We now further examine the significance of external account imbalances by analysing the macroeconomic conditions that define feasible limits for CADs, and for foreign debt to GDP levels, respectively. In preview, the theory suggests that the quantum of productive domestic investment essentially defines the feasible limit for CADs at any time, whereas an economy's capital to output ratio ultimately sets the limit for its foreign debt to GDP ratio. We can then ascertain the proximity to feasible limits of select advanced economies that have experienced significant external deficits and debt levels by comparing actual and estimated limits since 1990.

For an advanced economy, a limit on persistent foreign borrowing conceivably exists when an economy's domestic saving shrinks to zero. Beyond that point, additional foreign borrowing must fund additional consumption. This can not continue indefinitely, so the economy is inevitably unable to cover the total costs on invested foreign capital.

The following analysis explores and extends this basic solvency condition. However, in so doing, it abstracts from complications that arise, especially for developing economies, from the intermediation of funds between foreign lenders and ultimate domestic borrowers through the economy's banking and finance sector. Such financial sector problems are specifically related to the phenomena of adverse selection, where very poor credit risks obtain foreign loans, and moral hazard, where domestic borrowers undertake excessively risky activities.

The basic solvency condition for an advanced external debtor economy requires that the difference between domestic production, net of capital stock depreciation, and household consumption plus government spending, $Y_{t+1}-(C_{t+1}+G_{t+1})$, be at least sufficient to meet the servicing costs of foreign debt, i^*F_t, where F_t is the stock of foreign debt at time t. That is,

$$Y_{t+1} - (C_{t+1} + G_{t+1}) \geq i^*F_t \tag{4.6}$$

Net national output exceeds national income in debtor economies according to:

$$Y^{r}_{t-1} = Y_{t+1} - i^*F_t \tag{4.7}$$

where Y is net national output and Y^n is national income net of external debt servicing costs. This can be rewritten as

$$Y^{n}_{t+1} - C_{t+1} - G_{t+1} \geq 0 \tag{4.8}$$

or

$$S_{t+1} \geq 0 \tag{4.8a}$$

This fundamental solvency condition has implications for the size of the CAD, which over any period equates to the economy's saving-investment imbalance. The critical point beyond which a national problem arises is when residents' aggregate net saving disappears. Beyond this point, the domestic economy has to borrow externally to fund consumption in excess of income. The economy is then literally 'living beyond its means'.

In the national balance sheet, increased foreign liabilities in the form of debt are then no longer matched by the accumulation of real capital, as when foreign finance incrementally funds domestic investment for given positive saving. Under such circumstances only key currency economies may be able to fund excess consumption temporarily due to their strong creditworthiness.

Maximum feasible external deficits

External funding of consumption is unsustainable because no future income is attributable to any excess of consumption over present income. This condition is consistent with the No Ponzi Game condition that must be satisfied for intertemporal solvency. On the contrary, higher foreign debt incurred has to be serviced, which reduces future income. Accordingly, this suggests there is a maximum feasible

CAD, $CAD_{MAX\ t}$, that can be reached. It is simply defined by private investment undertaken by profit maximizing firms, net of capital depreciation.

$$CAD_{MAX\ t} = I_t \tag{4.9}$$

Figure 4.5 illustrates how a CAD that is solely defined by the volume of investment expenditure is theoretically sustainable. As in the previous analysis, the horizontal axis of this 45° diagram measures net national product, the output of final goods and services, made available for sale at home and abroad less capital depreciation, as well as national income defined as net output less income paid abroad. Assuming a given labour force, real output expands as the capital stock increases. Alternatively, the analysis could be undertaken by expressing all national accounting aggregates in per worker terms.

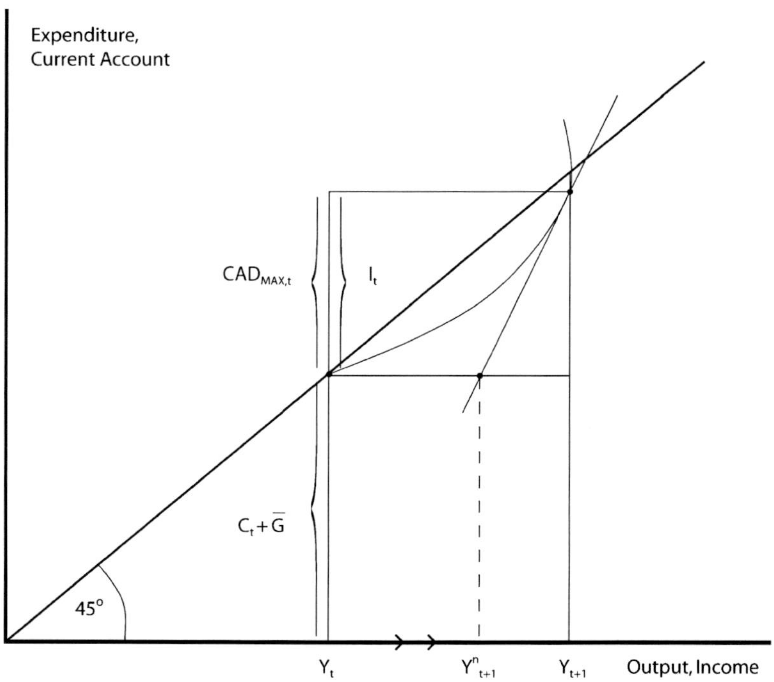

Figure 4.5 The maximum feasible CAD

As before, the vertical axis measures private consumption, public spending, private investment, national saving and the current account balance. Total spending, or absorption, in period t is the vertical sum of $C_t + G_t + I_t$, comprising expenditure by resident entities on domestic and imported goods and services, and where G_t represents government expenditure in the nature of consumption which detracts from national saving.

Hence, excess national expenditure over output again determines the size of the CAD.

Equivalently, CAD_t is the excess of investment, I_t, over national saving, S_t, at that same income level, assuming the pre-existing stock of foreign debt is zero. For a given value of output determined in period t, national saving varies as private and public consumption rise or fall. Normally, $Y_t - C_t - G_t = S_t > 0$. However, if $Y_t = C_t - G_t$, then $S_t = 0$, as shown at the point on the 45^0 directly above national income.

The investment opportunities frontier governs private investment, conveying again how additional capital expenditure in one period enlarges national output and income in the next.

$$Y_{t+1} = Y_t + g(I_t) \tag{4.10}$$

Investment depends positively on capital productivity, reflected in the slope of the investment opportunities frontier, and negatively on the exogenous world interest rate. Assuming static exchange rate expectations and abstracting from other risk factors that limit capital mobility, the exogenous world interest rate also determines the domestic interest rate, i.

Additional net investment undertaken by rational forward-looking agents and the associated rise in external liabilities enables higher subsequent production of Y_{t+1}. National income of Y^n_{t+1} is less than Y_{t+1} since the capital inflow in period t must be serviced at the given interest rate. The increase in national income attributable to CAD_t is $Y^n_{t+1} - Y_t$.

In sum, the CAD enables faster economic growth of national output and national income than otherwise, provided the return on foreign-funded capital exceeds the external debt servicing cost even at the maximum limit. Moreover, this analysis implies that an external deficit approaching its feasible limit can be narrowed directly through a reduction in government spending.

Feasible external debt limits

The maximum feasible CAD also suggests an upper bound for an economy's CAD that has a stock counterpart for foreign debt. The dynamic equations are:

$$F_{t+1} = F_t + CAD_{t+1} \tag{4.11}$$

$$K_{t+1} = K_t + I_{t+1} \tag{4.12}$$

where (4.11) and (4.12) are simply accounting relations that combine flows and stocks intertemporally.

Let k denote the economy's present capital–output ratio:

$$k_t = \frac{K_t}{Y_t} \tag{4.13}$$

Assume dynamic stability is characterized by a stable foreign debt to income ratio:

$$\frac{F_{t+1}}{Y_{t+1}} = \frac{F_t}{Y_t} \quad \text{or} \quad F_{t+1} = \frac{Y_{t+1}}{Y_t} F_t \tag{4.14}$$

For a given capital to output ratio,

$$k_{t+1} = k_t \Rightarrow \frac{K_{t+1}}{Y_{t+1}} = \frac{K_t}{Y_t} \Rightarrow \frac{Y_{t+1}}{Y_t} = \frac{K_{t+1}}{K_t} \tag{4.15}$$

Rearranging (4.14)

$$K_{t+1} - K_t = I_{t+'1} \tag{4.16}$$

Substituting (4.11) into (4.14),

$$F_t + CAD_t = \frac{K_{t+1}}{K_t} F_t \tag{4.17}$$

$$CAD_{t+1} = F_t \left(\frac{K_{t+1}}{K_t} - 1 \right) \tag{4.18}$$

$$CAD_{t+1} = \frac{F_{t+1}}{K_t}(K_{t+1} - K_t) \tag{4.19}$$

$$CAD_{t+1} = (I_{t+1})\frac{F_{t+1}}{K_t} \tag{4.20}$$

Since $CAD_{MAX\ t} = I_t$,

$$CAD_{MAX\ t+1} = (I_{t+1})\frac{F_t}{K_t} = CAD_{MAX\ t+1}\frac{F_t}{K_t} \tag{4.21}$$

Hence,

$$\frac{F_t}{K_t} = 1 \qquad \text{or} \qquad F_t = K_t \tag{4.22}$$

This means that a continuous series of maximum feasible CADs eventually results in foreigners holding claims to the economy's entire capital stock. Consequently, the maximum feasible limit in terms of the foreign debt to GDP ratio is ultimately equal to *k*, the capital–output ratio.

Benchmark estimates for advanced borrower economies

The foregoing theory suggests straightforward empirical measures for assessing how close deficit and indebted economies are to their limit values. In the case of current account imbalances, it implies that, *ceteris paribus*, economies with an external deficit may be able to tolerate a rise up to the extent of their positive net saving. Put differently, for given domestic investment opportunities domestic consumption could increase to eliminate net saving, thereby allowing domestic capital accumulation to be fully funded by foreign saving.

Charts 4.1–3 plot estimates of maximum feasible deficits for three advanced Asia-Pacific economies – the US, Australia and New Zealand – that have experienced significant CADs as a proportion of GDP since the 1990s. In the charts based on IMF national and external accounts data, the vertical distance between the value of actual deficits and maximum feasible deficits is equivalent to national saving, net of income paid abroad. The data reveal that external deficits recorded over this period were generally well below feasible limits, most recent New Zealand experience being the exception.

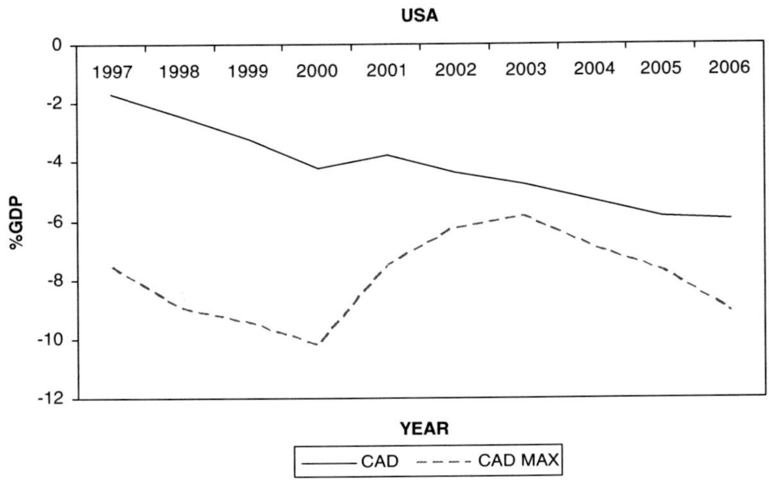

Chart 4.1 Feasible external imbalance, USA

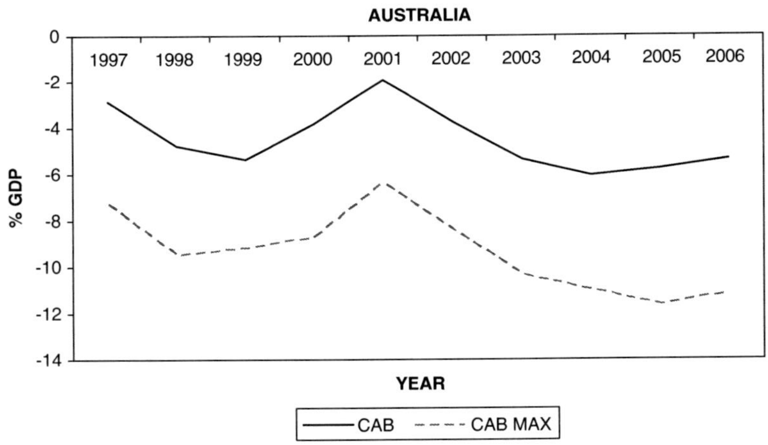

Chart 4.2 Feasible external imbalance, Australia

Foreign saving could temporarily fund excess domestic public and private consumption during periods of recession, allowing actual deficits to exceed feasible deficits as defined above, consistent with the consumption-smoothing role that the CAD may play in the short

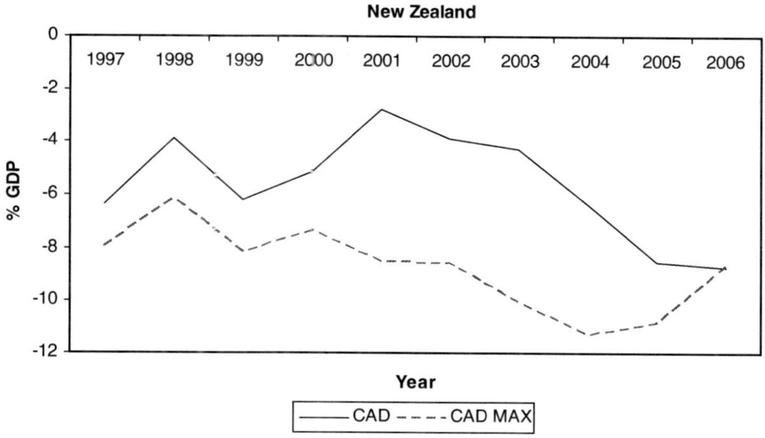

Chart 4.3 Feasible external imbalance, New Zealand

run (see Ghosh and Ostry 1995; Mansoorian 1998), but from which this approach has largely abstracted.

It is also likely that recorded net saving data are understated in advanced economies to the extent that national accounting convention treats most public expenditure on education and health as consumption. Yet such spending may alternatively be perceived as investment in human capital, and if reclassified as such in the national accounts, would yield higher measures of national saving. This would mean recorded saving rates and hence feasible limits would be higher than shown in the charts.

With regard to feasible foreign debt limits, we saw above that these were ultimately determined by the capital to output ratio, a readily available statistic for many debtor economies. For advanced economies, the k ratio ranges between 2.5–3.0. This implies a feasible upper limit for the external debt to GDP ratio of approximately 250–300 per cent for advanced economies. On the other hand, emerging economies tend to have lower k ratios, suggesting their maximum feasible limits are accordingly lower.

Qualifications

These limits are only supposed to be broadly indicative however and are subject to qualification. For instance, by focusing on saving, investment, national income, the capital stock and foreign debt, this chapter has abstracted from the state of the economy's financial system and the role it plays as the conduit for channelling domestic and foreign saving to the most productive investment opportunities.

In reality, information problems, such as asymmetric information between ultimate borrowers and lenders may prevent the optimal allocation of saving. In turn, this implies the additional income generating capacity of foreign-funded capital accumulation may not be as strong as theory suggests. Developing and emerging economies that experience large external deficits are also more vulnerable to sudden capital flow reversals than advanced economies, if foreign investors perceive their financial systems as poorly developed with inadequate prudential supervision.

Furthermore, by focusing on saving and investment rather than exports and imports as the measure of external imbalance, the modelling approach outlined above abstracts from the relative share of tradables relative to non-tradables in the economy. Obviously, the greater the proportion of GDP that entails tradable goods, the easier it would be for an economy to increase its current credits by a significant amount. For this reason, the ratio of the deficit to current credits provides useful supplementary information about the external position.

The above factors imply that the proposed limit measures for CADs and foreign debt may overstate the bounds of external sustainability, especially for emerging economies. At the same time, however, the proposed maximum CAD measure may understate the feasible limit as it does not allow for consumption smoothing during recessions, a phenomenon unsustainable beyond the short term.

Nonetheless the suggested limits would seem to improve on scant existing means to assess external sustainability, such as the arbitrary 5 per cent of GDP rule. They enable assessment of how near actual CADs and external debt levels are to unsustainable values, especially for advanced economies.

Conclusion

This chapter provided an international macroeconomic rendition of the familiar Keynesian cross-diagram showing how consumption, investment and the current account jointly affect successive national income outcomes. This framework is used to analyse the effects on the current account and national income of changes in the fiscal stance arising from altered government spending and taxing and their implications for the 'twin deficits' hypothesis.

Employing standard macroeconomic tools and relations, it yields results contrary to standard interpretations of CADs and the impact of fiscal activism on national income over the short and medium terms. Contrary to closed economy Keynesian theory, fiscal contraction can raise national income in the medium term. For instance, reduced public consumption narrows a budget deficit and increases national saving relative to investment, with subsequent national income gains.

Moreover, the model yields results at odds with the MF approach in which output remains aggregate demand driven and where fiscal deficits are either countercyclical or ineffective, depending on the exchange rate regime. Budget deficits arising from increased public consumption are never contractionary in Keynesian demand-oriented models, as they are shown to be above.

As an intertemporal approach, there are key points of difference with the two-period Fisherian approach to the open economy, based on utility and profit maximizing saving and investment behaviour (Frenkel and Razin 1996; Makin 2003; Obstfeld and Rogoff 1996). Unlike the conventional intertemporal paradigm, this framework invokes standard behavioural relations with the output-expenditure gap at the centre of the explanation of medium-term income variation.

Moreover, contrary to the two-period Fisherian approach to the open economy, the above framework shows the medium-run effects of internal and external shocks on the current account and national income over a sequence of discrete time intervals. While some results are consistent with precepts of long-run growth theory, it differs from that theory through its emphasis on open economy variables and medium-term income determination.

The above framework helps us understand why large CADs experienced over recent decades by advanced economies such as Australia, the US and New Zealand were easily sustained and coincided with periods of strong economic growth and very low saving in those economies. Foreign investors evidently concluded period by period, that the excess national expenditure they funded over output, as reflected in historically high CADs, was sufficiently productive.

Current account imbalances and external liability positions across major trading areas have changed markedly over past decades in many advanced and emerging economies. Yet an unresolved question about external deficits and debt is what fundamentally determines the bounds of sustainability. This chapter has also aimed to answer that question by proposing feasible limits that CADs and external debt levels may reach based on capital-theoretic relationships.

In summary, it contends that a feasible limit is reached for an economy's CAD when its net domestic saving reaches zero. Beyond this point, the economy would be borrowing externally to fund consumption in excess of its national income that would not be persistently possible. Hence, an economy's productive investment opportunities alone set a feasible upper limit for the external deficit.

The economy's capital-output ratio then ultimately sets the limit of its foreign debt ratio. Improved understanding of the feasibility of external positions would improve exchange rate forecasting by financial markets and enable policymakers to make better judgements when setting fiscal and monetary policies.

References

Adalet, M. and Eichengreen B. (2005) 'Current Account Reversals: Always a Problem?' in R. Clarida (ed.) *G7 Current Account Imbalances: Sustainability and Adjustment*, The University of Chicago Press, Chicago.

Alexander, S. (1952) 'Effects of a Devaluation on a Trade Balance', *IMF Staff Papers*, 1 (2), 263–78.

Edwards, S. (2005) 'Is the U.S. Current Account Deficit Sustainable? And If Not, How Costly is Adjustment Likely to Be?', *NBER Working Paper*, No. 11541.

Eichengreen, B. (2002) *Financial Crises and What to Do about Them*, Oxford University Press, Oxford, UK.

Fisher, I. (1930) *The Theory of Interest*, Macmillan, New York.

Fleming, J. (1962) 'Domestic Financial Policies under Fixed and Under Floating Exchange Rates", *IMF Staff Papers*, 12, 369–80.

Frenkel, J. and Razin, A. (1996) *Fiscal Policies and Growth in the World Economy*, MIT Press, Cambridge and London.

Ghosh, A. and Ostry, J. (1995) 'The Current Account in Developing Countries: A Perspective from the Consumption-Smoothing Approach', *The World Bank Economic Review*, 9, 305–34.

International Monetary Fund (2004) *International Financial Statistics*, International Monetary Fund, Washington.

Makin, A. J. (1994) *International Capital Mobility and External Account Determination*, Macmillan Press, Basingstoke, UK.

Makin, A. (2003) *Global Finance and the Macroeconomy*, Palgrave Macmillan, Basingstoke, UK.

Mann, C. (2002) 'Perspectives on the US Current Account Deficit and Sustainability', *Journal of Economic Perspectives*, 16 (3), 131–52.

Mansoorian, A. (1998) 'Habits and Durability in Consumption, and the Dynamics of the Current Account', *Journal of International Economics*, 44, 69–82.

Milesi-Ferreti, G. and Razin, A. (1996) 'Current Account Sustainability', *Princeton Studies in International Finance No. 81*, International Financial Section, Department of Economics, Princeton University, Princeton, NJ.

Mundell, R. (1963) 'Capital Mobility and Stabilization Policy under Fixed and Flexible Exchange Rates', *Canadian Journal of Economics and Political Science*, 29, 475–85.

Obstfeld, M. and Rogoff, K. (1996) *Foundations of International Macroeconomics*, MIT Press, Boston.

Sachs, J. (1981) 'The Current Account and Macroeconomic Adjustment in the 1970's', *Brookings Papers on Economics Activity*, 1, 201–82.

Solow, R. (1956) 'A Contribution to the Theory of Economic Growth', *Quarterly Journal of Economics* 70, 65–94.

Swan, T. (1956) 'Economic Growth and Capital Accumulation', *Economic Record*, 32 (November), 334–61.

5
Capital Mobility and National Income

Introduction

Since the demise of the Bretton Woods system of exchange rate management and consequent dismantling of a broad range of exchange controls, there has been enormous growth in the volume of international capital flows to advanced and emerging economies around the globe. Meanwhile, liberalized capital accounts have increased emerging economies' financial vulnerability to sudden international capital flow reversals of the magnitude witnessed in East Asia and other developing economies in the late 1990s.

In view of the economic and financial distress that short-term capital flow reversals may cause, particularly in light of financial crises, such as the Asian crisis of 1997–8, many economists (see, for example, Bhagwati 1998; Rodrik 1998; Wade 1998) favour the retention of capital controls for emerging economies, a policy position that implicitly presumes the costs of capital mobility exceed the benefits of capital mobility. Such thinking also underlies advocacy of the well-known Tobin tax (Tobin 1978).

The presumption that international merchandise trade was to be encouraged after the War through a supranational institution like the General Agreement on Tariffs and Trade, the WTO predecessor, did not extend beyond trade in goods to include freer international trade in saving or financial services.

Indeed, there was widespread antipathy towards free international capital movements at the time, as reflected, for instance, in a statement by John Maynard Keynes, an architect of the Bretton

Woods monetary system, that 'nothing is more certain than that the movement of capital funds must be regulated' (Keynes 1941).

Though exchange controls have been progressively dismantled since the early 1970s, their removal in emerging economies was accelerated significantly from the early 1990s, according to an index of capital controls devised by the IMF. Institutional investors in advanced economies increasingly became more aware of opportunities to diversify portfolios through the 1990s and more internationalized banks were readier to lend in emerging markets.

Interestingly, the IMF now promotes capital account liberalization for member economies, in contrast to its Bretton Woods era policy of sanctioning the earlier wide-ranging measures that restricted international capital flows. The size of current account balances around the world reveal the extent of recent international trade in saving, those countries running surpluses being net capital exporters and those with deficits, net importers.

In theory, greater international capital market integration can confer economy-wide benefits on advanced and emerging economies alike. For instance, international capital flows supplement domestic saving in recipient economies, allow more investment and higher economic growth in regions where profitability is higher, while simultaneously enabling savers in international creditor economies to gain from higher returns and portfolio diversification.

However, at the same time, it can increase the vulnerability of host economies to sharp international portfolio switches and accompanying capital flow reversals of the magnitude witnessed in East Asia and other emerging economies in the late 1990s. In light of the social, political and economic disruption that capital flow reversals can cause in the short term, it is not surprising that the earlier Keynesian-inspired aversion to highly mobile capital resurfaced through calls for the reimposition of Bretton Woods style capital controls for emerging economies.

Contemporary advocates of capital controls stress the differences between free financial flows and free trade in goods and services. These differences include the far greater volatility of financial asset prices compared to prices of goods and services, problems related to information asymmetries between borrowers and lenders and poor bank management. As a result, many economists presume the apparent costs of allowing international capital mobility outweigh the benefits.

Various theoretical approaches show that net capital inflow can allow more domestic capital accumulation, thereby raising the economy's overall productive capacity and in principle this yields greater national income. See, for instance, the neoclassical foreign investment model (MacDougall 1960; Grubel 1987; Ruffin 1984) and the Fisherian intertemporal model of international borrowing (Makin 2003). In short, if the productivity of the extra physical capital acquired through foreign borrowing exceeds the servicing costs on that borrowing, then national income can grow faster than otherwise.

Questions that hitherto have not been adequately addressed in the international literature are, how do we account for the contribution of foreign capital to national income growth, how can we identify it, and how significant is it empirically? To answer these important questions, this chapter first extends loanable funds analysis to assess the macroeconomic benefits of capital mobility and then invokes growth-accounting precepts to estimate capital flow related national income gains for Australia. Australia, one of the world's largest international borrowers for its size, makes a useful case study with its extensive high-quality macroeconomic and international investment data.

Capital mobility is measured with reference to the standard interest parity conditions, as well as the extent of the correlation between domestic saving and investment proposed by Feldstein and Horioka (1980). This stream of research links saving, investment and international capital flows and supposes that evidence of high correlation between domestic saving and domestic investment is indicative of low international capital mobility. However, numerous subsequent studies have shown that capital mobility by this measure has increased more recently, though by less than may be expected with highly liberalized international capital markets.

While considerable attention has also been given to examining how capital mobility affects the potency of monetary and fiscal policy as stabilization tools, relatively little attention has been paid to examining how capital immobility attributable to capital controls directly affects national income.

In interpreting the economic significance of international borrowing and lending for an open economy's national income, it is necessary to distinguish between long-run and short-run effects. However, first consider the significance of external account imbalances when cross-border returns equalize in the very long run.

Foreign capital and long-run national income

We first derive long-run equilibrium conditions in continuous time before shifting attention to period-to-period changes.

Assume GDP in real terms, *Y*, is generated by a standard production function of the form,

$$Y = f(A(t), K(t), \ell(t)) \tag{5.1}$$

where A is multifactor productivity, K is the capital stock and ℓ is hours worked by resident workers. On the aggregate demand side, available output is consumed or devoted to capital accumulation.

Differentiating (5.1) with respect to time

$$\begin{aligned}\dot{Y} &= \frac{\partial f}{\partial A}\dot{A} + \frac{\partial f}{\partial K}\dot{K} + \frac{\partial f}{\partial \ell}\dot{\ell} \\ &= \frac{\partial f}{\partial K}\dot{K} + \Gamma\end{aligned} \tag{5.2}$$

where $\Gamma = \frac{\partial f}{\partial A}\dot{A} + \frac{\partial f}{\partial \ell}\dot{\ell}$.

By accounting definition, national income in an open economy, Y^n, diverges from national output by net income earned from abroad, less capital stock depreciation.

For a borrower economy

$$Y^n = Y - r^* F - dK \tag{5.3}$$

where F is the accumulated stock of external debt, r* is the exogenous real world interest rate, d is the rate of depreciation and K is the total capital stock.

Differentiating (5.3) with respect to time,

$$\dot{Y}^n = \dot{Y} - \dot{r}^* F - r^* \dot{F} - d\dot{K} \tag{5.4}$$

Assuming the economy is too small to affect a given world interest rate (so that $\dot{r}^* = 0$) and substituting (5.2) and $\dot{K} = I$ (domestic investment) into (5.4)

$$\dot{Y}^n = \left(\frac{\partial f}{\partial K} - d\right) I + \Gamma - r^* \dot{F} \tag{5.5}$$

In the very long run, the net marginal product of capital in use domestically would equate in equilibrium to the real domestic and world interest rates with unrestricted international borrowing and lending. Hence,

$$\left(\frac{\partial f}{\partial K} - d\right) = r = r^* \tag{5.6}$$

It follows from national accounting that the current account balance and accumulated foreign debt, F, of a borrower country (or loans outstanding, Q, for a creditor country) reflect the difference between domestic investment, I, and saving, S. A CAD raises external debt for borrower economies, such that

$$(I - S) = CAD = \dot{F} \tag{5.7}$$

Substituting (5.6) and (5.7) into (5.5) therefore yields

$$\dot{Y}^n = \overset{*}{r}S + \Gamma \tag{5.8}$$

For a creditor economy,

$$\dot{Y}^n = \left(\frac{\partial f}{\partial K} - d\right)I + \Gamma + \overset{*}{r}\dot{Q} \tag{5.9}$$

and

$$(S - I) = CAS = \dot{Q} \tag{5.10}$$

Substituting (5.6) and (5.10) into (5.9) also yields expression (5.8). This provides an interesting general long run result. It is that when the marginal product of capital equates to the real domestic and foreign interest rate, whether an economy has an external deficit or surplus becomes irrelevant. The economy's growth rate, ι, is derived by dividing (5.8) by Y^n

$$\frac{\dot{Y}^n}{Y^n} = \frac{\overset{*}{r}S + \Gamma}{Y^n} = \iota \tag{5.11}$$

Hence, according to (5.11) a small economy's growth is essentially determined by fundamentals at home such as national saving, labour force growth and labour productivity and multifactor productivity, regardless of the economy's international borrower or lender status.

Turning now to the shorter term, we need to recognize that national income gains arise for borrower and lender economies, while discrepant rates of return are equalized on the path towards the very long-run equilibria just modelled.

An extended loanable funds framework

In the short run, international capital flows are not purely financial phenomena for they reflect international borrowing and lending which is ultimately tied to economic factors that determine saving and investment behaviour. Although intertemporal open economy models recognize this they usually assume perfect capital mobility prevails for longer-term flows to highlight linkages between international capital flows, intertemporal consumption, saving, and investment.

In what follows, consistent with the intertemporal approach, capital mobility is related to saving, investment and the transnational flow of funds. However, unlike standard intertemporal models, the analysis is limited to short-run effects so as to identify the welfare costs of capital controls explicitly.

Capital autarky versus perfect capital mobility

First, we assume autarky and that domestic saving, S, the residual from national income after private and public consumption plans have been satisfied, is fixed. Total investment spending, I, over a given period is funded out of available saving, with the real interest rate performing the balancing role.

The demand for loanable funds is a function of the real interest rate, and in equilibrium under autarky the domestic interest rate, r^A, is such that the market for loanable funds clears and investment equals saving. Consequently, the domestic saving schedule is drawn vertically, whereas the net domestic demand for investment purposes is a derived demand, depicted as a downward sloping schedule in interest rate-loanable funds space in Figure 5.1. This analysis restricts attention to borrowing, although foreign capital inflow also of course includes foreign ownership of equities issued by resident enterprises.

With perfect capital mobility, a small economy's domestic borrowing requirement over and above available domestic saving is fully met by foreign lenders (investors) at the exogenous real world interest rate, r^*. Therefore, let L^* be the foreign lending schedule, which is flat

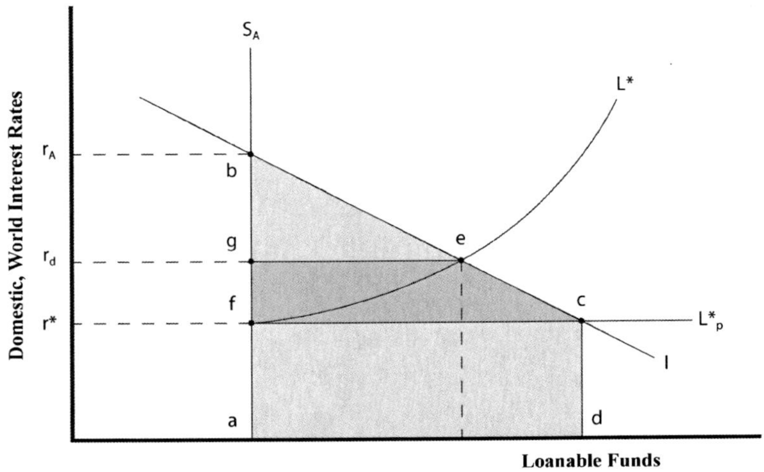

Figure 5.1 International capital mobility and macroeconomic welfare

when foreign lending schedule is infinitely elastic. The market for loanable funds must clear, so with perfect capital mobility

$$I(r^*) = S_A + L_P^* \tag{5.12}$$

where from the home economy perspective, L_P^* is foreign capital inflow in the form of borrowing.

Domestic investment therefore exceeds domestic saving at r* to the extent of foreign borrowing. This *ex ante* foreign borrowing requirement is shown by distance *fc* in the figure. Hence, if external debt is initially nil, it reaches level *fc* by period end. As the equilibrium real world interest rate is lower than the real autarky interest rate, investment under autarky is always lower than when international borrowing is permitted.

Here we abstract from the effect that changing exchange rate expectations have on interest differentials by assuming that foreign lending is denominated in the currency of the lenders, thereby nullifying exchange rate risk from foreigners' perspective.

This is consistent with the practice of advanced economy lending to emerging economies, the bulk of whose loans are denominated in foreign currency terms. Alternatively, it is possible to assume that exchange rate expectations are static throughout. International capital mobility is therefore perfect in this context if foreign lenders satisfy the excess domestic demand for funds and real interest parity prevails.

Short-run national income gains from foreign borrowing

Figure 5.1 also reveals how foreign borrowing raises national income, consistent with the neoclassical foreign investment model. The marginal product of capital determines the slope of the investment demand schedule, so that given r*, extra units of foreign-financed capital, times their marginal product, add to GDP to the extent of the area *abcd*.

However, of that the rectangular area, *afcd* is paid to foreign lenders, leaving a net national income gain equivalent to the triangular area *fbc*. International capital mobility therefore enables lower domestic interest rates and higher national income, provided the productivity of the extra foreign-financed capital exceeds its cost. Interest paid to foreign investors is equal to r**ad*.

The welfare costs of capital immobility

Yet if foreign lenders perceive high foreign debt as a sign of heightened country risk and diminished creditworthiness, they demand an interest premium, ρ, to compensate. This explains the convex foreign lending schedule rising from the world interest rate, r*, in Figure 5.1.

The more averse foreign investors are to rising foreign debt, the steeper the slope of the L* schedule and the higher the risk premium and interest differential will be. At some point, foreigners could judge the level of lending risk prohibitive, such that the foreign-lending schedule becomes vertical.

Hence, the foreign lending schedule is no longer perfectly elastic with the risk premium an increasing function of the stock of borrowing outstanding Of course, if the initial level of debt exceeded zero, the foreign lending schedule would rise from a point above r*. Alternatively, the risk premium, always positive, is the difference between the interest rate foreign lenders demand under imperfect capital mobility and the interest rate r* under perfect capital mobility. Hence,

$$r_d = r^* + \rho \tag{5.13}$$

where r_d is the equilibrium domestic interest rate.

Under imperfect capital mobility, investment is lower than with perfect capital mobility. Foreign debt related risk therefore causes macroeconomic welfare losses since potential national income gains from foreign borrowing are not realized. With reference to Figure 5.1, the welfare loss is area *fgec*.

Note, however, that foreign borrowing still confers a net welfare gain of *gbe*, provided the equilibrium interest rate allowing for risk is less than the autarky rate. Although international capital immobility limits an economy's growth, it also follows that the higher the interest risk premium, the slower foreign debt accumulates, suggesting that rising interest risk premia stabilize foreign debt levels.

Capital controls

In the above benchmark cases, foreign investors loaned funds through their purchases of debt instruments, without official restrictions of any kind imposed by the borrower economies. We now examine the macroeconomic welfare costs of imposing such restrictions. In practice, such controls range from those aimed at limiting the quantum of capital inflows to those in the form of taxes on capital inflows.

What becomes evident is that irrespective of the type of capital control, the minimum lending rate demanded by foreign lenders, or alternatively the minimum yield expected on bonds issued by the borrowing economy, will always be higher than the prevailing world interest rate, with adverse implications for national income.

Quantitative restrictions

First we consider the welfare costs of measures that restrict the quantum of capital inflows. The most common means by which the domestic monetary authorities may limit capital inflows is through mandatory unremunerated reserve requirements (URR). In the past, URR's have been most notably implemented by Chile, but also by monetary authorities in Argentina, Brazil, Columbia, Costa Rica, Czech Republic and Mexico.

A URR requires that a set percentage of funds borrowed from abroad be deposited with the central bank for a minimum period. As no interest is paid on the deposit, this effectively makes the reserve requirement an implicit tax on capital inflows. Under the Chilean

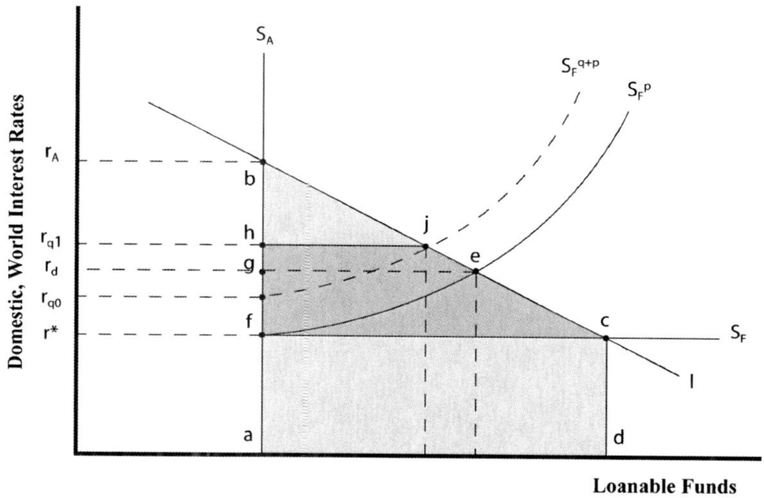

Figure 5.2 Macroeconomic welfare effects of unremunerated reserve requirements

system, foreign investors also had the option of paying the central bank an amount equal to the forgone interest without actually depositing funds, making the tax on capital flows explicit. (See Neely (1999) and Ulan (2000) for related discussion.)

Again, if investors continue to be averse to rising external indebtedness, the equilibrium interest rate will be r_{q_1}, inclusive of a risk premium, and the macroeconomic welfare effects will be as shown in Figure 5.2 above. The welfare loss from capital immobility is area *fhjc*, whereas the net gain compared with the autarky state is area *hbj*.

Taxes on foreign lending

Alternatively, capital controls may be in the form of explicit proportional taxes on principal loaned or interest earned by foreign lenders (sometimes called withholding taxes). Moreover, if foreign investors remain averse to the economy's rising external indebtedness, as discussed earlier, the equilibrium domestic interest rate will be r_{t1} as shown in Figure 5.3. The loss specifically due to the tax on capital outflows is the foregone national income *hjcf* less the taxation revenue gain for the economy, approximated by *hjmk*.

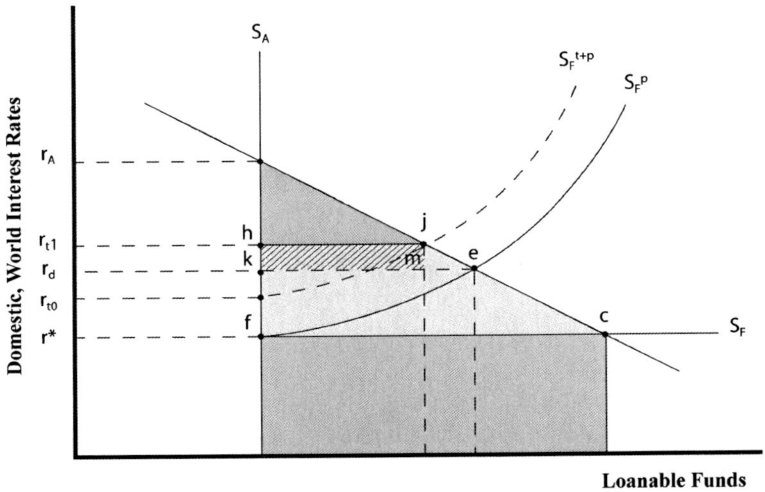

Figure 5.3 Welfare effects of taxes on capital inflows

Other things equal, this loss is less than would arise under a URR capital control regime.

It has been assumed implicitly that capital controls are not evaded, although empirical evidence suggests that evasion by emerging international borrower and lender economies in practice has been widespread (see Dooley 1996). Moreover, the above framework has abstracted from financial institutions and financial intermediation where, in reality, problems can arise due to information asymmetries between domestic borrowers and international lenders, as well as moral hazard problems stemming from official guarantees to lenders, explicit and implicit.

The contribution of foreign capital to national income

Ultimately the difference between the real marginal product of capital and the cost of borrowing abroad drives international capital flows and a useful distinction is that between home-funded and foreign-funded capital accumulation. For international borrower economies the real capital stock comprises capital funded by domestic saving plus additional capital accumulated through the use of external borrowing.

Hence, as originally proposed in Makin (2003) the macroeconomic production function may now be respecified as

$$Y = f(A, K^d, K^*, \ell) \tag{5.14}$$

where K^d is that part of the total domestic capital stock that has been funded by domestic saving and K^* is that part of the total domestic capital stock has been foreign financed.

By totally differentiating this open economy production function, the sources of increased GDP in the short run are shown to be

$$dY = f_A dA + f_K dK + f_{K^*} dK^* + f_\ell d\ell \tag{5.15}$$

where $f_{A,K,K^*,\ell}$ denotes the derivative of Y with respect to A, K, K*, ℓ.

For economies that are net borrowers, national output and national disposable income diverge to the extent of net income paid abroad. Hence,

$$Y^n = Y - r^* K^* \tag{5.16}$$

where Y^n is national disposable income and r^* is the effective servicing cost of foreign capital (inclusive of dividends) on external liabilities. So,

$$dY^n = dY - (r^* dK^* + dr^* K^*) \tag{5.17}$$

The effective interest rate paid to foreigners may vary from interval to interval as world interest rates fluctuate or as any risk premium varies through time.

From (5.15) and (5.17), the sources of national income growth can therefore be shown as

$$dY^n = \{f_A dA + f_L d\ell + f_K dK\} + \left\{f_{K^*} dK^* - (r^* dK^* + dr^* K^*)\right\} \tag{5.18}$$

The first set of braces captures the domestic sources of growth whereas the second set includes the foreign sources of central interest. Hence, national income gains can be attributed to domestic sources and foreign sources, such that

National Income Growth = *Domestic Contribution* + *Foreign Contribution*
(%) (%) (%)

To estimate the net contribution of foreign capital, it is necessary from (5.18) to derive values in real terms for each of the variables in the expression

$$(f_{K^*} - r^*)dK^* - dr^*K^* \tag{5.19}$$

where K* represents the capital funded from abroad.

Since foreign borrowing is usually intermediated through the commercial banking system of the economy, it is reasonable to assume that the productivity of capital in use domestically is invariant to the source of its funding. Therefore,

$$f_K = f_{K^*} \tag{5.20}$$

Next, we assume output is generated by a Cobb-Douglas function of the form

$$Y = AK^{\alpha}\ell^{1-\alpha} \tag{5.21}$$

where α is the share of capital in national income.

The Cobb-Douglas function remains a popular specification of the production process in international studies and this form is appropriate if the division of national income between capital and labour has been roughly constant over an extended period of time. As we will see shortly, this indeed has been the experience for Australia over the past decade.

When differentiated with respect to capital, the Cobb-Douglas production function yields

$$f_K = \alpha AK^{\alpha-1}\ell^{1-\alpha} \tag{5.22}$$

Dividing (5.20) by K,

$$\frac{Y}{K} = AK^{\alpha-1}\ell^{1-\alpha} \tag{5.23}$$

Hence,

$$f_K = \alpha AK^{\alpha-1}\ell^{\alpha-1} = \alpha\frac{Y}{K} \tag{5.24}$$

The marginal product of capital in use domestically is therefore the income share of capital in national income times the ratio of national output to capital.

Estimating national income gains: The Australian case

Using the comprehensive flow and stock data from Australia's national accounts, as first proposed in Makin (2006), it is possible to derive annual values of the marginal product of capital for each of the past ten years using expression (5.24). The data required for this purpose are included in Table 5.1. All value data are expressed in Australian dollars.

This data reveals minimal variation in the output/capital ratio and in the share of capital in national income, although there was a slight rise in the rate of capital consumption. Capital consumption now accounts for over half of gross investment and the higher rate of depreciation most likely reflects more intensive use of computers and information technology whose write-off period has diminished as innovation has intensified.

The marginal product of capital is the product of the capital share of income and output/capital ratio from expression (5.24). Net of depreciation, this yields annual values within the narrow range 8.2–9.2 per cent over the decade. These real values can then be combined with estimates of the real effective cost of foreign capital and the real external imbalance to yield real annual national income gains attributable to foreign capital.

To estimate the real servicing cost of capital, it is first necessary to derive implicitly the nominal effective cost of foreign capital using balance of payments and international investment position data. The implicit foreign interest rate is net interest paid abroad, as recorded in the current account balance, divided by the stock of net external debt as shown in Chart 5.1.

International evidence suggests that interest paid abroad is positively related to the stock of foreign debt, giving rise to an interest risk premium. A rising risk premium in Australia's case would, other things equal, increase interest paid abroad and hence be reflected in the implicit foreign interest rate.

Apart from debt, external liabilities are in the form of equities serviced through dividends and the profits of branches of transnational companies. Hence, to derive the total effective cost of foreign capital these payments are combined with interest paid abroad and divided by the weighted stock of net foreign liabilities, inclusive of equity investment.

Table 5.1 Estimating the marginal product of capital, 1995–6 to 2004–5

Year	Real capital stock[a] ($b)	Real GDP[b] ($b)	Output/Capital ratio[c]	Capital share[d]	Marginal product of capital[e] (%)	Capital consumption[f] (%)	Net marginal product of capital[g] (%)
1995–6	1806.0	621.8	0.34	0.39	13.3	4.7	8.5
1996–7	1857.6	646.0	0.35	0.37	12.9	4.7	8.2
1997–8	1918.2	674.9	0.35	0.38	13.5	4.8	8.7
1998–9	1981.0	709.9	0.36	0.38	13.5	4.9	8.6
1999–00	2050.6	738.1	0.36	0.38	13.7	5.0	8.8
2000–1	2098.5	752.4	0.36	0.38	13.7	5.0	8.7
2001–2	2155.6	780.8	0.36	0.39	14.1	5.1	8.9
2002–3	2231.8	806.2	0.36	0.39	14.1	5.2	8.9
2003–4	2318.3	838.3	0.36	0.40	14.4	5.2	9.2
2004–5	2407.9	857.8	0.36	0.40	14.3	5.2	9.1

Notes:

[a] Capital stock chain volume data in 2003–4 prices from Australian Bureau of Statistics, *Australian System of National Accounts, 2004–05*, Cat 5204.0, Table 69, p. 83.

[b] GDP chain volume data in 2003–4 prices from Australian Bureau of Statistics, *Australian System of National Account, 2004–05*, Cat 5204.0, Table 2, p. 16.

[c] The ratio of the real capital stock to real GDP.

[d] The ratio of gross operating surplus to the sum of compensation of employees and gross operating surplus; data from Australian Bureau of Statistics, *Australian System of National Accounts, 2004–05*, Cat 5204.0, Table 12, p. 26.

[e] The product of the output-capital ratio and the capital share of income.

[f] Estimated as the ratio of chain volume measures of consumption of fixed capital to end-year capital stock; data from Australian Bureau of Statistics, *Australian System of National Accounts, 2004–05*, Cat 5204.0, Table 69, p. 84.

[g] The difference between the marginal product of capital and the estimated depreciation rate.

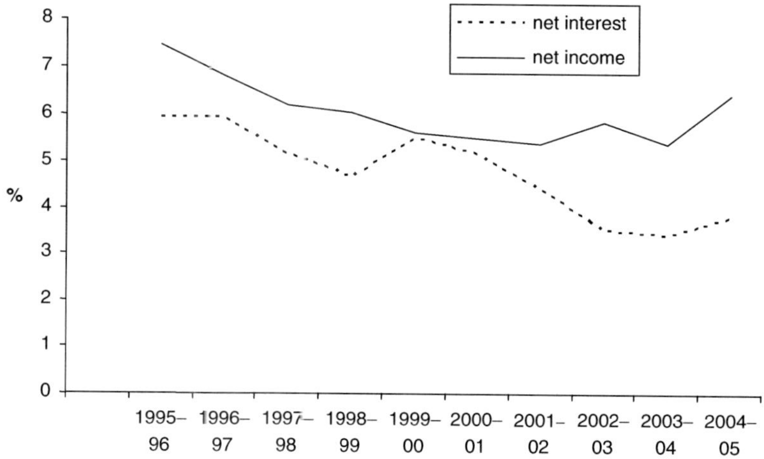

Chart 5.1 Implicit foreign interest rate and cost of foreign capital, 1995–6 to 2004–5[(a),(b)]

Notes:

[(a)] Based on data from Reserve Bank of Australia, *Bulletin*, Tables H5 and H7.

[(b)] Since the stock of debt changes through the year, the value of net external debt in the denominator should be a weighted average. The Australian Bureau of Statistics recommends a weight of two-thirds for the beginning of year value and a weight of one-third for the end of year value.

Chart 5.1 shows that the total effective measure persistently exceeded the effective interest rate on foreign debt in nominal terms over the period, implying an 'equity premium' existed for foreign investors in Australia. This equity premium widened significantly over recent years as the effective interest rate fell in line with global interest rates, thereby ensuring little variation in the nominal cost of foreign capital.

Table 5.2 presents estimates of the additional national income generated annually by foreign-financed capital that has accumulated over the past decade. In every year it is evident that the marginal product of foreign capital exceeded its servicing cost, the difference averaging over 5 per cent for the period.

This is not the full story, however, because the earlier relation (5.15) underpinning this estimation exercise also implies that further national income gains or losses arise from period-to-period

Table 5.2 National income gains from annual foreign capital inflow, 1995–2005

Year	Net foreign liabilities[a] ($b)	Net income payments abroad[b] ($b)	Real cost of foreign capital[c] (%)	Net marginal product less-real cost[d] (%)	Real CAB[e] ($b)	Real national income gain[f] ($b)
1995–6	262.0	19.5	4.0	4.5	24.7	1.1
1996–7	280.2	19.1	5.4	2.8	19.6	0.5
1997–8	292.4	18.1	4.7	4.0	25.2	1.0
1998–9	305.1	18.4	4.4	4.2	36.5	1.5
1999–00	324.0	18.2	3.2	5.6	35.2	2.0
2000–1	340.9	18.7	–0.4	9.1	18.7	1.7
2001–2	365.5	19.7	2.3	6.6	21.4	1.4
2002–3	386.0	22.5	3.8	5.1	42.0	2.1
2003–4	442.1	23.7	4.2	5.0	47.8	2.4
2004–5	485.8	31.2	4.6	4.5	56.1	2.5

Notes:
[a] Weighted average measures of net foreign liabilities based on data in current prices from Reserve Bank of Australia, *Bulletin*, Table H5.
[b] Current price data from Reserve Bank of Australia, *Bulletin*, Table H7.
[c] *Ex post* real cost of foreign capital is the ratio of net income payments to net foreign liabilities less annual inflation rate; inflation data from Reserve Bank of Australia, *Bulletin*, Table G1.
[d] The difference between the net marginal product of capital from Table 1 and the real cost of foreign capital.
[e] External account imbalances from Australian Bureau of Statistics, *Balance of Payments and International Investment Position, Australia, 2004–05*, Cat 5302.0, Table 1, p. 18; expressed in 2003–04 prices after deflating by the Implicit Price Deflator for investment from Australian Bureau of Statistics, *Australian System of National Accounts*, Cat 5204.0, Table 8, p. 22.
[f] The product of the net marginal product of foreign capital less real servicing cost and the external imbalance in 2003–4 prices.

movements in the implicit interest rate as applied to the stock of foreign debt. In other words, the total servicing cost of foreign capital also rises or falls from year to year as the foreign interest rate varies. Foreign interest rate falls add to net income gains, whereas rises, inclusive of any increase in interest risk premia charged by foreign lenders, subtracts from net income gains.

Year-to-year interest rate movements stem from changes in world interest rates, exchange rate swings affecting foreign currency denominated debt and any interest risk premium that may vary through time. Accordingly, Table 5.3 presents estimates of national income gains or losses arising from changes in the implicit foreign interest rate. World interest rates generally fell over the decade. Hence these interest-related income gains generally augment those shown in Table 5.2

As the average age of capital is 17 years, the new capital installed at the start of the decade in review could be expected to generate income throughout the entire period. For this reason the gains should also be considered cumulatively. On this basis, the extra real income stemming from foreign-funded capital over the decade was $A23.3 billion in constant prices, or $A24.2 billion in 2004–5 prices.

With a total workforce of around 9.8 million people in mid-2004–5, income per employed person in Australia was therefore approximately $A2500 higher in 2004–5 prices than it would have been without the net capital inflow that occurred between 1995–6 and 2004–5. With a total population around 20.5 million at the time, national income per head was close to $A1100 higher due to foreign capital inflow over the previous decade.

Finally, it is possible to estimate the annual contribution that foreign capital has made to growth in net disposable income. Interestingly, the gains approximate the size of the external imbalance as a proportion of GDP over the estimated time interval. Nevertheless it also suggests that purely domestic factors, especially multifactor productivity and labour force growth remain the primary sources of annual income growth.

While these results attest to the benefits of capital inflow to Australia, they do not imply that foreign-funded investment generated no losses or bankruptcies at the firm level over the period. If unproductive capital results in widespread losses in any year, the value of the net

Table 5.3 Total national income gains from foreign capital, 1995–2005

Year	Change in implicit foreign interest rate[a] (%)	Income gain from interest rate movements[b] ($b)	Real income gain from interest rate movements[c] ($b)	National income gain from foreign capital (from Table 2) ($b)	Total national income gain[d] (2003–4 prices) ($b)	Cumulative income gain (2003–4 prices) ($b)
1995–6	1.1	0.9	1.6	1.1	2.7	2.7
1996–7	0.0	0.0	0.0	0.5	0.5	3.2
1997–8	0.8	1.7	1.5	1.0	2.5	5.7
1998–9	0.5	1.2	1.0	1.5	2.5	8.2
1999–00	–0.9	–2.1	–1.9	2.0	0.1	8.3
2000–1	0.3	1.0	0.9	1.7	2.6	10.9
2001–2	0.7	2.3	2.2	1.4	3.6	14.5
2002–3	0.9	3.0	2.9	2.1	5.0	19.5
2003–4	0.1	0.4	0.4	2.4	2.8	22.3
2004–5	–0.4	–1.5	–1.6	2.5	1.0	23.3

Notes:
[a] The year-to-year change in the implicit foreign interest rate derived in Figure 4; data from Reserve Bank of Australia, *Bulletin*, Tables H5 and H7.
[b] The product of the weighted stock of net foreign debt and the change in the implicit foreign interest rate; data from Reserve Bank of Australia, *Bulletin*, Tables H5 and H7.
[c] The value of the income gain from interest rate changes deflated by the Implicit Price Deflator for GDP.
[d] The sum of the real national income gain from annual foreign capital inflow from Table 2 plus the real annual net gain from interest rate movements.

marginal cost less foreign servicing cost would conceivably be much lower. Under such circumstances financial crisis and recession could result, especially if accompanied by rising interest rates.

The macroeconomic methods and assumptions used above are of course subject to the standard criticisms that aggregative approaches attract. For instance, at the microeconomic level, saving and investment may be subject to various distortions that render them suboptimal and domestic and foreign capital controls could affect the volume of capital inflows.

Yet the economy-wide impact of microeconomic distortions is difficult to assess and should significant ones exist, they could have offsetting effects on the variables of most interest here. Microeconomic factors are therefore considered of second-order importance in this context. It may be that other functional forms of macroeconomic production, such as the CES production function, better reflect the relationship between labour and capital in the Australian context (for instance, with respect to the substitutability of labour and capital).

Examining whether alternatives to the Cobb-Douglas specification of output generation used here could be adapted to reconfirm the above estimates of national income gains from foreign capital inflow to Australia is a worthy topic for future research. Whether dwelling investment should be treated in the same way as other forms of investment may also warrant further consideration in this context.

In the expansive literature that examines the causes and consequences of international capital flows, there is a paucity of research that focuses on the direct impact that international borrowing in its various forms has on national income. This chapter contributes to that literature in two main ways.

First, it provides an open economy growth accounting framework that enables the contribution of capital inflow to be identified explicitly as part of the economic growth process in which the rate of capital accumulation exceeds the overall saving rate. Second, it uses raw national accounts data and standard assumptions about output generation to derive benchmark estimates of the benefits of capital inflow in the case of Australia.

By explicitly identifying the contribution of foreign capital to national income growth, it has shown that Australia's national income grew significantly faster due to the large CADs and higher debt levels of the past decade, yielding additional income on average of around $A2500 per worker.

At the same time, there is a risk that future income gains could diminish if world interest rates keep rising or if a higher interest risk premium emerged. Indeed, the above estimates show that sometimes annual movements in the implicit foreign interest rate have been at least as significant as new foreign capital inflow as a source of variation in national income.

On balance, the annual income gains over the decade most likely understate the total contribution of foreign capital and should be considered minimum values. This is because part of capital inflow is FDI which entails the transfer of technology, work practices and management techniques that boost multifactor productivity.

Hence, part of the multifactor productivity improvement over this time would be attributable to foreign capital rather than exclusively to domestic sources. Unfortunately, it is difficult to quantify exactly how much this would add to the foreign-contribution component of annual income growth.

The macroeconomic methods and assumptions used above are of course subject to the standard criticisms that aggregative approaches attract. For instance, at the microeconomic level, saving and investment may be subject to various distortions that render them suboptimal and domestic and foreign capital controls could affect the volume of capital inflows.

Conclusion

The main aim of this chapter is to highlight the national income gains that can stem from capital inflows over the medium term as cross-border rates of return on capital are being equalized and, as a corollary, examine the macroeconomic implications of capital controls that limit international financial flows to emerging economies.

Using a straightforward extended loanable funds framework, the above analysis has shown that exchange controls of different kinds reduce potential growth and hence economic welfare by raising an economy's external cost of capital. Capital controls in the form of taxes on inflows are preferable to quantitative controls known as unremunerated reserve requirements, since taxes impose smaller welfare losses due to revenue effects. This result mimics the well-known result from international trade theory that it is better to impose tariffs, rather than quotas, on imported goods and services.

Capital controls are advocated as a means of minimizing international capital flow reversals and hence as a means of preventing currency and financial crises that occur due to information and moral hazard problems. However, the above analytics suggest these problems are best addressed by focusing directly on unsuitable pegged exchange rate regimes and grave weaknesses in the domestic economy's financial system, not by reducing development potential and hence economic welfare via impediments to international trade in saving.

Employing a growth accounting method this chapter has shown that foreign capital inflow has contributed positively and significantly to national income in Australia because the additional production that capital inflow has made possible exceeded its servicing cost over a recent sample period. This evidence verifies the gains from international trade in saving and provides a counter to negative interpretations of CADs and international borrowing.

Yet there can be adverse implications for national income in developing countries that borrow whenever international monetary conditions unexpectedly change, or whenever *ex ante* expectations about the profitability of investment projects prove overly optimistic. Including these and political economy factors in theoretical international finance models remains a challenge for future research.

Emerging and transition economies in Europe, Latin America and East Asia that have liberalized their capital accounts over recent decades have recorded relatively large capital inflows and high external debt levels. But with relatively fragile domestic financial systems, many of these economies have experienced severe capital flow reversals, banking and currency crises and major recessions that have sporadically disrupted economic growth.

Not surprisingly, empirical studies using time series that include crisis years therefore fail to show strong evidence relating international capital market integration and economic growth in developing economies (see survey by Prasad et al. 2003). However, such results do not necessarily weaken the case for greater capital mobility. Rather they strengthen the case for identifying the underlying causes of currency and financial crises.

References

Australian Bureau of Statistics (2005) *Australian System of National Accounts, 2004–5*, Cat 5204.0, AGPS, Canberra.

Australian Bureau of Statistics (2005) *Balance of Payments and International Investment Position, Australia*, Cat 5302.0, AGPS, Canberra.

Bhagwati, J. (1998) 'The Capital Myth: The Difference between Trade in Widgets and Dollars', *Foreign Affairs*, 77 (3), May/June, 7–12.

Dooley, M. (1996) 'A Survey of the Literature on Controls over International Capital Transactions', *IMF Staff Papers*, 43 (4), 3–23.

Feldstein, M. and Horioka, C. (1980) 'Domestic Saving and International Capital Flows', *Economic Journal*, 90 (2), 314–29.

Grubel, H. G. (1987) 'Foreign Investment' in J. Eatwell, M. Milgate and P. Newman (eds) *The New Palgrave Dictionary of Economics*, vol. 2, Macmillan, London, 403–6.

Keynes, J. (1941) "The Origins of the Clearing Union, 1940–1942" in *The Collected Writings of John Maynard Keynes*, Macmillan for the Royal Economic Society, London.

Lane, P. and Milesi-Ferretti, G. (2002) 'Long-Term Capital Movements' in B. Bernanke and K. Rogoff (eds) *NBER Macroeconomics Annual 2002*, MIT Press, Cambridge, Massachusetts.

MacDougall, G. D. A. (1960) 'The Benefits and Costs of Private Investment from Abroad: A Theoretical Approach', *Economic Record*, Special Issue (March), 13–35.

Makin, A. (2003) Global Finance and the Macroeconomy, Palgrave Macmillan, Basingstoke.

Makin, A. (2006) 'Has Foreign Capital Made Us Richer?', Agenda, 13 (2), 225–37.

Neely, C. (1999) 'An Introduction to Capital Controls', *The Federal Reserve Bank of St Louis Review*, 81 (6), 13–30.

Prasad, E., Rogoff, K., Wei, S., and Kose, M. (2003) Effects of Financial Globalization on Developing Countries: Some Empirical Evidence IMF Occasional Paper 220, Washington, DC.

Reserve Bank of Australia, *Bulletin*, Reserve Bank of Australia, Sydney. http://www.rba.gov.au/Statistics/.

Rodrik, D. (1998) 'Who Needs Capital Account Liberalization?' in P. Kenen (ed.) *Should the IMF Pursue Capital Account Convertibility?*, Princeton Essays in International Finance No. 207.

Ruffin, R. (1984) 'International Factor Movements' in P. B. Kenen and R. W. Jones (eds) *Handbook of International Economics*, vol. 1, North-Holland, Amsterdam, Ch. 5, 237–88.

Tobin, J. (1978) 'A Proposal for International Monetary Reform', *Eastern Economic Journal*, 4, 153–9.

Ulan, M. (2000) 'Review Essay: Is a Chilean-Style Tax on Short-Term Capital Inflows Stabilizing?', *Open Economies Review*, 11 (2), 149–77.

Wade, R. (1998) 'The Asian Debt-and-Development Crisis of 1997–?: Causes and Consequences', *World Development*, 26 (8), 1535–53.

6
External Imbalances, Exchange Rates and Interest Rates

Introduction

This chapter examines the relationship between exchange rates, global imbalances, international borrowing and lending behaviour and long-term real interest rates. It establishes which domestic and international macroeconomic variables primarily influence exchange rates, external imbalances and global interest rates over any given time for both large and small borrower economies.

The current account, capital account and the exchange rate

This section aims to improve our understanding of exchange rate behaviour by advancing a model of the exchange rate that is uniquely premised on the macroeconomic fundamentals of national spending and production and international capital flows.

In the voluminous exchange rate literature, two broad streams characterize macro-oriented approaches to exchange rate determination. First, much research has sought to resolve the significance of changing national price levels for a multitude of currencies over different time horizons by testing purchasing power parity (PPP), although with mixed results. (See, for example, Imbs et al. 2005; Lopez 2008; Papell 2004; Taylor 2002.)

Second, a parallel literature has examined links between exchange rates and monetary variables, such as relative money supplies and interest rates, also with mixed results (see, for instance, Meese and Rogoff 1983; Flood and Rose 1999; Macdonald 1999; Engel et al. 2007).

In contrast, policymakers and participants in foreign exchange markets have long drawn links between current account outcomes and exchange rate movements. Moreover, researchers readily connect the consequences of exchange rate movements to current account adjustment in the spirit of the well-known Marshall-Lerner analysis (see Dornbusch 1996; Frankel and Rose 1995; Goldstein and Khan 1985; Hooper et al. 2000; Marquez 2002).

Yet surprisingly little theoretical or empirical work has been undertaken on the simultaneous influence of current account imbalances and international capital flows on the nominal exchange rate itself, over either the short or long run. What extant exchange rate modelling generally neglects is the important role the exchange rate plays in equilibrating flows across both the current and capital accounts of the balance of payments in financially open economies.

The emphasis in international monetary theory on asset markets and capital account transactions as primary influences on the nominal exchange rate contrasts with the traditional flow approach in which the exchange rate simultaneously equalizes net demand and supply of foreign currency arising from both current and capital account transactions.

A primary function of the balance of payments accounts is to provide a statistical record in flow terms of the supply and demand for an economy's currency. It is the nominal exchange rate itself which ensures the equality, in principle, between the current and capital balances in these accounts. As shown in Chapter 3, an economy with a CAD (CAS) has an excess demand (supply) for foreign currency that is satisfied by an excess supply (demand) of foreign currency, provided through the matching capital account surplus (deficit).

Hence, it follows that both current and capital account flows should simultaneously be taken into account when modelling exchange rate behaviour. Yet this has not been explicitly recognized in asset market models because of their focus on asset stock adjustment and financial flows only.

In what follows an alternative flow model of the exchange rate and the external accounts is developed and the basic framework then used to analyse current and capital account shocks on the exchange rate and external imbalance.

Output, expenditure and the current account

The following relations underpin a balance of payments framework that is central to subsequent analysis. Beginning with the current account balance, this is related to the real side of the economy via the macroeconomic accounting and behavioural relations below:

$$Y^n - AE = CA \tag{6.1}$$

$$AE = \overline{AE} - \theta e - \beta r \tag{6.2}$$

where $\overline{AE}$ is autonomous private and public spending by resident entities, θ is the responsiveness of absorption to exchange rate depreciation, e is the nominal effective exchange rate, β is the responsiveness of absorption to exchange rate depreciation and r is the domestic interest rate. CA is in surplus (CAS) when $Y > A$ and in deficit (CAD) when $Y < A$.

It is assumed that national output results from a macroeconomic production function and that the foreign and domestic price levels remain relatively stable. Hence, movements in the nominal exchange rate overwhelmingly account for real exchange rate variation over shorter periods, as normally presumed in other international macroeconomic models.

Absorption is negatively related to exchange rate depreciation because depreciations reduce spending on imports, whereas domestic interest rate rises contract the investment component of absorption in the standard way.

From the above relations

$$CA = Y^n - \overline{AE} + \theta e + \beta r \tag{6.3}$$

Since $dCA/de > 0$, the current account balance is positively related to the exchange rate in the short run. This implies an appreciating currency widens the CAD, as depicted by the downward sloping *CD* schedule in Figure 6.1. Furthermore,

$$dCA/dY^n > 0, \quad dCA/d\overline{AE} < 0, \quad dCA/dr > 0 \tag{6.4}$$

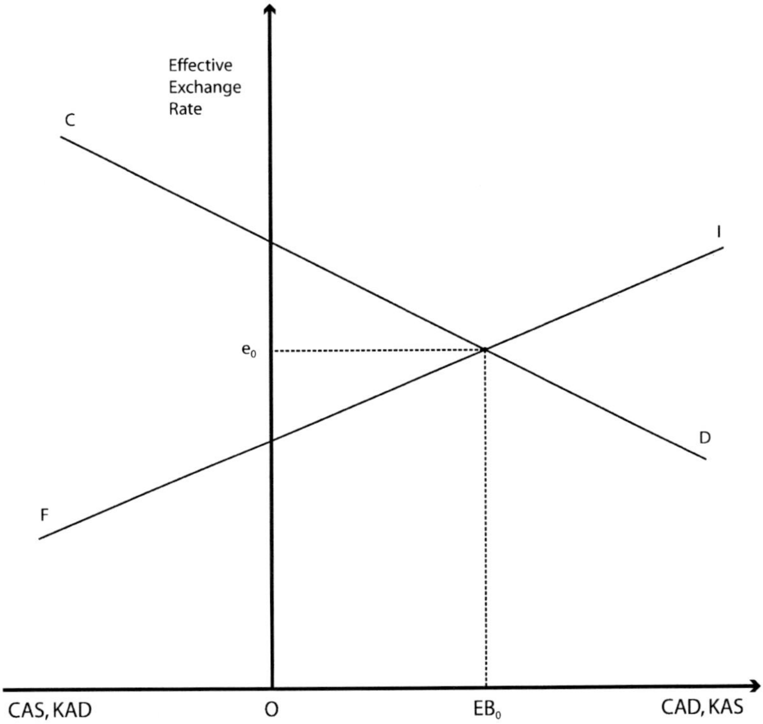

Figure 6.1 The current account, capital flows and the effective exchange rate

which suggests higher domestic spending relative to national income increases the CAD, whereas a lower domestic interest rate reduces it, other things equal.

The capital account, expectations and the exchange rate

Next consider the other side of the balance of payments accounts, the financial and capital account, usually referred to simply as the capital account. Here, recorded net capital flows are either in the form of foreign investment in equities, including FDI, or net foreign borrowing, involving cross-border purchase of interest-bearing instruments. Equity flows and bond purchases by foreign central banks stemming from foreign exchange rate intervention may be treated as autonomous.

However, net capital inflow also occurs whenever an interest differential opens up between domestic and foreign interest rates. Private cross-border capital flows respond to open interest differentials which are deviations from interest parity with such flows continuing until interest parity is restored. In turn, interest parity implies a stock equilibrium for the international investment position, characterized by the cessation of private capital flows.

Hence, we can state that

$$KA = \kappa + \varsigma\left[(r - (r^{*} + e + \rho)\right] \tag{6.5}$$

where KA is the capital account surplus, κ is net foreign equity investment and other autonomous capital inflows, including foreign reserves acquisition by foreign central banks, r is the domestic interest rate, r* is the foreign interest rate, ê is expected exchange rate depreciation, ρ is a time-varying interest risk premium and ς is the responsiveness of private capital flows to deviations from interest parity.

Since $\hat{e} = (f-e)/e = f/e - 1$, we can restate (6.5) as

$$KA = \kappa + \varsigma\left[(r - (r^{*} + f/e + 1 + \rho)\right] \tag{6.6}$$

where f is the expected future spot exchange rate.

Since $dKA/de = \phi f/e^2 > 0$, net capital inflow and hence the capital account surplus is positively related to the exchange rate in the short run. Moreover,

$$dKA/d\kappa > 0, \quad dKA/dr > 0, \quad dKA/dr^{*} < 0, \quad dKA/df < 0, \quad dKA/d\rho < 0 \tag{6.7}$$

The basic flow equilibrium condition for the balance of payments under a floating exchange rate regime is that the current account balance equals the capital account balance, but with opposite sign, such that

$$CAD\ (e; Y^{n}, \overline{AE}, r) = KAS\ (e; \kappa, r, r^{*}, f, \rho) \tag{6.8}$$

The above relationships underpin the *CD* and *FI* schedules depicted in Figure 6.2. This figure reveals how both current account flows

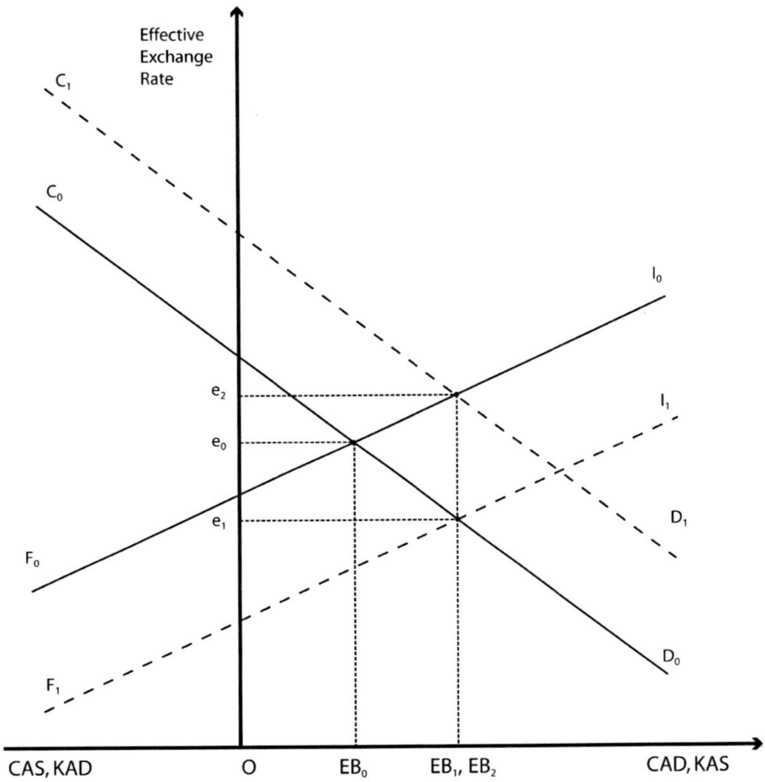

Figure 6.2 Current account versus capital account related shocks

and capital account flows jointly determine the nominal effective exchange rate with reference to macroeconomic fundamentals that include national output, expenditure, expectations and interest rates. Over any given period, numerous factors can shift the current account and capital account schedules, simultaneously varying the effective exchange rate and the external account imbalance.

Table 6.1 summarizes the outcomes of current account and capital account shocks predicted by the framework that depreciate the effective exchange rate, while simultaneously varying the size of the external imbalance. The interesting general result that emerges is this: if current account shocks predominate, the exchange rate

Table 6.1 The current account, the capital account and the exchange rate

Source of variation		Effect on:	
		External imbalance	*Exchange rate*
Current account			
National output	↓	↑	↑
Autonomous spending	↑	↑	↑
Interest rates	↓	↑	↑
Capital account			
Autonomous capital flows	↑	↑	↓
Domestic interest rates	↑	↑	↓
Foreign interest rates	↓	↑	↓
Expected exchange rate	↓	↑	↓

and the external imbalance will move in the same direction, with either depreciations associated with a widening external imbalance or appreciations associated with a narrowing.

On the other hand, if capital account shocks predominate, the exchange rate and external imbalance will move oppositely, with depreciations associated with a narrowing external imbalance and appreciations associated with a widening.

This central finding makes it possible to identify whether the current account or capital account has primarily influenced the exchange rate of any free-floating currency over given periods by examining whether and when external imbalances and effective exchange rates move together or oppositely. If the former (latter), the current (capital) account is the main driver of the exchange rate.

Saving, investment and capital flows

It is also important to understand the linkages between domestic and foreign saving and investment flows and real interest rates. In recent decades, the rise in the US external deficit and fall in long-term interest rate have strongly coincided with a major shift in the global pattern of saving and investment, particularly that between East Asia and the US.

The Asian financial crisis was a major catalyst for this shift, which has been abetted by the continued rise of China. Since the Asian crisis, saving in East Asian emerging economies has risen markedly with an especially strong increase in China's saving. Meanwhile, East Asian investment rates fell over the period compared to pre crisis rates (IMF 2005). Taking the period since 1985 as a whole, external factors have predominated also, consistent with enhanced international capital mobility following the progressive dismantling of exchange controls worldwide and the globalization of capital markets.

The intertemporal approach to external imbalances based on saving – investment gaps – provides a useful benchmark model for interpreting their policy significance. As shown in Chapter 4, this approach implies that foreign borrowing, arising from the forward-looking optimizing behaviour of private households and firms, can raise national income and intertemporal consumption, other things the same.

Critically, among these other things are presumptions of free private capital mobility and floating exchange rates, as well as a properly functioning banking and financial system that channels both domestic and foreign funds to their most productive use. If these presumptions are incorrect, sudden current account reversals can have business cycle implications, as seen during the 1997–8 Asian currency crisis and the 2007–8 US financial crisis.

Several authors have used intertemporal precepts to estimate the optimal level of the external imbalance by examining whether cycles in the CAD have been consistent with consumption-smoothing behaviour (see Ghosh and Ostry 1995). As argued by Mercereau and Minane (2004), however, time series analysis of the sustainability of external imbalances that tests consumption smoothing with reference to intertemporal budget constraints has serious limitations and fails to provide a reliable basis for assessing whether external imbalances are excessive.

Foreign borrowing, lending and interest rates

To understand the linkages between an economy's international borrowing, net foreign lending to that economy and long-term interest rate determination, an extended loanable funds framework is now introduced. Figure 6.3, which is in the spirit of the loanable funds approach of the previous chapter, graphically represents these key relationships. It assumes there are two economies, the US and the

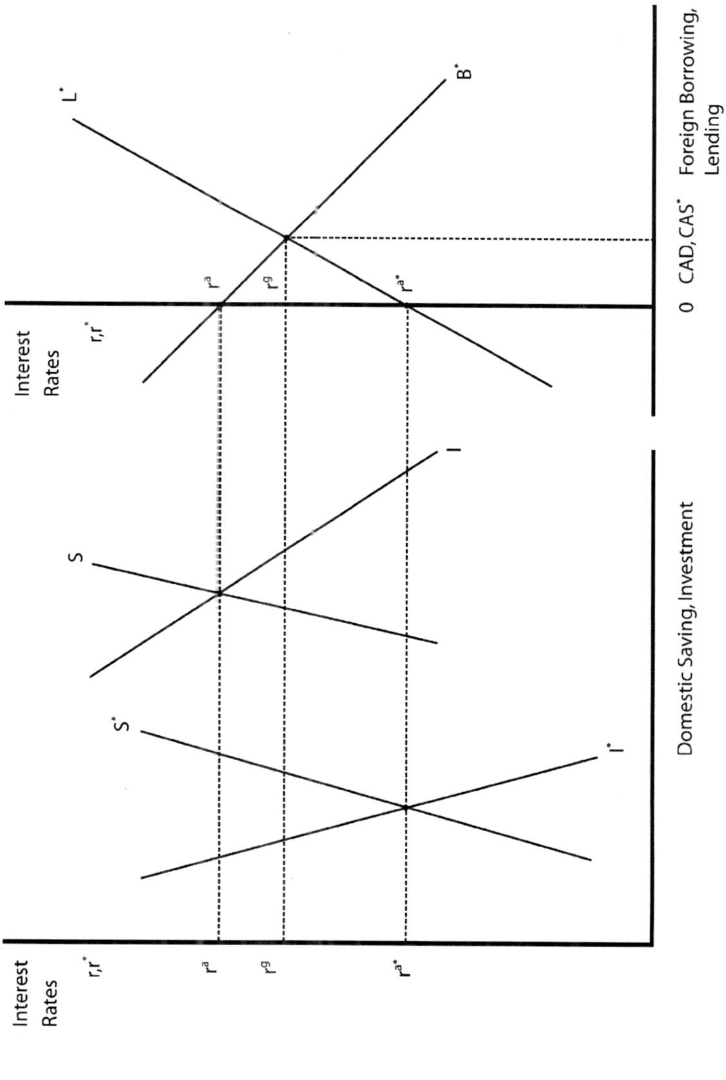

Figure 6.3 International borrowing, lending and interest rates

rest of the world (ROW), each comprised of three sectors – the private sector (households and firms), the government and foreign sectors, with all variables expressed in real terms.

Domestic saving is the residual between national income and consumption. Related positively to income and negatively to real interest rates, IMF (2005) and Deaton (1992), domestic saving is lent by exchanging funds for interest earning financial instruments. These instruments are typically bonds or certificates of deposit, issued by borrowers to fund real investment spending which is related positively to investment opportunities and negatively to real interest rates.

The left panel of Figure 6.3 shows the supply and demand for funds for a range of interest rates, given national income levels in the US and ROW. The S, S^* schedules reflect the positive relationship between domestic saving and interest rates. Domestic borrowers absorb saving by supplying interest earning financial investments on the other side of the market for loanable funds, issuing more instruments the lower the interest rate, as conveyed by the downward sloping I, I^* schedules.

External imbalances are here defined as the difference between regional saving and investment. In the US excess domestic demand for funds leads to an *ex ante* CAD and external borrowing requirement. The lower is the interest rate, the greater is the horizontal distance between US saving and investment in the left panel. This gap is replicated in the right panel as the foreign borrowing requirement.

Hence, the downward sloping B^* schedule shows net US demand for foreign funds in excess of domestic saving for a range of global interest rates. It intersects the vertical axis of the right panel at the point corresponding to the autarky interest rate. *Ex ante,* at global rates below the autarky rate, r^a , there is net foreign borrowing and associated CADs, whereas at global interest rates above r^a , the US would lend abroad experiencing CASs. Similarly, in ROW, schedule L^* shows the excess saving over investment for interest rates above r^a, the ROW interest rate prevailing absent capital flows between ROW and the US.

Ex ante, at global interest rates above r^a, there is net lending abroad and associated CASs. Below r^a, investment exceeds saving in ROW which then borrows from the US experiencing an external deficit. The global interest rate, determined at the intersection of the *ex ante* foreign borrowing and lending schedules, clears the international market for loanable funds, equilibrating borrowing by, and lending to, the US.

Domestic versus foreign shocks

This framework predicts the simultaneous impact on shared external imbalances and long-term interest rates of various internal and external shocks. If foreign saving rises relative to investment abroad (due, for example, to rapid income growth in China), the S^* and L^* schedules shift, as in Figure 6.4. This enlarges the US external imbalance lowering the global interest rate. *Ex post*, the rise in ROW's lending abroad matches the rise in the US CAD and its foreign borrowing.

Reduced investment abroad (due to a fall in β^*) also shifts L^* rightwards with the same effects as increased saving abroad – external imbalances rise and the global interest rate falls. Under these conditions, the US deficit and long-term interest rate are therefore determined exogenously by foreign saving and investment behaviour.

Alternatively, increased real investment or reduced saving in the US shifts B_0^* right to B_1^*. This simultaneously widens the external deficit and raises the global interest rate. Hence, from a US perspective, either internal or external factors can predominately alter its external imbalance and long-term interest rates over any given time. Fiscal activity can also be easily analysed within this framework with reference to the following relations.

$$S = S_p + S_g \tag{6.9a}$$

$$S^* = S_p^* + S_g^* \tag{6.9b}$$

$$S_p = Y - T - C \tag{6.10a}$$

$$S_p^* = Y^* - T^* - C^* \tag{6.10b}$$

$$S_g = T - G \tag{6.11a}$$

$$S_g^* = T_g^* - G^* \tag{6.11b}$$

where S_p, S_p^* is private saving, S_g, S_g^* is public saving, T, T^* is government tax revenue and G, G^* is government spending.

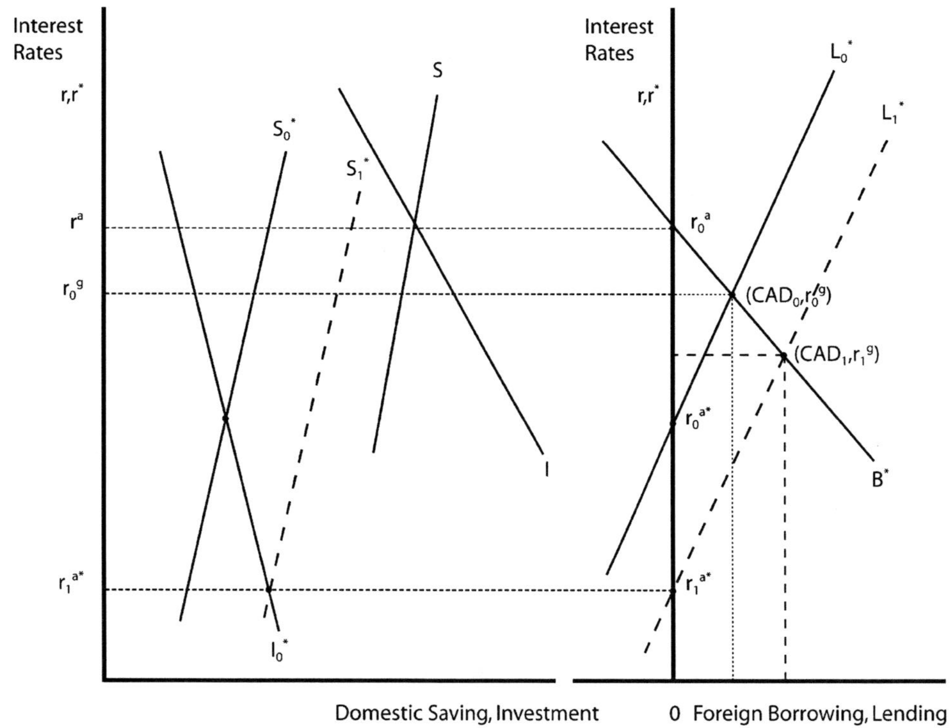

Figure 6.4 Increased foreign saving, the external imbalance and interest rates

Relations (6.9a) to (6.9b) define private and public saving for the US and ROW respectively. The Ricardian Equivalence proposition implies private saving can fully offset policy-induced changes in public saving, although empirical evidence suggests the offset is well under unity, Gale and Orszag (2004). Hence, a rise in G in the US that reduces public saving contributes to a fall in national saving relative to investment. The B^* schedule shifts right, widening the external imbalance and raising the global interest rate.

Alternatively, if public saving in ROW rises, due to lower public spending or higher taxes, L^* shifts right. External imbalances also widen, yet under these conditions, the global interest rate falls. In the contrary case of reduced public saving in ROW (due, for instance, to increased G*), the global interest rate rises, yet US borrowing falls. In sum, domestic fiscal expansion widens US borrowing only if the global interest rate simultaneously rises.

Table 6.2 includes all saving and investment shocks that could contribute to a rise in the US CAD. It yields the following interesting result: if the predominant shock to saving or investment is domestic, the US external deficit and global interest rates move in the same direction, whereas they move oppositely if the predominant shock is external. This general finding makes it possible to identify whether domestic or international factors have determined the US external deficit and borrowing over any period.

Using the real US 10-year government bond rate as a proxy for the global interest rate it is evident from Chart 6.1 that since the

Table 6.2 Effects of domestic and international shocks

Source of shock:	**Effect on:**	
	CAD	r
Domestic		
Private saving ↓	↑	↑
Public saving ↓	↑	↑
Investment ↑	↑	↑
International		
Private saving ↑	↑	↓
Public saving ↑	↑	↓
Investment ↑	↑	↓

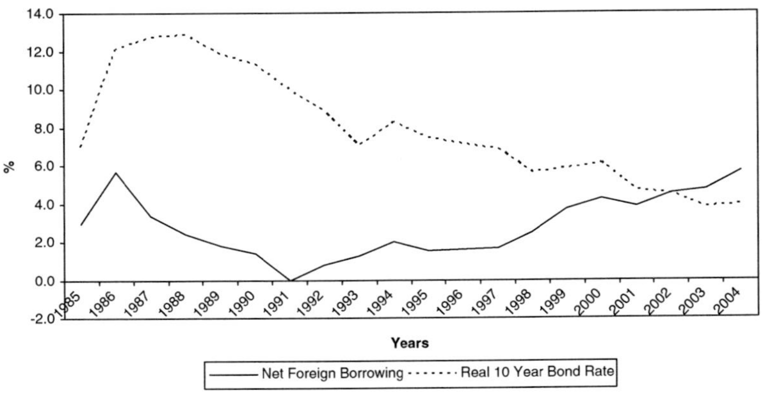

Chart 6.1 US net foreign borrowing and real ten-year bond rate, 1995–2004

early 1990s interest rates and the external imbalance have moved in the opposite direction. As more formally estimated in Makin and Narayan (2008), this suggests that external factors have predominated, whereas the opposite was true before this, suggesting internal factors were more important.

Identifying whether most of the variation in the CAS is sourced at home or abroad is important because, if domestic factors predominate, fiscal policy can in principle influence the external imbalance, whereas if foreign factors are responsible it is largely beyond control.

The small economy case

The above analysis has examined the case of an economy large enough to influence the global interest rate. However, many economies are too small to affect global interest rates and hence face an exogenous world interest rate. Taking the case of Australia and New Zealand ('Australasia') their external account imbalances remain central to analysis of their international economic performance and continue to influence macroeconomic policy.

CADs have averaged between 4 and 5 per cent of GDP since Australian and New Zealand exchange rates were floated and international capital flows liberalized in the early 1980s. These imbalances rank as the largest and most persistent in the world have been matched by equivalent net capital inflow (or CAS) and are unusually large by OECD standards.

An extensive literature on the significance of Australasian external imbalances has developed over recent decades covering many dimensions of the issue. In addressing the underlying causes, most studies have interpreted the imbalances as domestic saving–investment gaps and examined the major influences on national saving and investment from a home country perspective while assuming a highly interest elastic supply of foreign savings. This includes the role that federal fiscal settings have played in influencing domestic saving and investment behaviour.

By adapting the above analysis to the small economy case it is possible to examine whether domestic or foreign net saving has primarily influenced net capital inflow.

Incorporating interest risk premia

As in the large economy case, a common interest rate equilibrates the quantum of international borrowing and lending to the home country over any given period. If the home country is too small to affect the world interest rate, however, and if the ROW becomes increasingly averse to lending to it as foreign debt rises, then

$$r = r^{*} + \rho(\overset{+}{F}; \overset{+}{\Omega}) \qquad (6.12)$$

where ρ is the risk premium above the world interest rate, F is the stock of foreign debt and Ω captures other risk factors such as exchange rate risk and country risk.

Static exchange rate expectations are assumed as the normal case in the absence of any consensus about the short-to-medium term determinants of the exchange rate.

These relationships are graphically depicted in loanable funds – real interest rate space, as shown in the left panel of Figure 6.5. Following Makin (2002), the downward sloping schedule conventionally shows the domestic demand for funds arising for net investment purposes while the upward sloping schedule depicts net saving or the supply of domestic funds. The net international borrowing requirement *ex ante* is shown as the horizontal distance between the demand for funds and the supply of domestic saving for a range

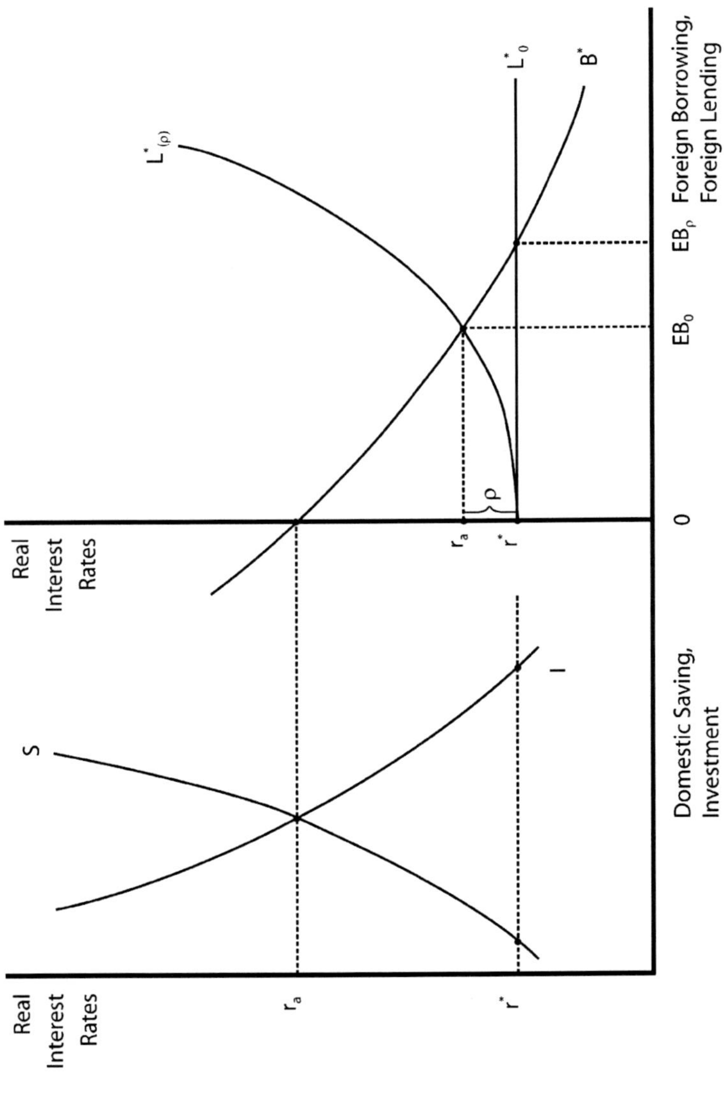

Figure 6.5 International borrowing, lending and real interest rates

of interest rates. The investment–saving gap is replicated by the B_0^* schedule in the right panel drawn in real interest rate – international borrowing and lending space.

A rise in the economy's borrowing requirement due, for instance, to increased real investment opportunities (a rise in *q*) or fall in public saving due to higher public consumption shifts the B^* schedule rightwards. Only if international capital mobility is perfect, will foreigners lend at r^*, the going world interest rate, as shown by the horizontal L_0^* schedule.

Yet in reality capital mobility is not infinitely elastic and lenders are averse to default and other forms of risk, including currency depreciation. Hence, the supply of foreign funds the home country can borrow depends not only on the excess of global saving over investment but also on risk perceptions.

This explains the upward sloping foreign lending or net capital inflow schedule, L^* in Figure 6.5. The more risk-averse foreign investors are to rising foreign debt, the steeper the slope of the L^* schedule. Changes in world saving relative to investment affect real global interest rates and shift the L^* schedule, downwards when net global saving rises, upwards when it falls. Other shift factors are expected appreciation/depreciation and heightened perceptions of political/country risk.

Domestic versus foreign net saving shocks

This international borrowing and lending framework can now be used to predict the effect of various domestic and foreign saving and investment shocks on both the external imbalance and real interest rates, as shown in Figure 6.6, based on the right panel of Figure 6.5.

For instance, an increase in domestic investment spending, other things the same, shifts the *ex ante* foreign borrowing schedule outwards. The real domestic interest rate rises from r_0 to r_1 and the external surplus increases from B_0 to B_1 *ex post*. Likewise, a rise in public consumption or investment has the same effect. These cases exemplify domestically sourced shocks that simultaneously influence the external imbalance and real interest rates.

Yet foreign saving and investment shocks emanating from abroad can also influence the home economy's external surplus and real

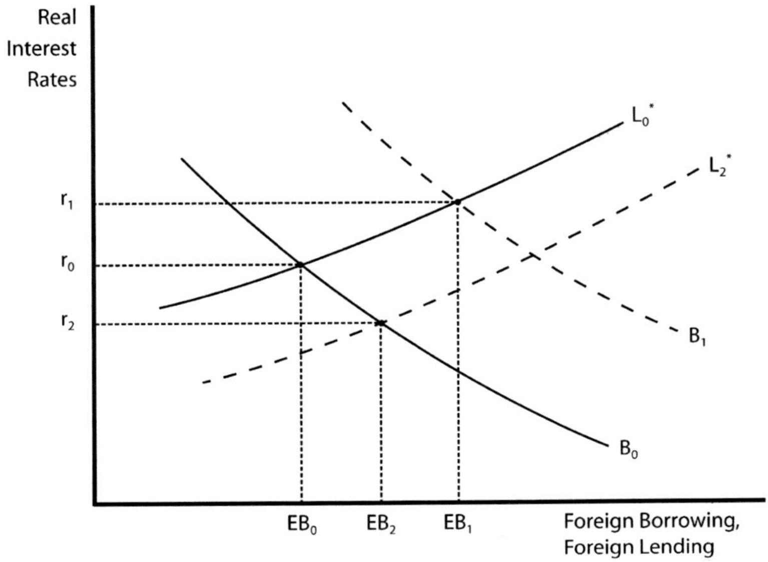

Figure 6.6 Domestic versus foreign net saving shocks

interest rate. For instance, assume the same initial equilibrium as before (at r_0,B_0) and that, other things equal, private investment overseas falls relative to private saving, raising net foreign saving. In this case, the foreign lending schedule shifts out, the capital account surplus widens from EB_0 to EB_2 and the equilibrium interest rate falls from r_0 to r_2.

Alternatively, with lower foreign public spending, public saving abroad rises, the external surplus also widens and the real interest rate falls. In the contrary case of reduced net private or public saving abroad due to increased consumption or investment, the home economy's external surplus falls and real interest rate rises.

All possible saving and investment shocks (domestic and foreign) that increase the external imbalance and vary real interest rates in the small economy case accord with those for the large economy as shown in Table 6.1. To restate the general result: if the predominant

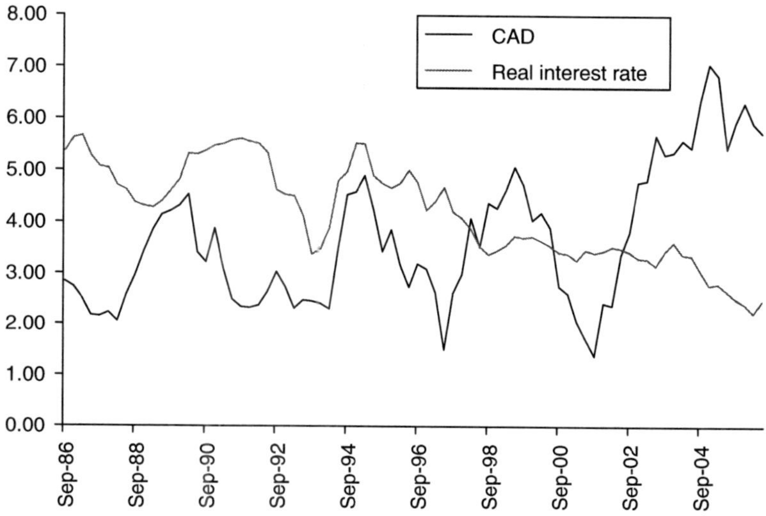

Chart 6.2 Australian net foreign borrowing and real ten-year bond rate, 1986–2004

net saving shock is domestic, the external imbalance and real interest rate move in the same direction, whereas if the predominant net saving shock is foreign, they move oppositely.

This central finding makes it possible to identify whether domestic or foreign factors have mainly influenced external imbalances by examining whether and when the external surplus and real interest rates have moved in the same or in opposite directions.

As Chart 6.2 reveals, in Australia's case prior to the late 1990s there was a high degree of co-movement of interest rates and net capital inflow suggesting internal factors were predominantly responsible for the external imbalance, but since then external factors have been.

Conclusion

This chapter provides an alternative perspective on global imbalances with explicit reference to the interplay between domestic and foreign influences on exchanges rates, external imbalances and the international flow of funds. It proposes straightforward frameworks that reveal the international macroeconomic conditions under which domestic and international factors govern external imbalances, exchange rates and long-term interest rates.

By examining links between relative domestic saving and investment patterns and international borrowing and lending, it shows how an economy's real long-term interest rates can be historically low when budget and CADs are simultaneously high. In this way it reveals how the increased international borrowing of the US over recent decades was primarily due to external factors, as suggested by Bernanke (2005).

Specifically, the rise in the US external deficit largely coincided with a major shift in the pattern of saving and investment in East Asia following the Asian crisis of 1997–8. Since that time, saving in crisis-affected East Asian economies rose significantly, accompanied by an especially rapid increase in saving by China. Meanwhile, East Asian investment rates fell over the period when compared to pre crisis rates (IMF 2005). Excess East Asian saving over investment was invested abroad with the US being a major recipient.

From a policy perspective, nothing in this analysis suggests that external deficits and borrowing are inherently undesirable if private capital is highly mobile and exchange rates are flexible. Nor does it deny that domestic factors, including fiscal and monetary policy, can play a role in limiting them. Nonetheless, it may be argued that an external deficit suggests domestic saving is 'too low' and that the external imbalance should be targeted by increasing saving relative to domestic investment via reduced private and public consumption. Yet at given income levels, higher private saving implies lower household consumption and hence living standards in the short term.

While scope may exist to raise overall domestic saving through fiscal measures that reduce public consumption, such policies may also unnecessarily reduce economic welfare. In any case, notwithstanding domestic macroeconomic policy initiatives, targeting the external account imbalance could prove elusive if it mainly results from international economic factors, such as misaligned pegged exchange rates (as we saw earlier in Chapter 3) that domestic policymakers are unable to affect.

References

Bernanke, B. (2005) 'The Global Saving Glut and the U.S. Current Account Deficit', remarks by Governor Ben S. Bernanke at the Sandridge Lecture, Virginia Association of Economists, Richmond, Virginia, March 10.

Deaton, A. (1992) *Understanding Consumption*, Oxford University Press, Oxford.

Dornbusch, R. (1996) 'The Effectiveness of Exchange-Rate Changes', *Oxford Review of Economic Policy*, 12 (3), 26–38.

Engel, C., Mark, N. and West, K. (2007) 'Exchange Rate Models Are Not as Bad as You Think' in D. Acemoglu and K. Rogoff (eds) *NBER Macroeconomics Annual* 2007, National Bureau of Economic Research.

Flood, R. and Rose, A. (1999) 'Understanding Exchange Rate Volatility without the Contrivance of Macroeconomics', *Economic Journal*, 109 (459) (November), 660–72.

Frankel, J. and Rose, A. (1995) 'A Survey of Empirical Research on Nominal Exchange Rates' in G. Grossman, and K. Rogoff (eds) *Handbook of International Economics*, vol. 3, Amsterdam, North-Holland.

Freund, C. (2005) 'Current Account Adjustment in Industrial Countries', *Journal of International Money and Finance*, 24, 1278–98.

Gale, W. and Orszag, P. (2004) 'Budget Deficits, National Saving and Interest Rates', Brookings Papers on Economic Activity, *Brookings Institution*, 2, 101–210.

Ghosh, A. and Ostry, J. (1995) 'The Current Account in Developing Countries: A Perspective from the Consumption-Smoothing Approach', *The World Bank Economic Review*, 9, 305–34.

Goldstein, M. and Khan, M. (1985) 'Income and Price Effects in Foreign Trade' in R. Jones and P. Kenen (eds) *Handbook of International Economics*, vol. 11, Amsterdam, North Holland, 1041–105.

Hooper, P., Johnson, J. and Marquez, J. (2000) 'Trade Elasticities for the G-7 Countries', *Princeton Studies in International Economics*, vol. 87, August, Princeton University, Princeton, New Jersey,.

Imbs, J., Mumtaz, H., Ravn, M. and Rey, H. (2005) 'PPP Strikes Back: Aggregation and the Real Exchange Rate', *Quarterly Journal of Economics*, 120 (February), 1–43.

International Monetary Fund (2005) *World Economic Outlook*, September, Chapter II, Washington, DC.

Lopez, C. (2008) 'Evidence of Purchasing Power Parity for the Floating Regime Period', *Journal of International Money and Finance*, 27 (1), 156–64.

MacDonald, R. (1999) 'Exchange Rate Behaviour: Are Fundamentals Important?', *The Economic Journal*, 109 (459), 673–91.

Makin, A. and Narayan, P. (2008) "Have US External Imbalances Been Determined at Home or Abroad?" *Economic Modelling*, 25(2), 520–531.

Makin, A. (2002) *International Microeconomics*, Pearson, London.

Marquez, J. (2002) *Estimating Trade Elasticities*, Kluwer Academic Publishers, Boston.

Meese, R. and Rogoff, K. (1983) 'Empirical Exchange Rate Models of the Seventies: Do They Fit Out of Sample?', *Journal of International Economics*, 13, 3–24.

Mercereau, B. and Miniane, J. (2004) 'Challenging the Evidence from Present Value Models of the Current Account', *IMF Working Paper 04/80*, International Monetary Fund Washington.

Papell, D. (2004) 'The Panel Purchasing Power Parity Puzzle', *Journal of Money, Credit and Banking*, 38 (2), 447–67.

Taylor, A. (2002) 'A Century of Purchasing Power Parity', *Review of Economics and Statistics*, 84, 139–50.

7
Money, Exchange Rates and the Balance of Payments

Introduction

This chapter presents an alternative monetary model of the exchange rate and balance of payments which yields several new results about the international adjustment process. For instance, it reveals that contrary to the traditional monetary approach to the balance of payments international adjustment under fixed rates is consistent with money market equilibrium, not disequilibrium. It also suggests a new chain of causality under floating rates that runs from domestic money market to exchange rate to price level, rather than from money market to price level to exchange rate.

An alternative monetary model

The traditional monetary approach to the balance of payments (MABP) and the monetary approach to the exchange rate (MAER) developed by numerous authors decades ago (Polak 1957; Frenkel 1976; Johnson 1977; Branson and Henderson 1985; Frenkel and Mussa 1985) proposed that the domestic money market should be at the centre of balance of payments and exchange rate analysis, an idea originally espoused by the classical economist David Hume (1752).

The MABP assumed national output was autonomous and suggested that balance of payments adjustment under a fixed exchange rate reflected temporary *disequilibria* between domestic money demand and supply. The MAER also presumed an invariant level of national income, focusing on money's role in determining nominal exchange rates rather than changes in the central bank's reserves. However, by taking national income as given, the MAER neglected the significance of the current account as an output – expenditure imbalance and the possibility of monetary shocks contributing to temporary variations in national income.

The still popular MF model explicitly addresses exchange rate and national income variation in the open economy, but as an aggregate demand-side model, it ignores national price level dynamics and has aggregate supply adjusting endogenously to total spending. Though other authors have tried to remedy this by positing an upward sloping aggregate supply function (Argy and Salop 1979; Bruce and Purvis 1985), all variants of the MF model rely on a specification of the external accounts that is unrelated to total spending and production.

This model also neglects that current account imbalances signify international borrowing and lending and the intertemporal use of foreign saving in the economy. More recently, the 'new open economy macroeconomics' (Lane 2001) has provided an alternative intertemporal paradigm, characterized by explicit microfoundations, nominal rigidities and imperfect competition. Unfortunately models developed within this paradigm remain highly sensitive to the specification of the microfoundations themselves, such as the nature of utility functions and the source of price stickiness (Sarno and Taylor 2003).

At the same time, unlike the MF model, it puts the output-expenditure relationship at the forefront and explicitly traces out the impact of monetary shocks on national expenditure, output, the exchange rate and price level. Moreover, unlike the new open economy macroeconomics, the current account imbalance is treated throughout as an output-expenditure rather than saving-investment phenomenon.

Monetary foundations

This section develops the basic linkages and framework to be used to model domestic monetary shocks. When modelling aggregate expenditure, extant open economy macroeconomic approaches, including the MF model, typically define aggregate demand as the sum of domestic spending on an economy's goods and services, net of imports, plus foreign demand for its goods and services, measured as exports. That is,

$$C + I + G + X - M = Y \tag{7.1}$$

The left side of the equation 7.1 shows domestic demand for home production, the bracketed term, plus foreign demand for domestic product. Defined this way, aggregate expenditure always equals aggregate supply. Alternatively, following Alexander (1952) here we define aggregate expenditure, as in previous chapters, as total spending by resident entities on goods and services, inclusive of imports, that is

$$C + I = AE \tag{7.2}$$

where AE is measured in real terms.

At the same time, it interprets aggregate supply as the total quantity of goods and services provided for sale at home and abroad, recognizing that part of aggregate supply is produced to satisfy export demand.

Since $Y - AE = X - M$, it follows that aggregate demand only equals aggregate supply when exports equal imports. Or in other words, only when the trade account is balanced with no net international flow of funds, such that the economy is neither incrementally borrowing nor lending abroad. *Ex post*, under a fixed exchange rate with limited capital mobility, the current account balance must also equal the central bank's change in foreign reserves.

Under a floating rate with capital mobility, foreign investors acquire home currency denominated bonds, to the extent of the private capital inflow; or if output exceeds expenditure, residents acquire foreign bonds and there is capital outflow. Increased net demand for foreign currency arising from a spending-output difference must be matched by a net supply of foreign currency made available from the central bank's reserves, or through private capital inflow. Otherwise, the exchange rate adjusts.

All goods and services are potentially tradable and in final equilibrium the domestic price level is simply the product of the exogenous world price and the nominal effective exchange rate, defined as the trade weighted price of foreign exchange, such that $P = eP^*$.

By setting the foreign price level at unity throughout, the domestic price level becomes

$$P = e \tag{7.3}$$

The domestic money stock, M^S, is determined by the home economy's central bank. Money market equilibrium prevails when residents' real demand for cash balances, λ, which is negatively related

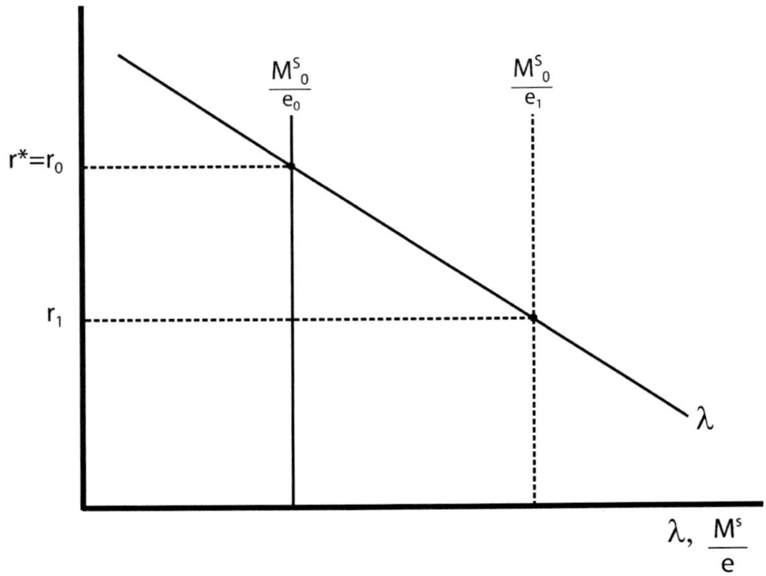

Figure 7.1 Domestic money market equilibrium

to the domestic interest rate and positively related to output, equals the real supply of money.

That is,

$$M^S/e = \lambda(\overset{-}{r}, \overset{+}{Y}) \tag{7.4}$$

The stronger the exchange rate, the lower is the price level, the larger is the real money stock and, for given money demand and nominal money supply, the lower is the real interest rate, as shown in Figure 7.1. Consumption and investment spending by residents is negatively related to the exchange rate, the price level and the real interest rate.

Hence,

$$AE = AE(\overset{-}{r}(\overset{-}{e}, \overset{-}{P}); \overset{+}{M^S}, \overset{-}{\lambda}) \tag{7.5}$$

This equation provides the basis for an AE schedule in exchange rate – expenditure and income space, as shown in Figure 7.2.

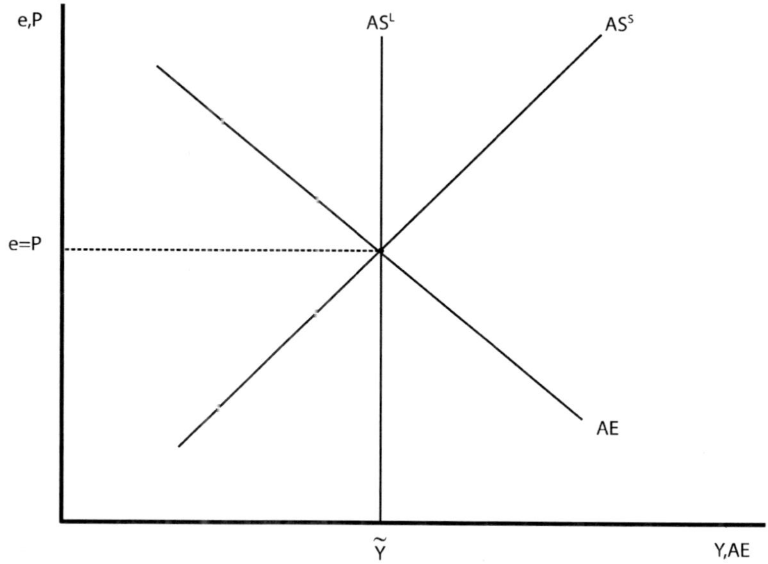

Figure 7.2 An international monetary framework

It is downward sloping because, other things equal, a stronger exchange rate (lower price level) raises the real money supply, which lowers the real domestic interest rate, thereby inducing higher domestic expenditure. The negative slope of this schedule can also be justified on the basis that a lower price level increases the economy's real wealth level, which induces higher expenditure for given real income.

Money supply or money demand shocks shift the AE schedule because it is drawn for a given nominal money supply and real money demand. Figure 7.2 also depicts short- and long-run aggregate supply functions. Long-run AS^L depends on the size of the labour force, the economy's capital stock and multifactor productivity in the standard way and it is assumed these are invariant over the time frame under scrutiny.

All domestic prices, including wages, are also presumed flexible over this time frame, enabling goods and services markets to clear and for the unemployment rate to stabilize at its natural rate. Hence, the longer-term aggregate supply schedule rises vertically above $\tilde{Y}$.

Nominal exchange rate depreciation makes home-produced goods and services cheaper from foreigners' perspective since domestic output is priced in the home currency. This creates additional demand for the home country's output, as determined in elasticities approach parlance by the elasticity of the ROW's demand for its exports, M*.

At the same time, production of additional output by home firms, or the elasticity of the supply of the home economy's exports, is constrained by domestic costs, including wages. For given wages, the rising short-run aggregate supply schedule, AS^S, will therefore reflect diminishing marginal capital productivity and rising marginal costs under competitive conditions.

Hence,

$$dM^* = Y - \tilde{Y} = dX \tag{7.6}$$

Production in the short run therefore behaves as depicted by the upward sloping aggregate supply schedule in Figure 7.2 where real appreciations (depreciations) temporarily lower (raise) output above its normal level. Eventually nominal wages, ω, will adjust as workers bargain to restore real wages, such that $\omega_0/e_0 = \omega_2/e_2$.

Alternatively, nominal wage adjustment is consistent with the equation

$$\omega = z(Y - \tilde{Y}) \tag{7.7}$$

where z is an adjustment parameter. As becomes apparent, the degree of wage stickiness is irrelevant to the international adjustment process under fixed exchange rates.

The economy is in initial general equilibrium in this framework where both the AD and AS schedules intersect. At this point, money demand equals money supply, national expenditure equals production, exports equal imports, the domestic interest rate equals the foreign interest rate and there is no net external financing requirement.

Monetary shocks under polar regimes

We now consider domestic and international adjustment in response to monetary shocks under fixed and floating exchange rates. The results for monetary contractions and expansions are symmetrical in this model. However, for variety, a monetary contraction is illustrated under floating rates and a monetary expansion under fixed rates.

Monetary contraction under floating rates

Consider first a monetary contraction under a floating exchange rate brought about by domestic bond sales by the central bank. Under these circumstances, the home economy's interest rate rises and reduces domestic spending. The AE schedule therefore shifts to the left as shown in Figure 7.3, appreciating the nominal exchange rate since the incipient CAS creates an excess supply of foreign exchange.

On the aggregate supply side of the economy, the appreciation decreases foreign demand causing domestic production to fall as exports fall and production moves down along the short run aggregate supply schedule. Meanwhile, the currency appreciation lowers

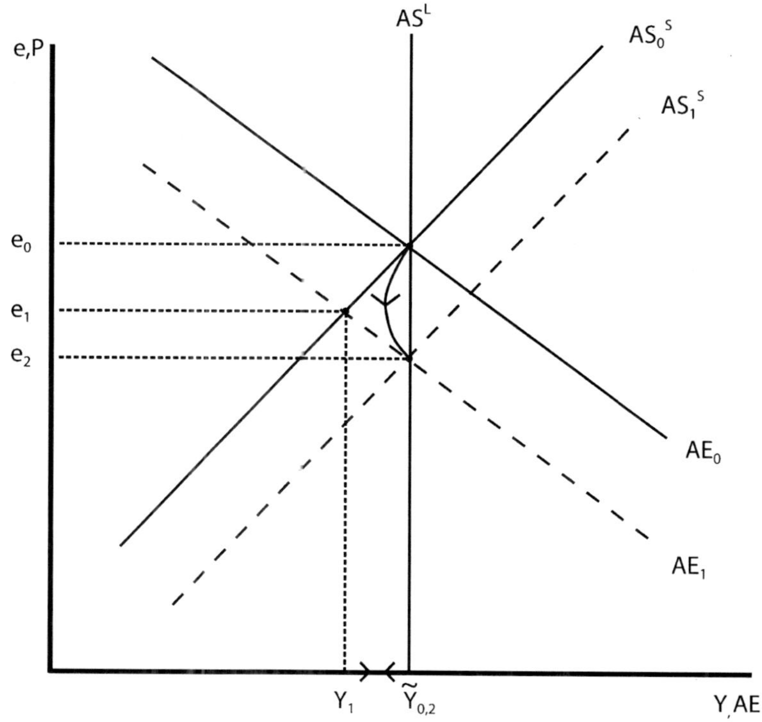

Figure 7.3 Monetary contraction under a floating exchange rate

the price level through its impact on the expenditure side, temporarily raising the real wage.

Yet as wage contracts are renegotiated, the equilibrium real wage is restored in the subsequent period. This shifts the short-run supply schedule down throughout the second period until eventual equilibrium is reached at $\tilde{Y}_2$.

Note, however, that while the nominal exchange rate appreciates throughout the first and second periods, the real money supply is also falling. Eventually, the real money supply schedule is restored to its initial level, such that the real interest rate again equals its initial equilibrium value and real interest parity prevails. At the same time, the economy's nominal interest rate would have fallen to the extent of the nominal appreciation.

In the opposite case of monetary expansion, the model predicts that the exchange rate would immediately depreciate as expenditure rises above output, eventually curbing excess expenditure but pushing up nominal wages and eventually raising the domestic price level with no lasting effect on output. In sum, contractionary or expansionary monetary policy only temporarily influences expenditure and output in this model through its effect on the real interest rate and competitiveness but only affects nominal variables in the long run, consistent with the neutrality of money proposition.

Monetary expansion under fixed rates

Consider next the economy-wide impact of a monetary expansion under a fixed exchange rate that results from a central bank purchase of bonds from residents. An exogenous rise in the nominal money supply initially lowers the domestic interest rate, thereby inducing greater consumption and investment expenditure by resident households and firms, shifting the AE curve rightwards as shown in Figure 7.4.

Since the domestic real interest rate temporarily falls relative to the foreign interest rate, foreigners would be unwilling to finance any CAD arising from domestic spending over output at exchange rate e_0. To maintain the exchange rate at $\bar{c}$, the monetary authorities must purchase domestic currency in the foreign exchange market by depleting foreign reserves.

This manifests as a temporary balance of payments deficit equivalent to the CAD. If left unsterilized, this foreign exchange market intervention necessarily offsets the original money supply decrease.

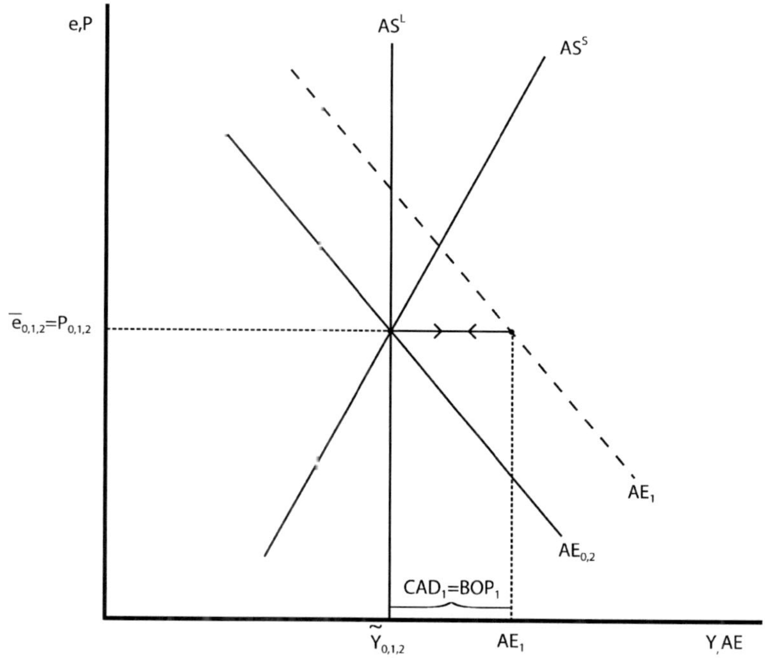

Figure 7.4 Monetary expansion under fixed exchange rate

Accordingly, the domestic interest rate reverts to its original level and the AE curve returns to its starting point in Figure 7.4.

Hence monetary expansion is impossible given the exchange rate constraint, though it does alter the composition of the central bank's balance sheet *ex post*. If the monetary shock is a fall in residents' demand for money, then the domestic interest rate would actually fall, shifting the AE curve rightwards, thereby creating excess demand for goods, services and foreign currency. Under these circumstances, the central bank then has to reduce the domestic money supply to the same extent as the fall in money demand to maintain the exchange rate at the fixed level.

It also follows here that sterilized foreign exchange market intervention by the central bank after expansionary open market operations would not stem exchange rate depreciation as it would not reverse the initial money supply increase and consequent fall in domestic interest rates and extra domestic expenditure.

Alternative chain of causation

Existing international monetary models provide an incomplete picture of the monetary transmission mechanism in open economies as they fail to explicitly trace out exchange rate and balance of payments adjustment with reference to the macroeconomic fundamentals of spending and production. In particular, standard approaches neglect the central role of the current account as an output-expenditure rather than a saving-investment phenomenon. Moreover, other models do not allow the exchange rate to be a major source of inflationary pressure for increasingly open economies.

Conclusion

By bringing discrepant output-expenditure behaviour to the forefront, the monetary model outlined above provides an alternative means of understanding the transmission of monetary shocks to domestic and international macroeconomic variables. Unlike the MABP, it treats international adjustment as a dynamic process consistent with continuous equality between residents' demand for the home money supply.

Moreover, under floating exchange rates, yet contrary to the MAER, it affords a major role to output-expenditure imbalances in determining the exchange rate. In so doing, it shows how causation runs from money through expenditure to the exchange rate to price level pressures, rather than from money to the price level to the exchange rate, even with PPP imposed as a long-run condition.

The importance of monetary factors as an influence on exchange rates has generated considerable empirical testing and debate. However, previous empirical work has been based on precepts of the original MAER (Cerra and Saxena 2008; Macdonald 1999; Rogoff 1999), whereas this chapter relates monetary foundations to the exchange rate and balance of payments directly through national expenditure and production aggregates, so it would be useful to test the alternative causality chain proposed above.

This could entail examining for a cross section of countries whether episodes of currency depreciation that are associated with excessive domestic money supply growth and high national expenditure actually precede inflationary surges, as the model proposes, or whether inflationary surges in fact precede bouts of depreciation, as the original MAER implies.

The approach is also pertinent to the perennial policy debate about the choice of exchange rate regime. In this approach, a fixed exchange rate regime effectively neutralizes the impact of a monetary shock on real output and employment, with the current account and overall balance of payments becoming the shock absorber. Lastly, the model implies that, other things equal, smaller economies susceptible to high inflation should adopt fixed, rather than a floating, exchange rates, given low and stable inflation in their main trading partners.

References

Alexander, S. (1952) 'Effects of a Devaluation on a Trade Balance', *IMF Staff Papers*, 2, 263–78.

Argy, V. and Salop, J. (1979) 'Price and Output Effects of Monetary and Fiscal Policy under Flexible Exchange Rates', *IMF Staff Papers*, 26 (2), 224–56.

Branson, W. and Henderson, D. (1985) 'The Specification and Influence of Asset Markets' in R. Jones and P. Kenen (eds) *Handbook of International Economics*, vol. 2, North Holland, Amsterdam.

Bruce, N. and Purvis, D. (1985) 'The Specification of Goods and Factor Markets in Open Economy Macroeconomic Models' in R. Jones and P. Kenen (eds) *Handbook of International Economics*, vol. 2, Holland, Amsterdam.

Cerra, V. and Saxena, S. (2008) 'The Monetary Model Strikes Back: Evidence from the World', *IMF Working Paper*, WP/08/73.

Frenkel, J. (1976) 'A Monetary Approach to the Exchange Rate: Doctrinal Aspects and Empirical Evidence', *Scandinavian Journal of Economics*, 78 (May), 200–24.

Frenkel, J. and Mussa, M. (1985) 'Asset Markets, Exchange Rates and the Balance of Payments' in R. Jones and P. Kenen (eds) *Handbook of International Economics*, vol. 2, North Holland, Amsterdam.

Hume, D. (1752) 'Of the Balance of Trade' in R Cooper (ed.) *International Finance: Selected Readings*, Penguin, Harmonsworth, 22–37.

Johnson, H. (1977) 'The Monetary Approach to the Balance of Payments: A Nontechnical Guide', *Journal of International Economics*, 7, 251–68.

Lane, P. (2001) 'The New Open Economy Macroeconomics: A Survey', *Journal of International Economics*, 54, 235–66.

MacDonald, R. (1999) 'Exchange Rate Behaviour: Are Fundamentals Important?', *The Economic Journal*, 109 (459), 673–91.

Polak, J. (1957) 'Monetary Analysis of Income Formation and Payments Problems', *IMF Staff Papers*, 6, 1–50.

Rogoff, K. (1999) 'Monetary Models of Dollar/Yen/Euro Nominal Exchange Rates: Dead or Undead?', *The Economic Journal*, 109 (459), 655–9.

Sarno, L. and Taylor, M. (2003) *The Economics of Exchange Rates*, Cambridge University Press, Cambridge UK.

8
Macroeconomic Policy, Interest Rates and National Income

Introduction

This chapter develops an alternative international macroeconomic model for evaluating the effectiveness of fiscal and monetary policy in stabilizing national income under fixed and floating exchange rates. It encompasses national output and income, saving, investment, the current account, interest rates and the money supply, while incorporating long-recognized linkages between the exchange rate, price levels and real interest rates, consistent with conventional international parity conditions.

It concludes that the exchange rate regime is ultimately not a critical determinant of the effectiveness of fiscal and monetary policy. Importantly, it predicts that fiscal expansion in the form of reduced public saving is counterproductive as a means of stabilizing national income, irrespective of exchange rate choice. Contrary to standard international macroeconomic theory, the model implies that fiscal consolidation strengthens the balance of payments, exchange rates and national income.

For many decades, the Keynesian-inspired MF model has proved the most durable vehicle for analysing the international macroeconomic impact of real and monetary shocks on globalized economies and remains central to textbook macroeconomics. What distinguishes this approach and its notable extensions such as Dornbusch (1976) and Bruce and Purvis (1985) is its lessons on the effectiveness of fiscal and monetary policies under fixed and floating exchange rate regimes. With highly mobile capital, fiscal policy is deemed very effective in stabilizing national income under fixed exchange rates, but is ineffective under floating exchange rates.

Contrariwise, monetary policy is supposedly ineffective for this purpose under fixed rates, yet very effective under floating rates. However, the MF model has numerous limitations that include its neglect of the supply side of the economy; its abstraction from price level changes; and its failure to adequately combine aggregate production, exchange rate passthrough and the implications of external account imbalances.

More recently, the 'new open economy macroeconomics' has provided an alternative intertemporal paradigm characterized by explicit microfoundations, nominal rigidities and imperfect competition. Models developed within this paradigm mostly use a two-country global economy set-up but are highly sensitive to the specification of the microfoundations themselves, such as the nature of utility functions and the source of price stickiness, about which no consensus exists.

Like the MF model that preceded it, much of the recent open economy literature emphasizes the aggregate demand side to the neglect of the output side and the role of the capital stock. Moreover, the intertemporal approach has been mainly used to analyse the effects of monetary policy on consumer welfare, as opposed to improving policymakers' understanding of how fiscal and monetary policy may work as income stabilization instruments under alternative exchange rate assumptions.

This chapter proposes an alternative international macroeconomic model for examining the effectiveness of fiscal and monetary policy in open economies which paradigmatically, has more in common with the MF model with its clear policy lessons than the more ambiguous 'new open economy macroeconomics'. Yet its focus on national income yields entirely different results to the MF model about the effectiveness of fiscal and monetary policy and the relevance of exchange rate choice.

For instance, it predicts that an 'expansionary' fiscal policy in the form of higher government spending and reduced public saving will contract national income under either fixed or floating exchange rates. This is essentially because public spending reduces domestic saving relative to investment with implications for foreign borrowing and national income. It also predicts that monetary policy is ineffective as a means of stabilizing national income over the medium to longer term, irrespective of prevailing exchange rate arrangements.

The basic underpinnings of the model are first developed by linking equilibria in the markets for goods and services, money and international capital. The framework is then deployed to analyse the transmission and effectiveness of fiscal and monetary policy. The last part concludes by summarizing the main results and highlighting key differences between this model and conventional international macroeconomic theory.

Theoretical framework

We start by examining the real sector through the behaviour of aggregate production, investment, saving and the external accounts of a small open economy. The domestic money market and international capital flows are in turn developed as the remaining building blocks of a general equilibrium model that is ostensibly similar to the MF framework, but which yields significant contrary results.

The real sector

On the aggregate supply side of the economy, national output, γ, the aggregate quantity of goods and services produced, is assumed to be generated in proportion, γ, to the economy's capital stock, K, such that

$$Y = \gamma K \qquad 0 > \gamma > 1 \tag{8.1}$$

This is consistent with the stylized fact that output-to-capital ratios are very stable in OECD economies over extended periods. Though recently much neglected, the stylized fact of relatively invariant output to capital ratios was in the past central to investment and growth theory (see Knox 1952). The economy is also assumed to be at its potential level of output with unemployment at the 'natural rate'. If the economy operates at below potential capacity, this is reflected in a temporary fall in λ and rise in unemployment above the natural rate.

The output to capital ratio can also be derived easily from specific production function forms, such as the standard Cobb-Douglas specification,

$$Y = AK^{\alpha}\ell^{1-\alpha} \tag{8.2}$$

where A is multifactor productivity and ℓ is the labour force. Under the assumption of constant returns to scale, α is the share of capital in national income and $(1 - \alpha)$ is the wages share. Dividing by K,

$$\frac{Y}{K} = AK^{\alpha-1}\ell^{1-\alpha} \tag{8.3}$$

and using the expression for the marginal product of capital

$$f_K = \alpha AK^{\alpha-1}\ell^{1-\alpha} \tag{8.4}$$

it follows that

$$Y = \left(\frac{f_K}{\alpha}\right)K = \gamma K \tag{8.5}$$

The Cobb-Douglas specification, though still widely used in macroeconometric models, has, of course, been strongly criticized by authors such as Fisher (1987, 1993) who argue that with given income shares this particular specification amounts to a tautology and that aggregating microeconomic production functions into macroeconomic production functions of this kind is problematic. Though consistent with the model to be developed, the specific Cobb-Douglas production function form is not essential to what follows.

National output differs from national income, Y^n, for open economies to the extent of net income paid or earned from abroad. If we presume a nil initial international investment position, then national income for an economy that has capital inflow, $S^* = CAD$, serviced at the world interest rate, r^*, is

$$Y^n = Y - r^*S^* = \gamma - K - r^*S^* \tag{8.6}$$

On the aggregate demand side of the economy, it is assumed that household consumption is proportionate to aggregate national income,

$$C = \upsilon Y^n \tag{8.7}$$

If the economy's private saving rate is defined as $\hbar$ (where $\hbar = 1 - \upsilon$), then the volume of private saving, consistent with the treatment of saving behaviour in the standard neoclassical growth model (Solow 1956; Swan 1956), is

$$S = \hbar Y^n \tag{8.8}$$

Private investment, I_p, is a simple linear function of the real domestic interest rate in accordance with both standard Keynesian and neoclassical theories of investment, such that

$$I_p = \bar{I}_p - br \tag{8.9}$$

where $\bar{I}_p$ is autonomous private investment and b reflects the sensitivity of private domestic investment to real interest rate movements. Empirical evidence suggests that investment is quite insensitive to interest rate movements (see Taylor 1999 for a survey), so the value of bis small.

Government s pending is either in the form of public consumption, or autonomous public investment, $\bar{I}_g$. Total investment, I, is therefore the sum of private and public investment, such that

$$I = \bar{I} - br \tag{8.10}$$

where $\bar{I} = \bar{I}_p + \bar{I}_g$.

With an initially balanced trade account, non-inflationary equilibrium requires that aggregate supply equals aggregate demand. As we will see, non-inflationary expansion in national income mainly occurs due to a rise in the rate of capital accumulation within any period.

Yet domestic investment itself, I, is constrained by the availability of saving, S, as investment must be funded, again consistent with the standard growth model. What differs here, however, is that domestic saving can be supplemented by foreign saving, S* = CAD, equivalent to the economy's net capital inflow, to yield a greater volume of investment than in the closed economy case.

Since domestic saving is the difference between private saving and public consumption, total domestic investment within any period is determined by

$$I = \bar{I} - br = S + S^* = (\hbar y - G) + S^* \tag{8.11}$$

Rearranging, the capital account surplus and matching CAD is also hereby shown equal to the domestic investment-saving gap

$$S^* = (\bar{I} - br) - (\hbar Y^n - G) \tag{8.12}$$

Returning to the supply side, the capital stock is comprised of that quantity of capital inherited from the previous period, K_0, plus new investment (net of depreciation) in the present period, I. Hence,

$$Y^n = \gamma K = \gamma(K_0 + I) = \gamma(K_0 + \bar{I} - br) \tag{8.13}$$

Using (8.6), (8.11) and (8.12), we can therefore express national income as

$$Y^n = \gamma(K_0 + \bar{I} - br) - \bar{I}r^* + brr^* + r^*\hbar Y - r^*G \tag{8.14}$$

or

$$Y^n = \frac{\gamma(K_0 + \bar{I} - br) - \bar{I}r^* + brr^* - r^*G}{(1 - \hbar r^*)} \tag{8.15}$$

Exactly the same relation can be derived for a lender economy experiencing a CAS and capital account deficit. This is because domestic saving exceeds domestic investment for lender economies, so that instead of equation (8.6)

$$Y^n = Y + r^* \, CAS \tag{8.16}$$

and instead of equation (8.12),

$$CAS = (\hbar Y^n - G) - (\bar{I} - br) \tag{8.17}$$

Combining these alternative equations with (8.13) also yields (8.15).

Expression (8.15) conveys the essentials of short-run national income generation in an open economy that either borrows or lends. Differentiating this expression with respect to the real domestic interest rate

$$\frac{dY^n}{dr} = \frac{-b(\gamma - r^*)}{(1 - \hbar r^*)} < 0 \tag{8.18}$$

This implies a downward sloping schedule, labelled the *NN* schedule, can be drawn in interest rate–national income (or r – Y^n) space, as shown in Figure 8.1.

In the limiting case of zero sensitivity of investment to real interest rate movements the *NN* schedule would of course be vertical. Moreover,

$$\frac{dY^n}{d\gamma} > 0, \quad \frac{dY^n}{d\bar{I}} > 0, \quad \frac{d\bar{Y}}{dG} < 0, \quad \frac{dY^n}{d\hbar} > 0 \tag{8.19}$$

Therefore, national income is negatively related to public consumption spending but positively related to rises in the private saving rate, autonomous private and public investment and capital productivity. Changes in these variables shift the *NN* schedule in Figure 8.1.

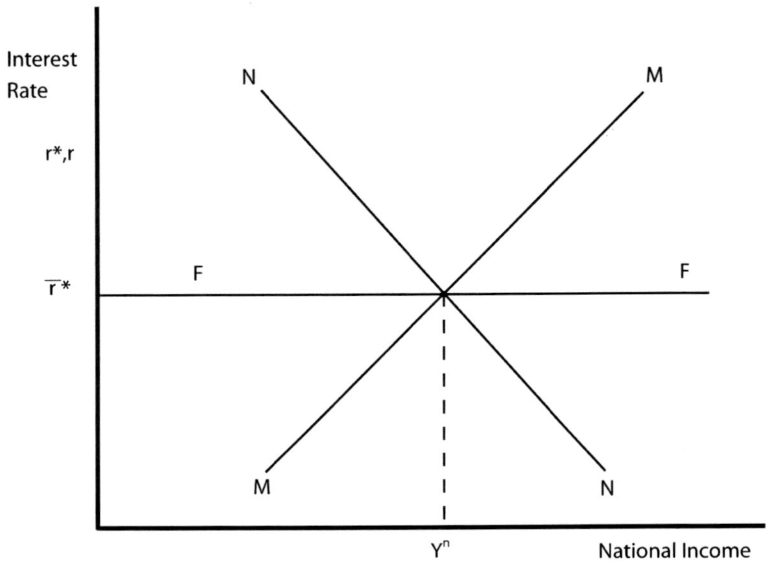

Figure 8.1 General equilibrium

Abstracting from exchange rate expectations and assuming the economy is small and that capital mobility is perfect, international capital market equilibrium also requires that the domestic (bond) interest rate equals the world interest rate, r*. Hence, eventual equilibrium must lie on the horizontal *FF* schedule, drawn for given world interest rate, $\bar{r}$*.

The monetary sector

The monetary side of the economy is modelled quite conventionally and centres on the interaction between residents' demand for money and its supply. The central bank controls the nominal money supply, M^S, which is matched in the central bank's balance sheet by bond holdings B, and foreign exchange reserves, Ψ. Hence,

$$M^S = B + \Psi \tag{8.20}$$

Central bank intervention in either the domestic bond or foreign exchange markets changes the domestic money supply, assuming the latter is unsterilized. With a fixed exchange rate, any excess supply of (demand for) foreign exchange reserves increases (decreases) the domestic money supply, whereas under a floating rate, the nominal exchange rate itself appreciates (depreciates) with no concomitant money supply change.

Real money demand, λ, depends positively on national income according to the proportion, χ, and negatively on the domestic interest rate according to the parameter δ.

Hence,

$$\lambda = \chi Y^n - \delta r \qquad 0 < \chi < 1 \qquad \delta > 0 \tag{8.21}$$

Assume the economy's goods and services are internationally tradable and that the foreign price level is invariant and normalized at unity. If absolute purchasing power parity (PPP) operates as a long-run equilibrium condition, then

$$P = e \tag{8.22}$$

In reality, nominal exchange rates adjust more quickly than the price level, which implies less than full pass through of exchange rate changes to the price level, causing real exchange rate variation over shorter periods. The macroeconomic implications of real exchange rate variation are considered subsequently when discussing the effectiveness of fiscal and monetary policy.

However, in what follows when assuming a floating exchange rate, the long run is defined as the hypothetical time it takes for full passthrough of exchange rate price effects. The empirical validity of PPP and the extent of exchange rate passthrough has been tested with mixed results over a long period. (See, for instance, surveys by Froot and Rogoff 1995; Isard 1995; Goldberg and Knetter 1997.)

In the domestic money market, the interest rate adjusts very quickly to ensure equality between the real money demand of residents, λ, and the real domestic money supply. Hence,

$$\lambda = \frac{M^S}{P} = (\chi Y^n - \delta r) = \left(B + \Psi\!\!\not{}_P\right) \tag{8.23}$$

This provides the following relationship between the domestic interest rate and national income.

$$r = \frac{\chi Y^n - (B + \Psi)}{\Psi} \tag{8.24}$$

Hence,

$$\frac{dr}{dY^n} > 0, \quad \frac{dr}{dB} < 0, \quad \frac{dr}{d\Psi} < 0, \quad \frac{dr}{dP} > 0 \tag{8.25}$$

Given the first condition in (8.25) above, it is possible to draw the *MM* schedule in Figure 8.1 as upward sloping in interest rate–national income space. Changes in the nominal money base always shift *MM*. If the exchange rate is fixed, rises (falls) in foreign currency reserves shift it rightwards (leftwards). Under a floating exchange rate, however, currency appreciations (depreciations) leave the nominal money supply unaffected, yet eventually raise (lower) the real money supply by changing the domestic price level.

International capital flows

Next, consider the nexus between the nominal exchange rate and international interest differentials. Relatively higher domestic interest rates induce capital inflow and tend to appreciate the nominal exchange rate, other things equal. Hence, it may be supposed that

$$e = e_0 - \Lambda(r - r^*) \tag{8.26}$$

where e_0 is the initial equilibrium exchange rate and Λ sets the rate of appreciation.

The nominal exchange rate stabilizes and international capital flows cease when $r^* = r$. In Figure 8.1 this occurs at points on the horizontal *FF* schedule drawn at the given world interest rate. If the domestic interest rate falls below the world interest rate, under a floating exchange rate, capital outflow immediately depreciates the exchange rate. This raises the domestic price level, thereby contracting the real money supply. Alternatively, under a fixed exchange rate, exchange rate pressures lead to central bank intervention. Hence, capital outflow reduces official currency reserves and the real money supply.

Figure 8.1 combines the schedules that have been derived to depict equilibrium in the real, monetary and the foreign exchange market sectors of the economy. General equilibrium prevails at the point where the *NN*, *MM* and *FF* schedules intersect. This framework can be used to examine a wide range of internal and external shocks to the economy. For instance, under a fixed exchange rate an improvement in capital productivity or the saving rate would shift the *NN* schedule rightwards in the first instance.

The domestic (bond) interest rate would then momentarily exceed the exogenous world rate creating an excess supply of foreign exchange. Given the foreign exchange market intervention required to fix the exchange rate, an unsterilized money supply increase shifts *MM* out until interest parity is restored.

The focus of what follows, however, is the general equilibrium effects of changes in the stance of fiscal and monetary policies under alternative exchange rate regimes. In the case of comparative static exercises under fixed exchange rates, the exchange rate and price level remain invariant, such that the key results of any shock are determined within the period.

Yet under the assumption of a floating exchange rate, as we will see, the extent and speed of passthrough of exchange rate changes to the price level has major implications for the impact of policy shocks on the economy. Therefore at this juncture, the short run is defined as time during which no passthrough occurs, the medium run the time during which partial passthrough occurs and the longer run when passthrough is complete.

The effectiveness of monetary policy

Next consider monetary expansion under a fixed exchange rate following central bank intervention in the domestic bond market. In the first instance, the nominal money supply increase shifts *MM* right, lowering the domestic interest rate below the world rate as shown in Figure 8.2. This causes capital outflow, an excess demand for foreign currency and contraction of the nominal money supply.

As a result, *MM* returns to its former equilibrium, at which point real interest parity prevails. Monetary policy is therefore ineffective under a fixed exchange rate and is also ineffective in the longer run under a floating rate. This is because currency depreciation induced by relaxed monetary policy eventually raises the domestic price level, contracting the real money supply and shifting *MM* back to its original position.

Again, however, in the presence of slow passthrough of exchange rate variation to the domestic price level, it is possible for real exchange rate movements to delay movement of *MM*, ensuring real interest rates can deviate from equilibrium levels for prolonged periods.

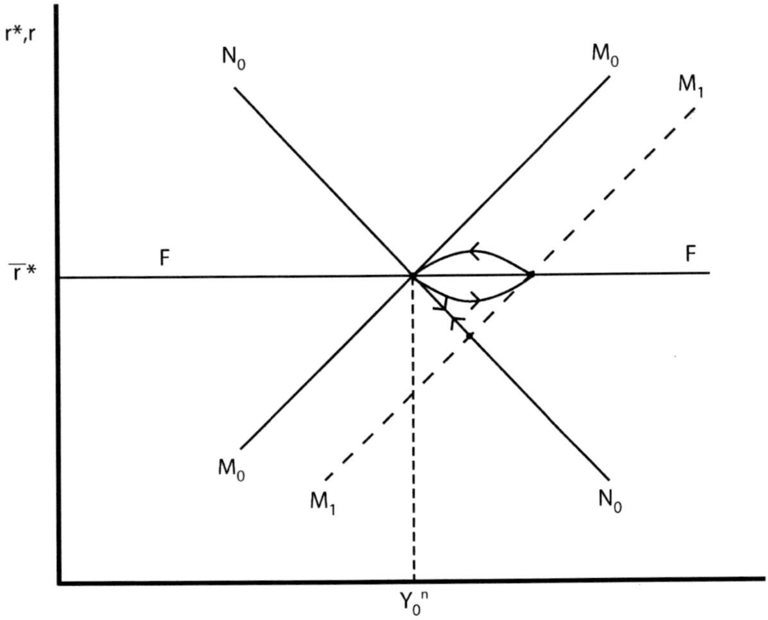

Figure 8.2 Monetary expansion

Real sector shocks

We now consider shocks that emanate from the real side of the economy. These are in the form of public sector spending shocks and productivity shocks.

Public consumption versus public investment

First, consider the effects of a fiscal expansion under a fixed exchange rate involving higher government consumption expenditure. A rise in public consumption reduces public and national saving. For given investment opportunities, this increases the external account imbalance via international borrowing.

Since this new borrowing must be serviced at the going world interest rate, fiscal expansion in this form implies lower national income. Hence, the *NN* schedule shifts to the left, as shown in Figure 8.3. Money demand accordingly falls for the given money supply, causing

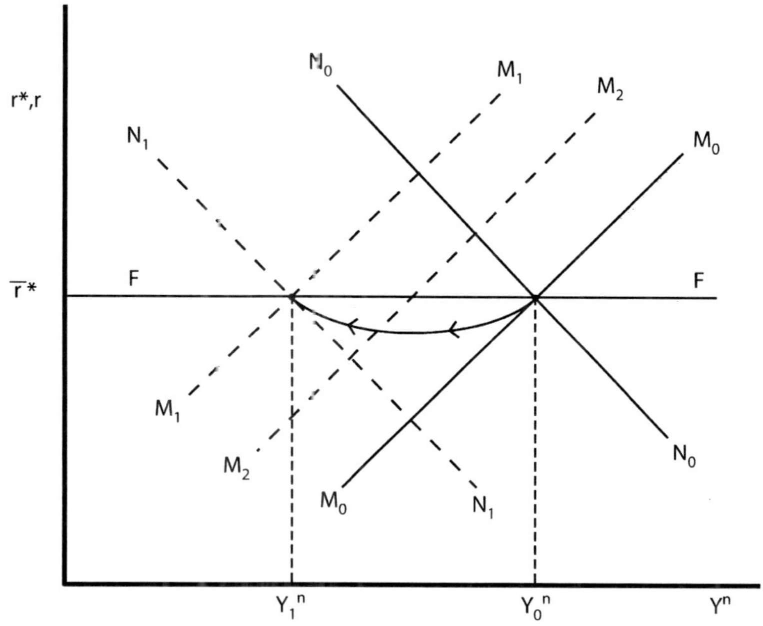

Figure 8.3 Higher public consumption

an incipient fall in the domestic interest rate below the world rate which induces capital outflow.

To maintain the fixed exchange rate, the central bank purchases foreign exchange, thereby contracting the domestic money supply absent sterilization. Consequently, the *MM* schedule will continue to shift to the left until intersecting the new *NN* schedule at the point where interest parity is restored in the asset markets.

If the exchange rate floats, the same conclusions just derived about the pro-cyclical impact of additional public consumption spending still hold in the long run when the full passthrough of exchange rate effects on the domestic price level has occurred. Indeed, over the longer term whether exchange rates are pegged or float becomes irrelevant to the question how effective fiscal policy is.

For instance, in the case of fiscal expansion in the form of increased public consumption *NN* would still shift left lowering the domestic interest rate as money demand falls. But under a floating regime, the exchange rate itself depreciates, eventually raising the price level and shrinking the real money supply, which shifts *MM* leftwards until real interest parity again prevails. Meanwhile, the rate of passthrough of exchange rate changes to the domestic price level governs the speed at which the *MM* schedule shifts out until it reaches the point where real interest parity is restored.

Hence, an easier fiscal stance resulting from higher public consumption ultimately proves counterproductive as a means of boosting real national income. This is contrary to the standard MF result that fiscal policy is very effective when used counter-cyclically under a fixed exchange. Of course, Ricardian effects are possible in the wake of spending increases.

In the extreme, though empirically unsupported case, a one-for-one offset of private consumption by resident households mindful of future tax obligations would neutralzse the contractionary impact of fiscal expansion by preventing the saving-investment gap widening in the first instance (Barro 1989; Masson et al. 1998).

Consider now the effects of a rise in government investment, resulting from increased infrastructure spending. Other things equal, this raises the autonomous investment term, $\bar{I}$, in Equation 8.13 and thereby shifts the *NN* schedule to the right, as shown in Figure 8.4. Money demand rises for given money supply, putting upward pressure on the domestic interest rate, thereby inducing short-term capital inflow.

To maintain the fixed exchange rate, the central bank has to purchase excess foreign exchange, so enlarging the domestic money supply. Consequently, the *MM* schedule shifts rightwards until it intersects with the new *NN* schedule at the point where interest parity is restored in the asset markets. Hence, increased infrastructure spending raises national income, whereas greater public consumption lowers it.

Again, if the exchange rate floats, the domestic interest rate rises and this induces capital inflow and appreciates the currency. The impact of the public expenditure boost is therefore slower than for the fixed exchange rate case, governed by the rate of passthrough and hence the speed at which *MM* shifts right due to an expanding real money supply.

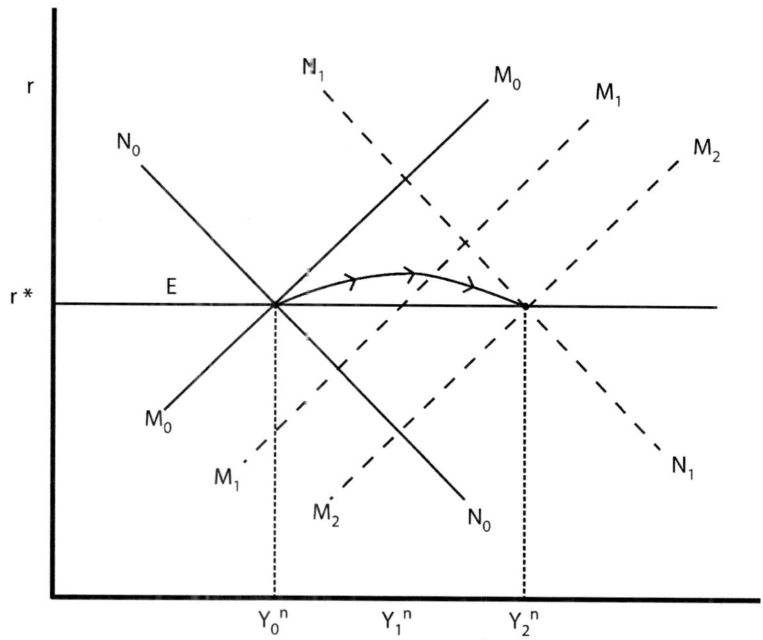

Figure 8.4 Increased public investment

In sum, the nature of the public expenditure being manipulated by the fiscal authorities becomes central to interpreting the overall impact of fiscal policy and whether changes in the fiscal stance are effective, non-effective, anti-cyclical or pro-cyclical. Moreover, this approach demonstrates that over the longer term, the exchange rate regime has no bearing on the longer run effectiveness of fiscal policy.

Productivity improvement

Turning lastly to an improvement in capital productivity (a rise in γ) under a fixed exchange rate, this would shift the *NN* schedule rightwards in the first instance from N_0N_0 to N_2N_2 as Figure 8.4 also shows. The domestic interest rate would then momentarily rise above the world rate creating an excess supply of foreign exchange. Central bank purchases of foreign exchange would increase the domestic money supply shifting the *MM* schedule out until real interest parity was restored at the intersection of the N_2N_2 and M_2M_2 schedules.

Alternatively, under a floating rate, a productivity shock would raise the domestic interest rate, appreciate the currency and also eventually shift the schedules to M_2M_2 and N_2N_2. Slow passthrough acts as a drag on the short-term expansion of national income although equilibrium is eventually reached at the intersection of N_2N_2 and M_2M_2 , the equilibrium reached if there was quick reversion to PPP.

Short-term variation in the capital–output ratio, reflecting lower economy-wide capacity usage, may also stem from aggregate demand-induced slumps in production. The macroeconomic consequences of such slumps would be the reverse of those just outlined for a productivity improvement that raises the capital–output ratio.

Conclusion

Methodologically, the framework of this chapter departs from recent macroeconomic approaches founded on microeconomic principles and optimizing representative agents. However, it provides a straightforward framework for addressing practical policy issues in open economy macroeconomics with reference to the key variables of interest. It is also consistent with earlier aggregative macroeconomic methods that are the mainstay of macroeconomics textbooks and as realistic as optimizing approaches based on microeconomic foundations.

In addition to focussing directly on macroeconomic aggregates at the outset rather than microeconomic foundations, this chapter assumes that domestic goods and services originate on the production side of the economy through a macroeconomic production function whose arguments are the key factor inputs. Within each time interval, domestically produced goods and services are exchanged along with imported foreign goods and services and are either consumed or used for investment on the aggregate demand side.

Macroeconomic activity therefore runs at the outset of the short run from aggregate supply to aggregate demand, rather than the orthodox line of causality of aggregate demand to aggregate supply. Nonetheless the quantum of output made available by domestic firms is still generated in light of expected within-period aggregate demand. This fine distinction about the aggregate demand–aggregate supply nexus alters results about the effects of changes in the stance of macroeconomic policy, particularly for the efficacy of fiscal policy.

Existing international macroeconomic theory unsatisfactorily explains the general equilibrium impact of monetary and fiscal policies on national income, interest rates, the external accounts and exchange rates. This is because it underemphasizes the significance of saving-investment imbalances and their implications for net foreign borrowing and national income. In addressing this deficiency, the model outlined in this chapter overturns some standard results about the effectiveness of macroeconomic policy under both fixed and floating exchange rate regimes.

Table 8.1 summarizes the effects of expansionary fiscal and monetary policies and productivity improvement on the balance of payments, exchange rates (a rise indicating depreciation) and national income.

With fiscal policy, higher government spending that lowers public saving weakens the external position and contracts national income. An easier fiscal stance resulting from higher public consumption spending therefore proves counterproductive as a means of boosting national income. Indeed, this model suggests that such a policy would actually be pro-cyclical, contrary to the MF result that changing the fiscal stance is an ineffective means of stabilizing national income under a floating exchange rate.

An important corollary to this is that fiscal consolidation that targets unproductive public consumption spending will raise, rather than lower, national income, consistent with limited empirical work on this

Table 8.1 Key results

	Exchange rate regime			
	Fixed		Floating	
	Balance of payments	**National income**	**Exchange rate**	**National income**
Source of shock				
Public consumption ↑	↓(*)	↓(*)	↑(*)	↓(*)
Public investment ↑	↑	↑	↑	↑
Productivity ↑	↑(*)	↑(*)	↓(*)	↑(*)
Money supply ↑	↓	0	↑	0(*)

(*)indicates a result different to the MF model.

issue (see IMF 2001). Nonetheless productive infrastructure investment and productivity improvement perhaps resulting from government-assisted R and D programmes still raises national income.

Another key point of difference between this model and conventional MF analysis is that the nature of the exchange rate regime becomes less relevant as a factor influencing the long-run (in)effectiveness of macroeconomic policy over the medium to longer runs.

References

Barro, R. (1989) 'The Ricardian Approach to Budget Deficits', *Journal of Economic Perspectives*, 3, 37–54.

Bruce, N. and Purvis, D. (1985) 'The Specification of Goods and Factor Markets in Open Economy Macroeconomic Models' in R. Jones and P. Kenen (eds) *Handbook of International Economics*, vol. 2. Elsevier, Amsterdam.

Dornbusch, R. (1976) 'Expectations and Exchange Rate Dynamics', *Journal of Political Economy*, 84 (6), 1161–76.

Fisher, F. (1987) 'Aggregation Problem' in P. Eatwell, M. Milgate and J. Newman (eds) *The Palgrave Dictionary of Economics*, Macmillan, Basingstoke, 53–5.

Fisher, F. (1993) *Aggregation, Aggregate Production Functions and Related Topics*, MIT Press, Cambridge, Masachusetts.

Froot, K. and Rogoff, K. (1995) 'Perspectives on PPP and Long-Run Real Exchange Rates' in G. Grossman and K. Rogoff (eds) *Handbook of International Economics*, vol. 3, Elsevier, Amsterdam.

Goldberg, P. and Knetter, M. (1997) 'Goods Prices and Exchange Rates: What Have We Learned?', *Journal of Economic Literature*, 35 (3), 1243–72.

Knox, A. (1952) 'The Acceleration Principle and the Theory of Investment: A Survey', *Economica*, 19, 269–97.

Masson, P. Bayoumi, T. and Samiei, H. (1998) 'International Evidence on the Determinants of Private Saving', *World Bank Economic Review*, 12, 483–501.

Solow, R. (1956) 'A Contribution to the Theory of Economic Growth', *Quarterly Journal of Economics*, 70, 1 (February), 65–94.

Swan, T. (1956) 'Economic Growth and Capital Accumulation', *Economic Record*, 32 (November), 334–61.

Taylor, M. (1999) 'Real Interest Rates and Macroeconomic Activity', *Oxford Review of Economic Policy*, 15, 95–113.

9

Monetary Policy and the Real Exchange Rate

Introduction

The conduct and effectiveness of monetary policy has changed markedly over recent decades as capital markets have become more internationally integrated, external imbalances have widened and exchange rates have become more variable. Inflation targeting is also now a primary goal of monetary policy in many advanced and emerging economies. Yet in this financially globalized context, many unresolved questions remain about the nature of the monetary policy transmission mechanism under floating exchange rates.

For instance, how does a change in the monetary stance influence real exchange rate adjustment and external imbalances? How do inflationary expectations at home and abroad affect inflation and the real economy? How important are changing interest risk premia and foreign interest rate movements to domestic monetary policy settings? And how do cyclical and productivity shocks in the real sector affect competitiveness, the current account and inflation over the medium term?

This chapter aims to provide clear-cut answers to these questions with reference to an international macroeconomic framework that links aggregate production, aggregate demand, interest rates, exchange rates, expectations, domestic and foreign price levels and external account imbalances.

This distinct approach contrasts with more traditional international monetary models that incorporate transnational capital flows, such as the MF framework which is widely used for interpreting the impact of real and monetary shocks in open economies. The MF model remains central to textbook macroeconomics and has proven so durable because it delivers clear macroeconomic policy prescriptions about national income stabilization under alternative polar exchange regimes.

Yet the standard MF model does not relate the direct effects of monetary and real sector shocks to national price levels, real exchange rates and external account imbalances, nor does it explain international macroeconomic behaviour with reference to deviations from the standard parity theorems of international finance. Moreover, as an aggregate demand oriented approach, the MF approach is unable to highlight the impact of aggregate supply-side phenomena, such as productivity shocks on exchange rates, the price level, competitiveness and current account imbalances.

Another dominant international macroeconomic paradigm, the more recent micro-founded intertemporal approach primarily relates consumption, saving, investment and international borrowing in economies populated by forward-looking, representative-agent, consumers and producers. Yet, as argued previously in this work, the macroeconomic policy implications of extended versions of the microfoundations approach that introduce money, price levels and exchange rates depend on the way the microfoundations themselves, such as the nature of utility functions and sources of price rigidities, are specified.

The complexity of the prevailing paradigm makes it considerably less tractable than the MF model for international macroeconomic policy analysis, a reason it is not widely used by policymakers as a vehicle for interpreting international macroeconomic linkages. To fill a gap in our understanding of international monetary linkages, this chapter proposes another alternative schema founded on aggregate output and expenditure relations and on the macroeconomic consequences of deviations from interest parity and PPP.

This distinct framework delivers new results about the transmission and effectiveness of monetary policy in financially globalized economies, with reference to the adjustment of nominal exchange rates, aggregate demand, price levels, real exchange rates and external imbalances.

The chapter proceeds as follows. The basic international monetary framework emphasizing the role of the real exchange rate is first developed, and then used to analyse the international macroeconomic effects of various domestic and foreign monetary and real shocks. This approach yields key results that differ from extant open-economy models, but are compatible with those of the models outlined earlier in this book.

Theoretical framework

The real sector

Real output or GDP is produced proportionate to the economy's capital stock, such that

$$\tilde{Y} = \gamma K \tag{9.1}$$

where $\tilde{Y}$ is full employment GDP, γ is the output to capital ratio and K is the capital stock, consistent with the stylized fact that output-to-capital ratios are remarkably stable for advanced economies over extended periods.

As in the previous chapter we use the inverse of the capital-output ratio, once central to investment and growth theory. In initial equilibrium the economy is assumed to be at its potential level of output with unemployment at the 'natural rate'. If the economy operates below potential capacity, this is reflected in a rise in unemployment above the natural rate.

Central to what follows is a distinction between full employment national output (or output consistent with the natural rate of unemployment) and total expenditure on that output which varies with real exchange rate fluctuations. The real exchange rate, or competitiveness, is defined as

$$R = \frac{eP^*}{P} \tag{9.2}$$

where e is the nominal effective exchange rate, defined as the price of foreign exchange; P* is the exogenous world price level; and P is the domestic price level. If in initial equilibrium the real exchange rate is normalized at unity,

$$R = \frac{eP^*}{P} = 1 \tag{9.3}$$

This implies that deviations from the unity value of the real exchange rate also measure deviations from PPP. Nominal exchange rate movements primarily drive real exchange rates since national price levels are sticky in the short run. A real depreciation due to nominal depreciation ($R > 1$) therefore instantly improves competitiveness.

This raises domestic demand for domestic product and net exports, thereby raising aggregate demand AD, above normal full employment output in the short run, whereas a real appreciation due to nominal appreciation ($R < 1$) worsens competitiveness and lowers AD below normal. This notion of aggregate expenditure by resident and non-resident entities accords with the traditional textbook interpretation of AD. However, in earlier chapters we defined aggregate expenditure as absorption in the Alexander (1952) sense and used the acronym AE to denote it. To avoid confusion it is important to note the changed use of terms at this juncture.

The positive relationship between exchange rates and aggregate spending can be further explained with reference to the following expression, based on the demand aggregates from the national accounts

$$AD = C_D + C_F + I_D + I_F + (X - C_F - I_F) \tag{9.4}$$

or,

$$AD(\overset{+}{R}) = C_D(\overset{+}{R}) + I_D(\overset{+}{R}) + X(\overset{+}{R}) \tag{9.5}$$

where C_D is demand for domestically produced consumption goods, C_F is demand for imported consumption goods, I_D is demand for domestically produced investment goods, I_F is imported investment goods and X is exports. $C_D + I_D$ is expenditure on domestic product by resident entities. Total imports equal $C_F + I_F$, whereas X is exports or expenditure on domestic product by foreign entities.

C_D, I_D and X are positively related to the nominal and real exchange rate in the short run, as a rise (fall) in the exchange rate improves (worsens) competitiveness, making domestically produced consumption and investment goods more attractive to resident entities and exports more attractive to foreigners.

Since C_F and I_F are negatively related to the exchange rate in the short run, a rise in total spending induced by improved competitiveness, per relation (9.5), is accompanied from a point of initial balance by a rising trade and CAS ($X - (C_D + I_F) > 0$).

Due to the relative price changes that follow currency depreciation, domestic spending switches to home-produced consumption and investment goods from imports, while foreign spending on domestic product also rises via higher exports. Hence, from initial equilibrium at which AD = $\tilde{Y}$, currency depreciation unambiguously raises total expenditure on domestic product above the full employment level of national output, so that

$$AD > \tilde{Y} \tag{9.6}$$

Hence from initial equilibrium, aggregate spending will vary according to

$$AD = AD_0 + \xi\left(\frac{eP^*}{P} - 1\right) \qquad \xi > 0 \tag{9.7}$$

where ξ represents the short-run responsiveness of aggregate spending on domestic product to real exchange rate changes. When aggregate spending exceeds the full employment level of output, the domestic price level will rise such that

$$\dot{P} = \upsilon(AD - \tilde{Y}) \qquad \upsilon > 0 \tag{9.8}$$

where υ is a parameter governing the rate of price level adjustment.

Following nominal depreciation, price level stability again prevails when $\dot{P} = 0$ or when R = 1. Hence, domestic inflation arising from depreciation-induced excess aggregate expenditure tends to erode competitiveness gains, reswitching net foreign demand as the real exchange rate tends to revert to its equilibrium unity value.

At the same time the price level rise is re-enforced by the passthrough of sustained changes in the nominal exchange rate (Froot and Rogoff 1995; Isard 1995; Frankel and Rose 1996; Wu 1996; Goldberg and Knetter 1997; Lopez 2007, *inter alia*, examine the theory and evidence of PPP and exchange rate passthrough).

Since $dAD/dR > 0$, we can depict the short-run behaviour of aggregate spending and national income in real exchange rate – aggregate expenditure space by the upward sloping DD schedule in Figure 9.1. Initial equilibrium is characterized by equal spending and potential output ($AE_0 = \tilde{Y}$), a stable price level ($\dot{P} = 0$) and a balanced trade and current accounts (CA = 0).

Above the R = 1 line competitiveness improves. The economy then experiences excess total expenditure on domestic product and trade and CASs (CA > 0).

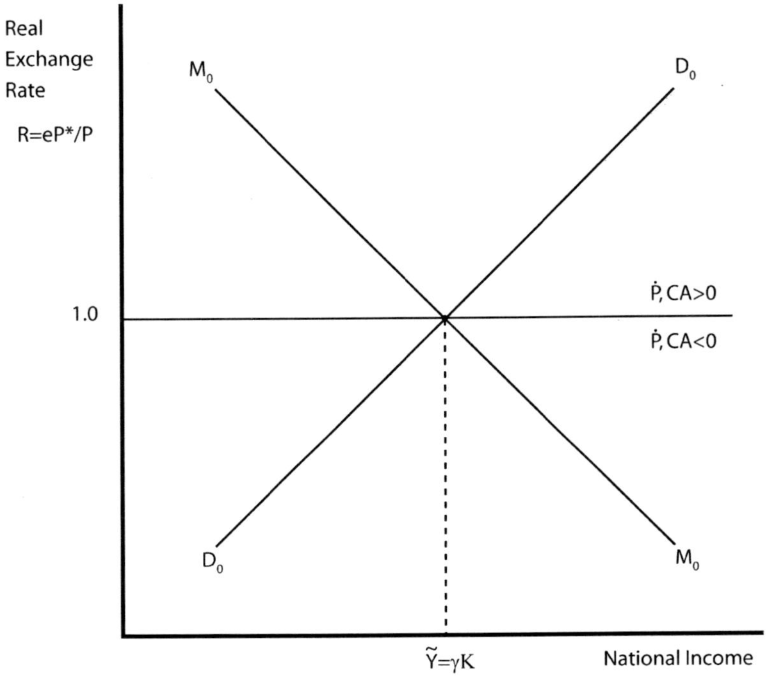

Figure 9.1 General equilibrium

However with a rise in R, production of additional output to meet higher demand from home and abroad above the full employment level is constrained by rising domestic costs, including wages which, combined with exchange rate passthrough, generates higher domestic inflation. This reverses the competitiveness gain.

The contrary case is real appreciation. Here competitiveness worsens, aggregate spending falls below 'full employment' output and there are temporary trade and CADs ($CA < 0$) below the $R = 1$ line. Positive (negative) productivity shocks shift *DD* rightwards (leftwards) since they alter the level of potential output.

The monetary sector

In the monetary sector, there are two assets: money and bonds, and the domestic interest rate depends on the money demand–money supply relationship. More formally, real money demand, λ, is positively related to total spending via parameter χ, and negatively related to the domestic interest rate via parameter δ, such that

$$\lambda = \chi AD - \delta r \qquad 0 < \chi < 1 \qquad \delta > 0 \tag{9.9}$$

The central bank alters the nominal money supply, M^S, via changes in its holdings of government bonds and foreign exchange reserves. Hence,

$$M^S = B + \Psi \tag{9.10}$$

Under a fixed exchange rate, unsterilized central bank purchases (sales) of foreign exchange raise (lower) the money supply, whereas under a float the money supply is invariant with the nominal exchange rate itself depreciating (appreciating). Using the equilibrium condition that real money demand equals real money supply,

$$M^S/P = \chi AD - \delta r \tag{9.11}$$

Now assume the nominal interest rate is related to the exogenous world interest rate according to uncovered interest parity and allowing for a risk premium

$$r = r^* + \hat{e} + \rho \tag{9.12}$$

where r^* is the world interest rate, $\hat{e}$ is expected exchange rate depreciation and ρ is the time-varying risk premium.

Further note that

$$\hat{\epsilon} = \frac{f - e}{e} = \frac{f}{e} - 1 \tag{9.13}$$

where f is the spot exchange rate expected next period. Initial equilibrium implies static exchange rate expectations, such that the expected future exchange rate can be set at $f = e_0$. The rational expectations case is discussed subsequently.

By substitution and algebraic manipulation, (9.11) can be solved as

$$e = fP^* \left[\frac{\chi AD - M^s P^{-1}}{\delta} + 1 - r^* - \rho \right]^{-1} \tag{9.14}$$

Dividing by the domestic price level and substituting $R = ep^*/P$

$$R = fP^* \left[\frac{\chi AD - M^s P^{-1}}{\delta} + 1 - r^* - \rho)P \right]^{-1} \tag{9.15}$$

Differentiating (9.15) with respect to national income yields

$$\frac{dR}{dAD} = -\frac{fP^{*}\chi P}{\delta} \cdot \left[\frac{\chi AD - M^{s}P^{-1}}{\delta} + 1 - r^{*} - \rho)P \right]^{-2} < 0 \qquad (9.16)$$

This expression justifies the downward sloping money-related schedule labelled *MM* in real exchange rate – national income space shown in Figure 9.1, the centrepiece diagram of this approach. Given a sticky domestic price level in the short run and an exogenous foreign price level, the nominal exchange rate drives real exchange rate movements in the first instance.

We assume that at the initial equilibrium where *DD* and *MM* intersect, PPP and real interest parity prevail, spending equals full employment output and the external accounts are balanced. Movement away from initial equilibrium implies spending deviates from the level of spending that is consistent with full employment output and a stable price level. Moreover, it implies deviations from the parity conditions.

From initial equilibrium, movement along the *MM* schedule conveys that a rise (fall) in total spending raises (lowers) money demand and the domestic interest rate in the short run, appreciating (depreciating) the nominal exchange rate, *ceteris paribus*. It also follows from (9.15) that

$$\frac{dR}{dM^{S}} > 0, \quad \frac{dR}{dP^{*}} > 0, \quad \frac{dR}{dr^{*}} > 0, \quad \frac{dR}{d\upsilon} > 0 \qquad (9.17)$$

The above signs imply that monetary expansion due to bond market or foreign exchange market intervention, as well as rises in the foreign price level, foreign interest rates and the risk premium shift *MM* right. Unstable money demand that manifests, for instance, as a rise in the responsiveness of money demand to spending can also shift this schedule.

It is now possible to incorporate exchange rate expectations by presuming the future exchange rate reflects expected PPP. Under these conditions, since absolute PPP is $e = P/P^{*}$, it follows that the future exchange rate reflects expected future price levels at home and abroad, where ε denotes expected values, so that

$$\varepsilon e_{+1} = f = \varepsilon\left(P_{+1} / P^{*}_{+1} \right) \qquad (9.18)$$

Equation (9.15) may then be rewritten as

$$R = \varepsilon\left(P_{+1}/P^*_{+1}\right)P^*\left[\frac{\chi AD - M^s P^{-1}}{\delta} + 1 - r^* - \rho)P\right]^{-1} \tag{9.19}$$

This yields the further results that

$$\frac{dR}{d\varepsilon\left(P_{+1}/P^*_{+1}\right)} > 0 \tag{9.20}$$

Hence, higher anticipated domestic inflation immediately shifts the *MM* schedule upwards whereas higher anticipated foreign inflation shifts it downwards.

Monetary shocks

This framework can now be used to analyse numerous monetary policy shocks.

Monetary policy, national income and the current account

First, consider the case of a monetary contraction. Central banks in advanced economies adopt official interest rates as intermediate targets for inflation control with direct liquidity implications such that increasing (decreasing) a target interest rate decreases (increases) the nominal money supply. With monetary contraction, *MM* shifts downwards, as shown in Figure 9.2.

Given relatively more sluggish adjustment in the product markets than in asset markets, money market equilibrium is instantly re-established and the nominal exchange rate overshoots in the Dornbusch (1976) sense, with the real exchange rate immediately dropping to R_1.

Thereafter, total spending on domestic output falls and a trade and CAD emerges; exports fall due to lower foreign spending on exports and imports rise due to residents switching spending from domestic to foreign-produced goods and services. Capital inflow in response to a relatively higher domestic interest rate matches the rise in the external deficit.

Hence, tight monetary policy increases rather than decreases a CAD, while simultaneously slowing the economy. This contrasts with the traditional view that tighter monetary policy reduces

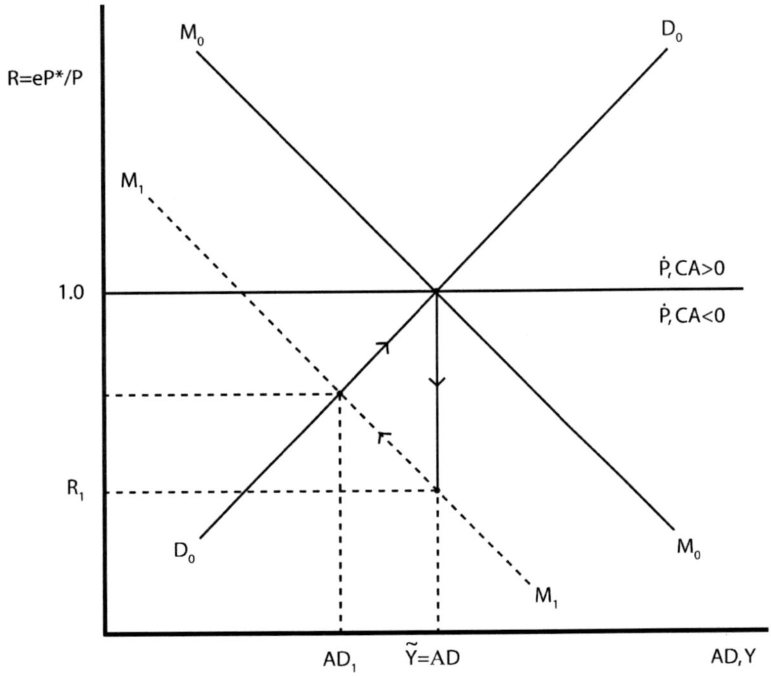

Figure 9.2 Monetary contraction

external deficits by curbing national spending and import demand, a policy frequently prescribed by the IMF.

Over the medium term, the domestic price level will tend to fall because, other things equal, total expenditure falls relative to full employment output. Re-enforcing the downward pressure on the price level are passthrough effects from the nominal appreciation. A lower price level expands the real money supply, shifting *MM* back towards its original position. The real exchange rate therefore tends to track back to unity, reversing the initial competitiveness losses from nominal appreciation.

Under a pegged exchange rate system, monetary policy becomes ineffective as a stabilization tool. For instance, a monetary expansion leads to a domestic interest rate fall below the initial parity rate which generates excess demand for foreign currency, immediately depleting foreign exchange reserves. This offsets any intended monetary expansion, with no lasting *MM* shift.

Monetary policy is therefore ineffective under a fixed exchange rate as expenditure and national output remain at y_0. Nonetheless the framework also usefully illustrates that a fixed exchange rate may be the best means of attaining price level stability for a small open economy under circumstances where the foreign price level is significantly more stable than the domestic one.

Higher inflation expectations

This approach also highlights the importance of controlling inflation expectations as a means of keeping inflation within any specified target range. In this framework, changed expectations about the future domestic price level can have as much impact on the economy as changes in the monetary stance itself.

For instance, if markets suddenly expect a higher future domestic price level (a rise in εP_{+1}), the *MM* shifts out, immediately depreciating the exchange rate, raising aggregate spending and generating inflationary pressures. To counter this, the central bank then has to tighten liquidity and raise official interest rates.

Increased inflation and interest rates abroad

How central banks should react to expectations of rising world inflation (a rise in εP^*_{+1}) is a monetary policy issue that existing macroeconomic models are not well equipped to address. However, in this framework a rise in expected inflation abroad leads to a leftward *MM* shift, appreciating the nominal exchange rate and real exchange rate. If domestic inflation is within its target range, it becomes necessary to relax monetary policy to avert a slowdown in domestic spending arising from any loss of competitiveness.

On the other hand, official interest rate increases abroad generate capital outflow and depreciate the exchange rate. This, in turn, boosts net exports and generates upward price level pressure, as shown in Figure 9.3. If inflation is presently within its target range, this implies that the domestic central bank also needs to lift interest rates at home by restricting liquidity.

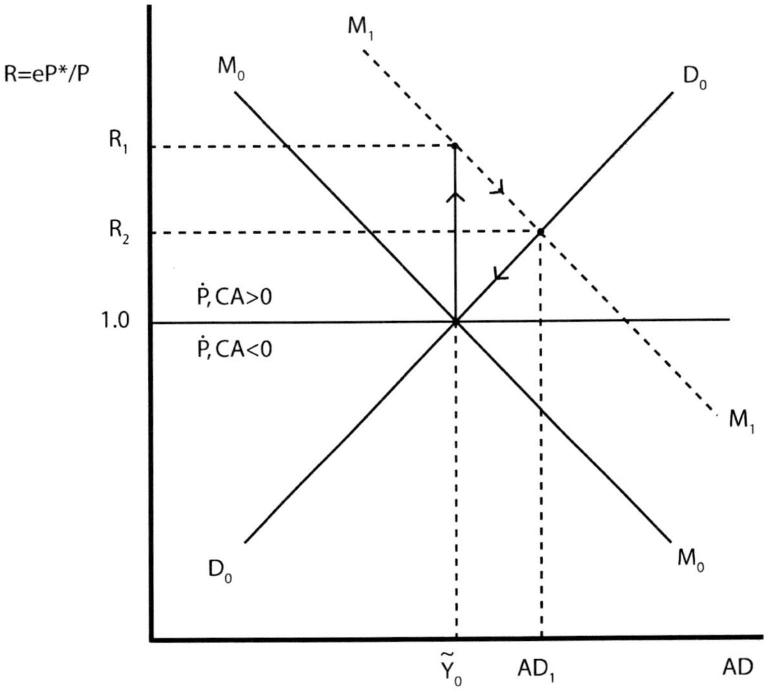

Figure 9.3 Increased interest rates abroad

Real sector shocks

Now consider the international macroeconomic implications of some real side shocks in the form of productivity improvement and investment booms as shown in Figure 9.4.

Productivity gains

Under a floating exchange rate, a positive productivity shock raises productive capacity and hence potential national output, shifting the *DD* schedule right. Yet, other things (including nominal money supply) the same, rising money demand appreciates the currency and tends to lower competitiveness to R_1 at the intersection of D_1D_1 and M_0M_0. This loss of competitiveness limits the medium-term expenditure increase to AE_1 and gives rise to an external deficit.

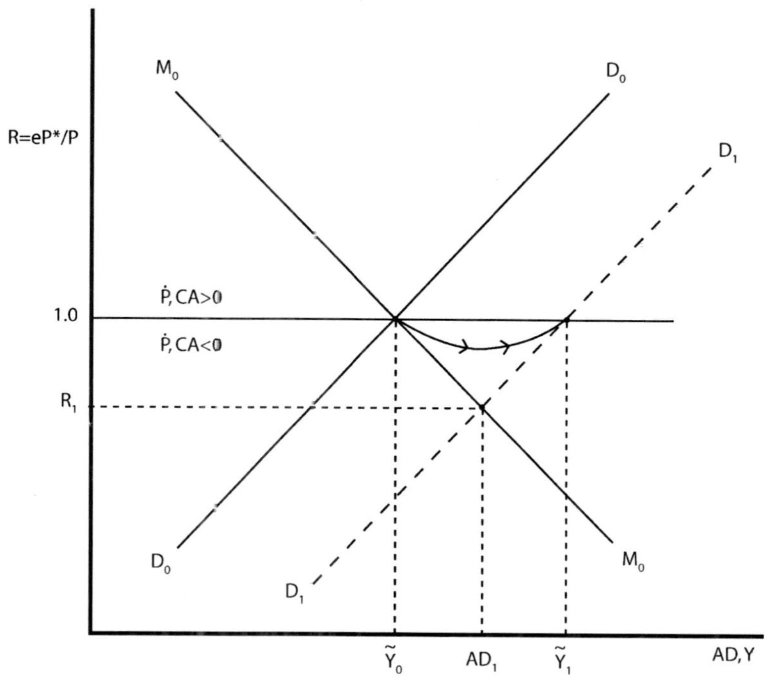

Figure 9.4 Productivity improvement, investment boom

However, over time downward pressure on the price level stemming from the productivity induced output expansion, as well as exchange rate passthrough effects, tend to push *MM* rightwards until the real exchange rate is unity. Full employment output and total spending once again coincide (above $\tilde{Y}_1$). Of course, the slower the price level reacts to nominal exchange rate passthrough, the more prolonged are deviations from purchasing power and real interest parity.

Investment fluctuations and cyclical movements

Investment fluctuations drive business cycles and this framework can model their economy-wide impact by examining their impact via changes in the rate of capital stock growth. Since full employment output is $\tilde{Y} = \gamma K$, a rise in investment expands productive capacity and shifts *DD* right. The demand for money rises as national spending increases.

For a given money supply, the interest rate will therefore exceed the foreign rate. This creates excess supply of foreign exchange which appreciates the nominal and real exchange rates with the same economy-wide results as a productivity improvement. That is, higher domestic investment generates medium-term currency appreciation, a CAD and downward price level pressure.

If the nominal exchange rate was fixed, however, unsterilized purchases of foreign exchange by the central bank would automatically increase the domestic money supply and shift *MM* rightwards. As a result, under a fixed exchange rate regime monetary policy would accommodate productivity improvements and extra real investment by raising national income without attendant price level effects.

Implications for exchange rate choice

Choosing the exchange rate regime that best suits the characteristics of an economy is one of the most significant policy decisions a national government must make and, at critical times, reassess. Exchange rate regime choice is a perennial issue and, given the heterogeneity of extant international monetary arrangements, has generated a literature aimed mostly at identifying empirical regularities associated with different exchange rate systems.

Reflecting the inconclusive empirical results of this literature *in toto* and the lack of consensus on a theoretical framework for evaluating the international macroeconomic effects of alternative regimes in developing, emerging and advanced economies, the IMF has concluded that there are no simple prescriptions for implementing any particular exchange rate system.

Nonetheless in view of the pivotal role of the exchange rate in open economies and their potential to spark financial crises, the need to understand the macroeconomic consequences of exchange rate choice remains as important as ever. Contrary to the bipolar view of exchange rate regimes (Fischer 2001), exchange rate regimes lying between the polar extremes of free floating and hard peg remain the most prevalent, especially in developing and emerging economies, accounting for around half of all regimes based on recent de facto rather than de jure classifications (see Rogoff et al. 2004).

What straightforward theoretical model explains this? And do economies necessarily progress in moving from pegged to free-floating regimes, as inferred by the supposition that there is widespread 'fear of floating' in developing economies (Hausmann et al. 2001 and Calvo and Reinhart 2002)? Or, might the absence of bi-polarism instead imply that intermediate regimes confer significant macroeconomic benefits on developing economies?

The degree of passthrough also has profound implications for exchange rate regime choice because the more completely and rapidly pass-through occurs, the greater the similarity of the international macroeconomic effects of real and monetary shocks and the less relevant the issue of exchange rate regime choice becomes.

Indeed, the hypothetical extreme of complete and immediate passthrough of nominal exchange rate changes to the price level is equivalent to instantaneous PPP in a small economy producing only tradables. Under these circumstances, the real money supply adjusts as quickly through its numerator under a fixed regime, as through its denominator under a free float.

In reality, however, the price level reacts quite slowly to exchange rate changes, and passthrough is likely to be minimal in the short to medium term, the less open the economy, the smaller the share of tradables and the more differentiated are its goods and services from its trading partners. If passthrough is negligible within the period, and manifests quite slowly afterwards, then deviations from purchasing power and real interest parity would be prolonged (Sarno and Taylor 2002). With reference to the floating rate case of the framework, the *MM* schedule would therefore shift only minimally, if at all, within the period under scrutiny.

Under these conditions, the model can now be used to prescribe which exchange rate system is more suitable for economies buffeted by diverse internal and external shocks. In particular, does the source of shocks, real or monetary, have implications for exchange rate choice? And is it relevant whether the shocks are symmetrical or asymmetrical?

Assume the economy is relatively more susceptible to real shocks than monetary shocks and that these are either in the form of symmetrical fluctuations in seasonal conditions, volatile world commodity prices affecting the terms of trade, or swings in the saving rate. As shown in Figure 9.5, the *DD* schedule would then shift around its mean value within a given short-run period, with the *MM* schedule remaining relatively stable throughout.

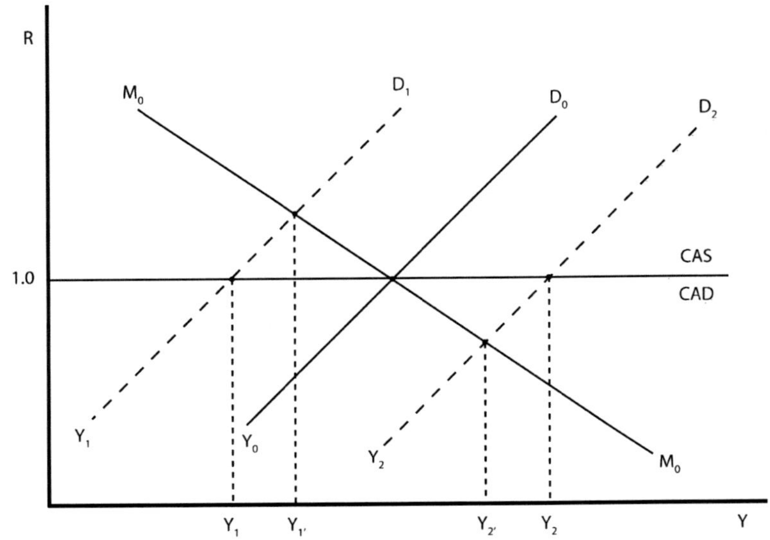

Figure 9.5 Real shocks and exchange rate choice

If the exchange rate is fixed, the money supply is endogenous and national income varies between Y_1 and Y_2 around the mean, whereas if the exchange rate floats, income would vary less, between Y_1 and Y_2. The floating exchange rate acts as a real shock absorber, insulating the economy from excessive income fluctuation and so is preferable to a pegged system.

Alternatively, assume the economy is more prone to monetary shocks, such as oscillating money demand and volatile exchange rate expectations than to real disturbances. Under these conditions, the *MM* schedule shifts about its mean value relative to the *DD* schedule, as shown in Figure 9.6.

In this case, a fixed exchange regime simultaneously stabilizes competitiveness and national income (at Y^0), whereas a floating regime leads to variation in both, especially in the real exchange rate due to overshooting. Under such conditions, it is clearly preferable to peg the exchange rate, not only as a means of minimizing national income but as a means of stabilizing the future price level, consistent with an inflation-targeting regime.

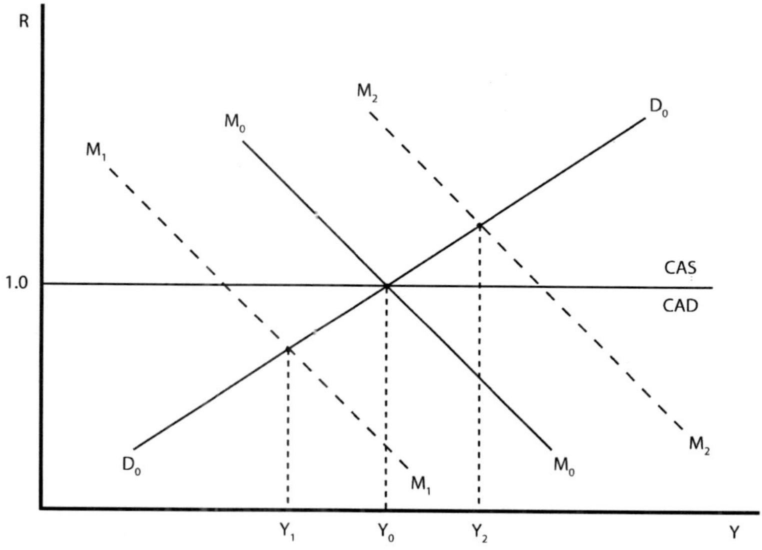

Figure 9.6 Monetary shocks and exchange rate choice

The general conclusion from this analysis is that a floating exchange rate best minimizes national income variation if the goods and services markets are most vulnerable to shocks, whereas a fixed exchange rate best minimizes such variation if the monetary sector is relatively more unstable. Importantly, however, this analysis presumes that negative shocks are of the same magnitude and as probable as positive shocks period to period.

With respect to the real sector, this is implausible for economies experiencing steady economic growth driven by productivity improvements, investment gains and exports. Persistent output growth not only appreciates the currency but creates a CAD and subsequent deflationary pressures from eventual passthrough. Yet why would domestic policymakers accept a combination of CADs, restricted output expansion and deflationary pressures, when these problems can easily be avoided via judicious exchange rate management?

Accordingly, in a growing economy, it may be optimal from a domestic monetary policy viewpoint to stabilize the nominal exchange rate through monetary expansion, thereby accommodating positive non-reversible real shocks and maximizing non-inflationary national income gains.

On the contrary, if an economy is frequently subjected to terms of trade problems beyond its control, it may be preferable to allow currency depreciation. This prevents larger real income losses than necessary, even at the risk of future inflationary pressures.

Conclusion

This chapter combines national and external accounting behaviorial relationships with precepts of international finance to yield a novel diagrammatic framework for analysing the monetary transmission mechanism in financially globalized economies. The main predictions of the approach are shown in Table 9.1.

Contrary to textbook paradigms, this framework reveals that changes in liquidity engineered by shifts in the stance of monetary policy have major implications for nominal and real exchange rates, the domestic price level and external account imbalances. Moreover it shows that macroeconomic fundamentals can be key drivers of exchange rate fluctuations over the short and medium terms.

Significantly, it also demonstrates that, contrary to the orthodox IMF view, central banks cannot use restrictive monetary policy to narrow an economy's trade and CADs. Indeed, monetary tightening

Table 9.1 Key Results

	Nominal exchange rate	**Expenditure, national income**	**Current account balance**	**Domestic price level**
Expansionary monetary policy	↑	↑	↑	↑
Rising inflation expectations	↑	↑	↑	↑
Higher expected world inflation	↓	↓	↓	↓
Higher world interest rates	↑	↑	↑	↑
Improved productivity	↓	↑	↓	↓
Increased domestic investment	↓	↑	↓	↓

in response to a growing external deficit would, other things equal, tend to further widen the imbalance. Additionally, this approach highlights the importance of keeping inflationary expectations low as a means of inflation control, as well as showing how higher foreign inflation and interest rates can be transmitted to the domestic economy under floating exchange rates.

These findings have important implications for the way monetary policy is conducted in internationally integrated economies that adopt inflation targeting. It suggests it is imperative for central banks to maintain credibility to sustain low and stable inflation expectations. Moreover, in setting official interest rates, central banks explicitly have to take world inflation and world interest rate behaviour into account.

Another novel finding is that productivity improvement in the home economy tends to appreciate nominal and real exchange rates, induce CADs and put downward pressure on the price level. This is consistent with the behaviour over much of the period since the early 1990s of OECD economies such as Australia, New Zealand and the US, each of which simultaneously experienced relatively high productivity growth and lower inflation, accompanied by large external deficits.

This framework, which is compatible with tenets of standard growth theory and the international parity conditions, also allows us to examine the issue of exchange rate choice with reference to real and monetary shocks. Among other things, it implies that the best exchange rate regime for any economy depends on the size and speed of exchange rate passthrough to the domestic price level, which is related to its openness, as well as the relative stabilities of its real and monetary sectors.

Importantly, the framework demonstrates that to achieve high real national income in an international environment of low inflation, there are grounds for managing the nominal exchange rate when exports and productivity are driving growth and the monetary sector is relatively unstable. These circumstances most likely apply to emerging economies with relatively weak financial systems.

Hence, the model implies that emerging economies may rationally choose to peg their exchange rates, not because they exhibit a fear of floating *per se*, due, for instance, to concerns about policy credibility and currency mismatches, but because managed exchange rates enable them to maximize macroeconomic welfare through higher real income. At the same time, a degree of flexibility may be necessary to lower real income variation in the face of unexpected negative real shocks.

Accordingly, many economies would understandably vary the extent of exchange rate management over time, with a bias towards pegging when macroeconomic conditions were favourable. This is consistent with the fact that intermediate regimes are the most prevalent in developing and emerging economies (Rogoff et al. 2004). Alternatively, a free-floating system may still better suit relatively closed economies, such as Japan and the US, that have more robust monetary sectors, yet more frequently experience negative internal and external real shocks.

References

Calvo, G. and Reinhart, C. (2002) 'Fear of Floating', *Quarterly Journal of Economics*, 117, 379–408.

Dornbusch, R. (1976) 'Expectations and Exchange Rate Dynamics', *Journal of Political Economy*, 84 (6), 1161–76.

Fischer, S. (2001) 'Exchange Rate Regimes: Is the Bi-Polar View Correct?', *Journal of Economic Perspectives*, 15 (Spring), 3–24.

Frankel, J. and Rose, A. (1996) 'A Panel Project on Purchasing Power Parity: Mean Reversion within and between Countries', *Journal of International Economics*, 40, 209–24.

Froot, K. and Rogoff, K. (1995) 'Perspectives on PPP and Long-run Real Exchange Rates' in G. Grossman and K. Rogoff (eds) *Handbook of International Economics*, vol. 3, Elsevier, Amsterdam.

Goldberg, P. and Knetter, M. (1997) 'Goods Prices and Exchange Rates: What Have We Learned?', *Journal of Economic Literature*, 35 (3), 1243–72.

Hausmann, R., Panizza, U. and Stein, E. (2001) 'Why Do Countries Float the Way They Float?', *Journal of Development Economics*, 66 (4), 387–414.

Isard, P. (1995) *Exchange Rate Economics*, Cambridge University Press, New York.

Lopez, C. (2007) 'Evidence of Purchasing Power Parity for the Floating Regime Period', *Journal of International Money and Finance*, 27 (1), 156–64.

Papell, D. (2004) 'The Panel Purchasing Power Parity Puzzle', *Journal of International Economics*, 43 (3), 313–32.

Rogoff, K., Husain, A., Mody, A., Brooks, R. and Oomes, N. (2004) *Evolution and Performance of Exchange Rate Regimes*, IMF Occasional Paper 229, Washington, DC.

Sarno, L. and Taylor, M. (2002) 'Purchasing Power Parity and the Real Exchange Rate', *IMF Staff Papers*, 49, 65–105.

Wu, Y. (1996) 'Are Real Exchange Rates Non-Stationary? Evidence from a Panel Data Test', *Journal of Money, Credit and Banking*, 28, 54–63.

10
Select Stabilization Policy Issues

Introduction

This chapter examines two issues of relevance to macroeconomic stabilization policy, one relating to monetary policy, the other to fiscal policy. The first concerns the impact of unexpected inflation on domestic borrowers and lenders in the economy and what this implies for the conduct of monetary policy.

Previous research on inflation has mainly concentrated at the economy-wide level on such questions as its principal causes; how best to control it in practice; the welfare costs of ongoing inflation and the costs, in terms of activity and employment, of eliminating high inflation through disinflation. Much less attention has been paid to the redistributive effects of inflation and deflation.

The second part of the chapter focuses on the macroeconomic significance of public debt and what it implies for the stance of fiscal policy. It reveals that a fiscal stance is ultimately unsustainable if it leads to an ever-increasing ratio of public debt to income. This part develops approaches that national fiscal authorities can adopt to manage excessive public debt levels that centre on the importance of controlling primary (non-interest) budget balances. There is also discussion of problems associated with activist fiscal policy, with an emphasis on the detrimental effects of excessive public consumption spending.

Unexpected inflation and interest rates

After long periods of relative price stability, the onset of higher inflation surprises borrowers and savers (lenders) and enables a transfer of income to occur from savers to borrowers, including governments running sizeable fiscal deficits, as occurred in the 1970s. For periods up to several years from the start of a higher inflation regime, nominal interest rates can remain relatively stable, resulting in real interest rates turning negative.

Hence, the notion that, at the outset, higher than anticipated inflation is a form of 'theft' because it erodes the real value of wealth whenever savers are not fully compensated for their lost purchasing power via higher nominal interest rates. As households and firms come to anticipate higher inflation as the norm, however, real interest rates begin to rise and the misappropriation of wealth ceases.

Inflation outcomes in advanced, emerging and developing economies improved markedly in the 1990s and early 2000s compared to previous decades. Yet, because of relatively poor inflation histories hitherto, inflation expectations were slow to adjust to reality in many of these countries. This arbitrarily redistributed income, benefited some citizens at the expense of others. In particular, during the early 1990s disinflation episode domestic borrowers bore the cost of the central bank's poor credibility on inflation control, while savers experienced a reversal of the misfortunes that had been suffered by savers during the unexpected rise of inflation in the 1970s.

As a general rule, real interest rates are lower than necessary during a transition to a new higher inflation regime, but higher than necessary during a transition to a lower inflation regime. When inflation unexpectedly rises this bestows significant income losses on savers, but confers gains on savers when inflation unexpectedly falls. The following section proposes a new framework for understanding how and why such redistributions between domestic borrowers and lenders occur.

Arbitrary income transfers

A changing domestic price level affects income distribution and household welfare in a number of ways. For instance, inflation can lower real disposable income in circumstances where nominal wages are not fully indexed, or even if wages are indexed, when marginal income tax rates are not. Indirectly, inflation can also worsen inequality by slowing output growth and hence employment through channels which distort relative prices and harm allocative efficiency.

It has also long been recognized that a changing price level can arbitrarily redistribute income and wealth between savers and borrowers when it is unanticipated. Households must be either net savers or borrowers of funds, except for those whose expenditure always coincides exactly with their income. Surprisingly, however, the impact of unanticipated inflation on borrowers and lenders has to date not been well developed analytically.

As first argued by Irving Fisher (1930), the prevailing interest rate structure of an economy should reflect the expectations of borrowers and lenders about the direction of future inflation. With accurate inflation forecasts and well-founded expectations, only real influences, such as changes in saving behaviour that shift the supply of funds, or changes in the productivity of capital that shift the demand, should affect real interest rates over time.

Yet real interest rate variation measured on an *ex post* basis also arises when changes in inflation are unexpected. Arbitrary income transfers between borrowers and savers are associated with this source of real interest rate fluctuation, especially during transitions from low inflation to high inflation regimes and vice versa. Figure 10.1, relating interest rates, inflation, borrowing and lending, illustrates this graphically.

Lending is shown to be positively related to the interest rate and borrowing negatively related. Saver-lenders exchange funds for interest-earning financial instruments, such as bonds or certificates of deposit, issued by borrowers. Hence the upward sloping lending schedule can also be interpreted as a demand for interest earning assets schedule. For a given level of wealth, the higher the interest rate, the higher is the demand for interest earning assets relative to the demand for other financial and real assets, such as equities and real estate.

On the other side of the market, borrowers supply the interest earning assets and issue more the lower the interest rate is. In reality of course a spectrum of rates reflects different maturity terms and the relative riskiness of financial instruments. Here, 'the' interest rate is an average of market rates, all of which are affected by inflationary

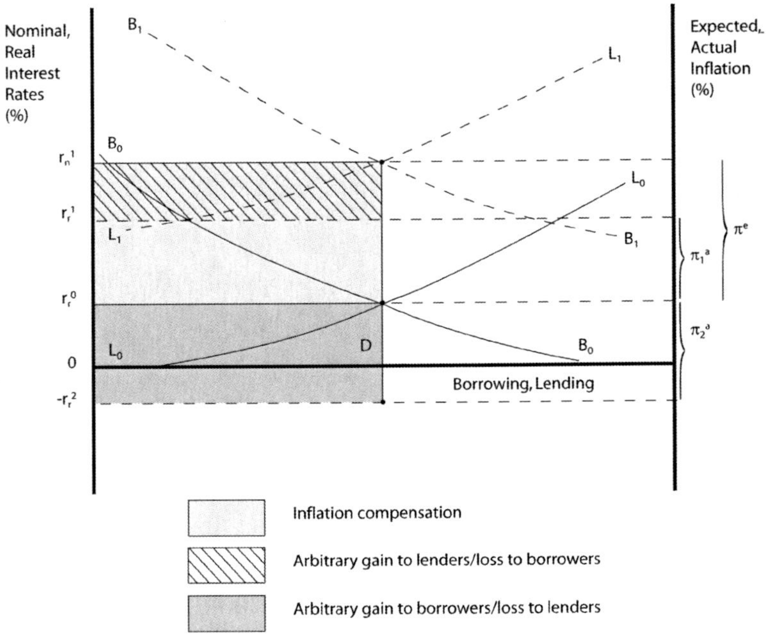

Figure 10.1 Inflation, interest rates and income transfers

expectations. With reference to Figure 10.1, if there is no inflation initially with none expected, the equilibrium interest rate is r_r^0, also the real interest rate.

However, with the onset of inflation, assumed to be generated by a monetary process for which the central bank is responsible, saver-lenders in the economy demand a higher nominal rate of return at all quantities of funds supplied as compensation for erosion in the value of principal. Hence, once inflation is expected to persist, the lending schedule shifts upwards by the amount of expected inflation, π^e, as shown.

At the same time, borrowers realize that under inflationary conditions they can repay less principal in real terms in the future, so the present period demand for available funds rises. If lenders and borrowers have the same initial expectations about inflation, the new equilibrium interest rate in the funds market would therefore be r_n^1, as illustrated on the left-side vertical axis of Figure 10.1.

Hence, in accordance with the Fisher effect, the difference between the initial real rate, r^0, and the new nominal interest rate, r_n^1, is the anticipated rate of inflation, π^e, as measured on the right-side vertical axis or $r^0 = r_n^1 - \pi^e$. That is, the rise in the nominal interest rate paid by borrowers and earned by saver-lenders is equal to the anticipated inflation rate, such that the real interest rate remains unchanged, *ex ante*. Although the exact expression for the *ex ante* real interest rate is $r_n^i - \pi^e/1 + \pi^e$, the denominator approximates unity if inflation is not excessively high.

Of course, in the unlikely event of expected deflation, the borrowing and lending schedules would shift down and the nominal interest rate would then be less than the real interest rate (Ball 1992; Barsky 1987; Mishkin 1992). The value of the additional nominal interest income received by lenders and paid by borrowers, as compensation for the erosion in the purchasing power of the principal loaned is the product π^e x OD, where OD is the quantity of funds actually loaned or borrowed over a given time.

Now consider what happens when the expected inflation rate, subsumed in the observed nominal interest rate, differs from the *ex post* inflation rate. In the figure, if *ex post* inflation, π_1^a, is less than expected inflation, π^e, then there is an arbitrary income transfer from borrowers to lenders as indicated. This results from incorrect inflation forecasts yielding a higher effective real interest rate than was necessary. In general, it becomes clear that whether inflation is higher or lower than anticipated has contrary welfare implications for lenders and borrowers.

On the other hand, if higher inflation comes as a complete surprise and the nominal interest rate remains stable, as was the case in the late 1970s, the *ex post* real interest rate could fall to r_r^2. This real rate is the difference shown between the stable nominal interest rate and the actual amount of inflation. If the unexpected inflation outcome is sufficiently high, then the real interest rate can become negative as depicted, as indeed it was for many industrial economies under similar circumstances in the late 1970s.

This was opposite to actual inflation being less than previously expected, as was the experience in many economies during the disinflation of the early 1990s and which gave rise to unwarranted high, real interest rates. Under these circumstances, income was not transferred from lenders to borrowers as in the 1970s, but from borrowers to lenders. In general terms, from Figure 10.1 the arbitrary income transfer, Θ, can be expressed as

$$\Theta = OD \text{ x } (\pi^{e} - \pi^{a}) \tag{10.1}$$

If $\Theta < 0$, borrowers gain and lenders lose, whereas if $\Theta > 0$, borrowers lose and lenders gain.

Estimating redistributional effects

The magnitude of the arbitrary income transfers between borrowers and lenders arising from divergences between *ex ante* and *ex post* inflation outcomes could be estimated using data from nations' flow of funds accounts and from alternative series on inflation expectations (see Makin 2003).

The flow of funds accounts record the value of outstanding financial credit in an economy, a proxy for borrowing and lending in the economy as a whole. Interest is payable on all forms of credit and the rates charged by lenders and paid by borrowers across the spectrum should at any time reflect inflation expectations. The key exception is interest rates payable on inflation-indexed bonds issued by some governments in advanced economies which provide a safeguard against arbitrary income transfers. However, the stock of indexed bonds presently on issue around the world is relatively small.

The main long-term series on inflation expectations for the US, for example, are the Livingston Survey, the Michigan Institute of Social Research Survey of Households (the Michigan Survey) and the Survey of Professional Forecasters. These surveys of inflation forecasts over recent decades reveal that households and businesses have usually expected inflation to be either significantly higher or lower than eventually recorded.

Presuming nominal rates reflected expected inflation according to the Fisher effect, it would be possible for any economy, data permitting, to obtain the product of the difference between expected and actual inflation and the stock of outstanding credit as an estimate of an arbitrary income transfers attributable to unanticipated inflation or disinflation.

Conceivably, the redistributional effects of unanticipated inflation may also affect income inequality within an economy, as measured, for instance, by the Gini coefficient. Unfortunately, such measures are not routinely published by national statistical agencies. Nonetheless it is possible to infer that if high income earners save more and borrow less than low income earners, other things the same, overall inequality could be expected to improve following an unexpected rise in inflation and worsen in the wake of an unexpected fall. Moreover, as inflation tends to be more variable when it is higher, year-to-year arbitrary transfers would be more random under a high-inflation regime than under a low-inflation regime.

In terms of specific groups, unexpected rises in inflation adversely affect the aged and those saving for retirement, for instance, though at the same time benefit younger generations borrowing during the low-saving period of the life cycle. Hence, this inflation-linked source of income redistribution has an inter-generational dimension.

Implications for monetary policy

What then do the redistributive effects of unexpected inflation imply for the conduct of monetary policy? It suggests that adopting an inflation-targeting regime is advisable in order to minimize arbitrary redistribution that arises when unpredictable inflation rates make real interest rates lower or higher than justified. Under inflation targeting central banks build credibility on the issue of inflation control and this acts to anchor inflation expectations at a low level (Bernanke and Mishkin 1997).

In practice this means that central banks aim to keep inflation within a stipulated low range on average over the business cycle. Countries that have adopted such inflation target ranges as the centrepiece of their monetary policies include Australia (2–3 per cent), New Zealand (0–3 per cent), Canada (1–3 per cent), Sweden (1-3 per cent) and Spain (0–3 per cent). Alternatively, the analysis suggests that to minimize arbitrary income transfers, it may be even more desirable for central banks to announce point-specific inflation targets of say, 2.2 per cent, as prescribed in the United Kingdom, or in Finland, although point targets could hinder policy from dealing with other shocks.

In sum, the above underscores the importance of keeping inflation low and stable. To the extent that under present monetary policy arrangements central banks underachieve by allowing inflation to exceed previously announced goals, they are responsible for bestowing windfall gains on borrowers. Alternatively, if they overachieve in relation to their stipulated inflation targets by lowering inflation beneath target, then savers arbitrarily benefit.

Managing public debt

High public debt levels raise numerous macroeconomic risks, especially for emerging economies. For instance, excess public sector demand for domestic funds raises net international borrowing and effective interest rates that crowd out of private investment and limit economic growth. Moreover, an escalating stock of public debt increases the probability of default, raising the interest risk premium charged by creditors. This further enlarges public debt interest obligations, accelerating budget outlays. Governments facing uncontrollable interest servicing costs are tempted to default or monetize public debt.

Outright debt default makes further government borrowing on reasonable terms very difficult, whereas monetization subsequently generates higher inflation. Should default or monetization occur, either course of action is likely to precipitate capital flight, sparking possible financial crisis. Indeed, capital flight can occur before the domestic authorities actually default or monetize if investors suddenly judge such events inevitable, or when they realize crowding out is retarding economic growth.

Using a range of mathematical methods, numerous authors have examined the dynamic macroeconomic interrelationship between budget balances and public debt (see, for instance, Bohn 1998; Buiter 1985; Fischer and Easterly 1990; Frederiksen 2001). In what follows, we focus strictly on the sustainability dimension. This is first outlined algebraically, then interpreted using graphical techniques.

Since the primary budget balance (the conventional fiscal balance less interest payments) determines the rate at which new debt accumulates or old debt can be retired, it plays the central role in assessing fiscal sustainability. Fiscal authorities directly control the primary fiscal balance through discretionary fiscal measures affecting public expenditure and revenue.

Stabilizing public debt

A straightforward method for assessing the fiscal effort required to stabilize or lower this ratio is founded on the government intertemporal budget constraint, whereby the stock of public debt in the current period equals pre-existing debt plus the primary budget surplus (or minus the primary budget deficit) plus accrued public debt interest. Budget deficits are not money-financed by the central bank. In other words, there is no seigniorage, since money financing can be highly inflationary.

The budget accounting relation can be expressed algebraically in discrete time as

$$D_t = D_{t-1} + iD_{t-1} + PB_t \tag{10.2}$$

where D is public debt, i is the nominal interest rate, and PB is the primary balance.

Dividing by nominal GDP (or Y_t)

$$\frac{D_t}{Y_t} = (1+i)\frac{D_{t-1}}{Y_t} - \frac{PB_t}{Y_t} \tag{10.3}$$

$$\frac{D_t}{Y_t} = \frac{(1+i)}{(1+g)}\frac{D_{t-1}}{Y_{t-1}} - \frac{PB_t}{Y_t} \tag{10.4}$$

where g is the rate of GDP growth.

Taking the change in the public debt to national income ratio

$$\frac{D_t}{Y_t} - \frac{D_{t-1}}{Y_{t-1}} = \frac{(1+i)}{(1+g)}\frac{D_{t-1}}{Y_{t-1}} - \frac{D_{t-1}}{Y_{t-1}} - \frac{PB_t}{Y_t} \tag{10.5}$$

Setting

$$\Delta\left(\frac{D}{Y}\right) = \frac{D_t}{Y_t} - \frac{D_{t-1}}{Y_{t-1}} \tag{10.6}$$

and simplifying

$$\Delta\left(\frac{D}{Y}\right) = \left[\frac{i-g}{1+g}\right]\frac{D_{t-1}}{Y_{t-1}} - \frac{PB_t}{Y_t} \tag{10.7}$$

Equation (10.7) shows that public debt to GDP rises, the higher the primary deficit, the higher the interest rate and the lower the rate of growth, whereas the public debt to income ratio falls, the lower the interest rate, the higher the rate of growth and the higher the primary surplus. If GDP growth is relatively small, the (1+g) term may be omitted to simplify the expression.

To stabilize public debt to national income,

$$\frac{PB_t}{Y_t} = \left[\frac{i-g}{1+g}\right]\frac{D_{t-1}}{Y_{t-1}} \tag{10.8}$$

or simply

$$pb = \mu\left[\frac{i-g}{1+g}\right] \tag{10.9}$$

where pb is the primary balance to income ratio and μ is the previous period debt to income ratio.

The relationship between nominal and real interest rates is

$$i = (1+r^*)(1+\pi)-1 \tag{10.10}$$

where r^* is the real interest rate and π is the inflation rate, and the relationship between nominal and real growth, g^*, is

$$g = (1+g^*)(1+\pi)-1 \tag{10.11}$$

Hence, through substitution, and assuming small product terms are negligible (10.9) can also be written as

$$pb = \mu\left[\frac{r^*-g^*}{1+g^*+\pi}\right] \tag{10.12}$$

If the interest rate exceeds the growth rate, a primary surplus is required for debt stabilization, whereas if the growth rate exceeds the interest rate, a primary deficit is possible. If a primary surplus is necessary for debt stabilization, its size rises directly with the magnitude of the initial debt to income ratio. Hence, the higher is the initial debt stock, the more difficult it is to stabilize the debt to income ratio and the higher this ratio, the greater is the fiscal effort required.

The relationship between primary balances, interest rates, growth and debt stabilization can usefully be illustrated with reference to Figure 10.2. In the figure, the horizontal axis shows possible primary budget balances ranging from deficit to surplus that the fiscal authorities can choose for time *t*.

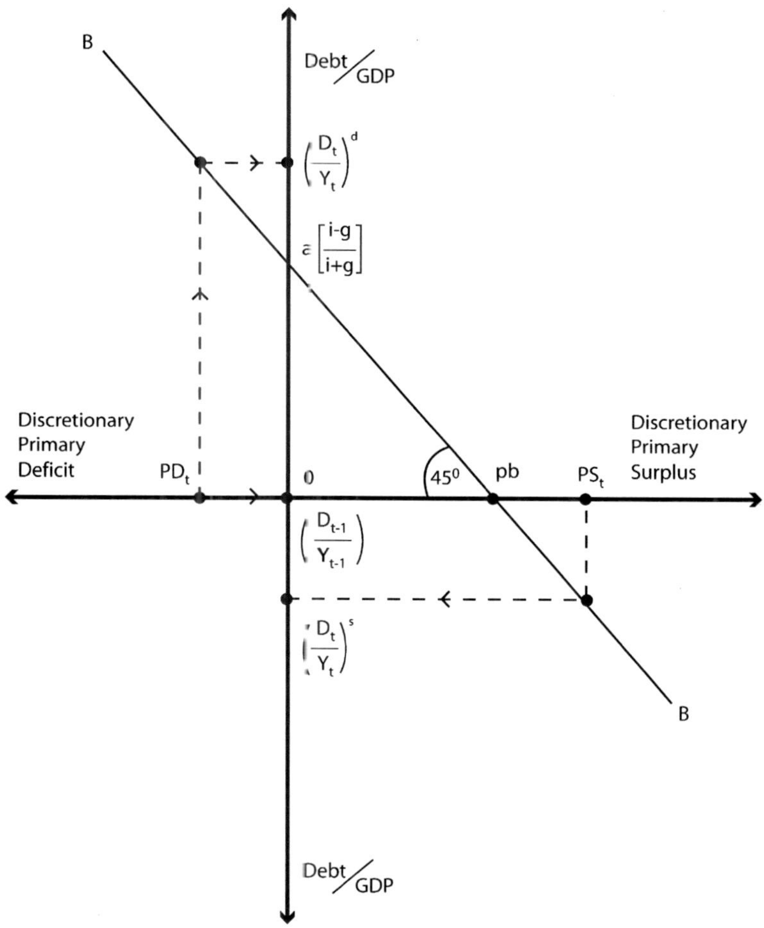

Figure 10.2 The primary budget balance and debt to income ratio

The vertical axis shows public debt to GDP values over the same period, with debt levels rising above the horizontal axis and falling below it. At the origin, the primary budget balance is zero and the debt ratio is D_{t-1}/Y_{t-1}. The *BB* schedule passing through the intersection point a $(i - g)/1 + g$ on the vertical axis and through the point pb on the horizontal axis relates discretionary primary balances for period *t* to corresponding changes in the debt ratio, for given interest and economic growth rates.

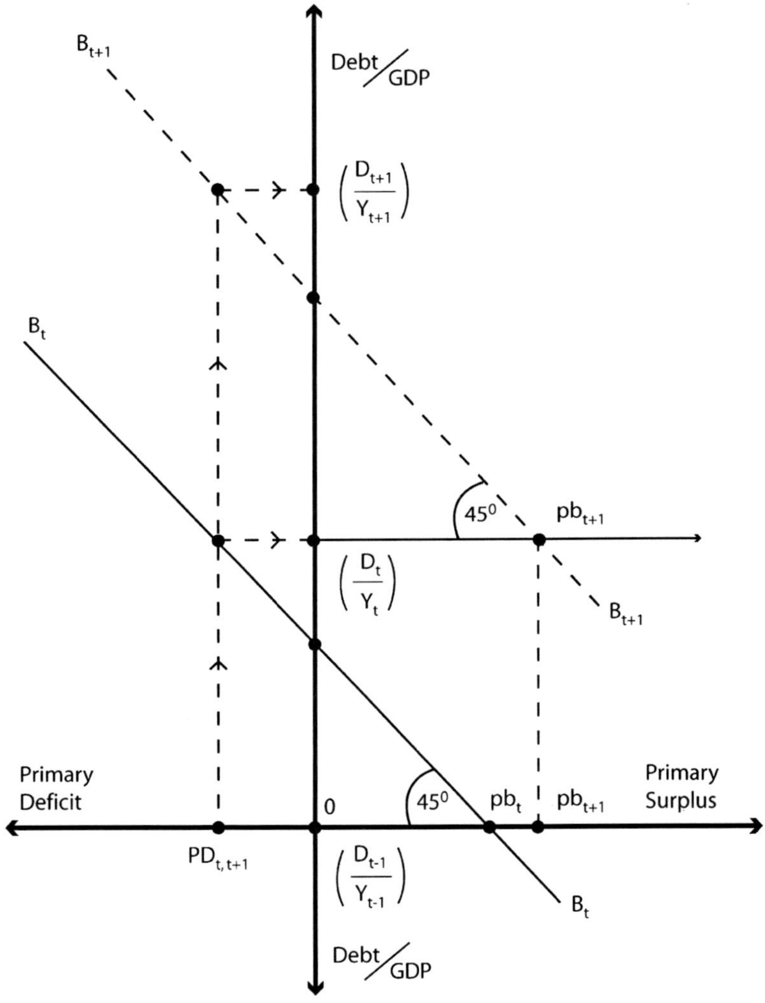

Figure 10.3 Persistent primary deficits and debt instability

The negative slope of the *BB* schedule, derived by differentiating (10.5), has a value of minus one and intercepts the vertical axis above intersection point D_{t-1}/Y_{t-1} if $i > g$, and would intercept below this point if $i < g$. Taking the case where $i > g$, the figure shows that a primary deficit of say PD_t in excess of the stabilizing primary balance *pb* implies a rising debt ratio of $(D_t/Y_t)^d$, whereas a surplus of PS_t in excess of *pb* reduces the debt ratio to $(D_t/Y_t)^s$. In the opposite case where $i < g$, the *BB* schedule would intersect below the horizontal axis as $a(1 - g)/1 + g$ would be negative. Although not drawn in the figure, a lower *BB* schedule reflecting a lower interest rate and/or higher growth rate could show that it is possible to run primary deficits without raising the debt ratio, up to the point where the *BB* line intersects the deficit section of the primary balance line.

This analysis can also be used to highlight the vicious cycle effects of higher deficits and debt as shown in Figure 10.3.

For instance, a primary deficit in period t of pb_t raises the debt ratio to D_t/Y_t. As creditors become more concerned about public sector solvency and the probability of default, a higher risk premium for holding the larger debt stock in period $t+1$ raises the interest rate for that period. Other things equal, a higher interest rate and increased uncertainty would reduce private investment and hence g for $t+1$.

The $B_{t+1}\ B_{t+1}$ schedule of Figure 10.3 has a larger intercept value than the $B_t\ B_t$ schedule, implying an even larger primary surplus of pb_{t+1} is necessary to stabilize higher public debt level at end t+1. The debt trajectory is therefore unstable and primary fiscal deficits of $PD_{t,\,t+1}$ (or larger) repeated in t+2, t+3 .... t+n make a fiscal and financial crisis inevitable. On the contrary, a virtuous cycle can arise if a sufficiently large primary surplus in *t* reduces the debt ratio. In this case, lower debt implies a lower interest rate, reduced uncertainty, higher investment, higher economic growth and a shrinking debt to income ratio.

Reducing public debt

Solvency requires that present debt, D_t, can eventually be repaid at some time in the future, t−n, such that $D_{t+1} = 0$. This means that the present value of budget surpluses over the period must equal the debt stock at t. Hence,

$$D_t = \frac{PB_{t+1}}{(1+i)} + \frac{PB_{t+2}}{(1+i)^2} + \frac{PB_{t+3}}{(1+i)^3} + \ldots + \frac{PB_{t+n}}{(1+i)^n} \qquad (10.13)$$

or

$$D_t = \frac{\sum_{j=1}^{n} (1+i)^{n-j} PB_{t+j}}{(1+i)^n} \qquad (10.14)$$

Solving for the constant primary balance $\overline{PB}$ to achieve solvency,

$$\overline{PB} = \frac{D_t(1+i)^n}{\sum_{j=1}^{n}(1+i)^{n-j}} \tag{10.15}$$

Since $D_{t+n} = D_t\,(1+i)^n$, it follows from (10.14) that the solvency condition is

$$D_{t+n} = D_t(1+i)^n - \sum_{j=1}^{n}(1+i)^{n-j}PB_{t+j} = 0 \tag{10.16}$$

Dividing (10.16) by Y_{t+n} and noting that

$$(1+g)^n Y_t = Y_{t+n} \tag{10.17}$$

yields

$$\frac{D_{t+n}}{Y_{t+n}} = \frac{D_t(1+i)^n - \sum_{j=1}^{n}(1+i)^{n-j}PB_{t+j}}{(1+g)^n Y} \tag{10.18}$$

If the debt to income ratio is reduced to a proportion ν of the existing ratio between t and $t + n$

$$\frac{D_{t+n}}{Y_{t+n}} = \nu\left(\frac{D_t}{Y_t}\right) \quad \text{where} \quad 0 \leq \nu \leq 1 \tag{10.19}$$

Hence, substituting in (10.18)

$$\nu\left(\frac{D_t}{Y_t}\right) = \frac{D_t(1+i)^n - \sum_{j=1}^{n}(1+i)^{n-j}PB_{t+j}}{(1+g)^n Y_t} \tag{10.20}$$

Solving for D_t and redividing by Y_t, it follows that

$$\frac{D_t}{Y_t} = \frac{-\sum_{j=1}^{n}(1+i)^{n-j}PB_{t+j}}{\left[\nu(1+g)^n - (1+i)^n\right]Y_t} \tag{10.21}$$

Solving (10.21) for the constant primary balance ($\overline{PB}$) as a proportion of national income that would satisfy condition (10.19)

$$\frac{\overline{PB}}{Y_t} = \frac{D_t}{Y_t} \cdot \frac{\left[(1+i)^n - (1+g)^n \cdot \nu\right]}{\sum_{j=1}^{n}(1+i)^{n-j}} \tag{10.22}$$

This formula allows governments to compute the primary balance necessary to reduce public debt to a target level as a per cent of GDP, by a specified future time.

A given fiscal stance becomes untenable if public debt to income exceeds a level financial markets will tolerate. Precisely what this level is in percentage terms is a matter for judgment however and may vary from country to country, given levels of economic development and the underlying strength of financial systems.

Faced with rapidly rising public debt, fiscal authorities need to decide whether merely stabilizing debt to national income is sufficient to safeguard against financial crises. If not, the primary budget balance as the main instrument fiscal policy needs to be used more aggressively to achieve a lower public debt to GDP ratio within an acceptable time frame.

Gains from fiscal consolidation

Students of introductory economics absorb the Keynesian doctrine that fiscal stabilization is central to macroeconomic policy management. Governments are supposed to use their discretionary spending and income tax powers to smooth business cycle fluctuations for employment purposes. By altering economy-wide activity, fiscal stabilization allegedly raises employment levels during recessions and curbs excessive aggregate expenditure and inflationary pressures during booms.

Although there are several well-known counterarguments to the Keynesian view of the macroeconomic impact of fiscal activism, it is still surprisingly popular among academic economists and remains influential in economic policy circles. As previously argued (Makin 1998), Keynesianism provides governments with an intellectual, as well as an electoral, rationale for fiscal expansion, such as during the major recessions of recent decades. The most obvious example is Japan, where numerous budgetary measures were aimed at stimulating macroeconomic activity in the light of Japan's negligible economic growth from the 1990s. Yet Japanese fiscal activism was seemingly to no avail.

The main arguments that have been mounted against fiscal stabilization over the years, in both closed and open economy settings, have hinged on the offsetting behaviour of households and firms to budgetary shocks and fiscal deficits, as eventually reflected in private spending, interest rates and exchange rates.

In one way or another, three quite different approaches predict that an increase in public spending will be offset by a fall in private spending, implying that higher public spending has no effect on the size of national income, at least in the short term. As a general rule, they each imply that government spending is more appropriately seen as a substitute for, rather than a complement to, private sector spending.

First, the Ricardian Equivalence proposition, the oldest non-Keynesian argument, suggests that forward-looking households should expect higher future taxes to follow rises in public spending when this spending is financed by running large budget deficits and increased levels of public debt. Under these circumstances, households would save more today (that is, consume less) in anticipation of higher future tax rises that will become necessary when the public debt matures.

In effect, this means that additional public spending 'crowds out' household consumption spending, leaving aggregate expenditure unchanged. Empirical evidence for a range of advanced economies suggests, however, that such offsetting spending behaviour by households has at most been partial. In other words, an extra dollar of public spending is matched by much less than a dollar of increased private saving.

Second, there is the standard investment 'crowding out' argument. This asserts that because higher government spending raises the public sector borrowing requirement, other things equal, it pushes up interest rates and thereby 'crowds out' private sector investment spending. Hence the pattern of expenditure shifts away from private investment towards government consumption. This implies that the opportunity cost of fiscal expansion is lower future economic growth because the rate of real domestic capital accumulation falls.

Like the fundamental Keynesian model against which it was originally set, this proposition is severely limited by its closed economy assumptions. The scale of international transactions has grown to such an extent that it is no longer appropriate to think about macroeconomic linkages without explicitly taking into account international factors such as foreign investment flows, CADs and exchange rates.

Earlier demand side oriented aggregative models for open economies in the spirit of MF continue to be the mainstay of textbook international macroeconomics and remain the most widely used means of analysing the impact of fiscal and monetary policy on exchange rates, the balance of payments and national income by policymakers.

Yet as proposed in Chapters 4 and 8 of this book and contrary to the Keynesian idea that tight fiscal policy can depress an economy's performance, there are theoretical grounds for believing that bouts of fiscal consolidation actually improve macroeconomic performance by eventually accelerating investment and GDP growth. This is what has happened following numerous fiscal consolidation episodes in many advanced economies over recent decades. However, it critically depends on whether the extra government spending is in the nature of consumption or investment.

Several empirical studies of fiscal episodes (Alesina and Ardagna 1998; Giavazzi and Pagano 1990; Giavazzi et al. 2000; Gupta et al. 2005) have also concluded that bouts of fiscal consolidation actually improve macroeconomic performance, contrary also to the closed economy Keynesian premise that fiscal policy is an effective countercyclical instrument. Such improvement occurs through lower interest rates, accelerated real investment and national income, as well as stronger exchange rates and external positions.

The above discussion suggests that the macroeconomic terminology that is widely used to describe changes in the stance of fiscal policy is often contrary to what it suggests. For instance, fiscal 'expansion', or worse fiscal 'stimulus' does not necessarily imply higher overall economic activity, especially if it stems from a rise in government consumption. On the other hand, fiscal consolidation that targets unproductive spending is likely to be expansionary for the economy.

Conclusion

This chapter proposed a straightforward analytical framework for understanding how arbitrary income transfers between domestic borrowers and lenders arise from unexpected inflation or disinflation episodes. Specifically, it showed how income is transferred at the economy-wide level, either in an environment where the rate of inflation is changing systemically, as during major changes in an inflation regime, or where inflation is highly variable from year to year.

It also derives key relationships between budget balances, interest rates and public debt levels and presents graphical techniques for understanding and assessing the sustainability of public debt and its significance for stabilization policy. Finally, this chapter canvasses arguments about the limitations of using activist fiscal policy as a macroeconomic stabilization tool and highlights economy-wide benefits that accrue from judicious fiscal consolidation.

References

Alesina, A. and Ardagna, S. (1998) 'Tales of Fiscal Adjustment', *Economic Policy*, 27, 489–545.

Ball, L. (1992) 'Why Does High Inflation Raise Inflation Uncertainty?', *Journal of Monetary Economics*, 34 (3), 371–88.

Barsky, R. (1987) 'The Fisher Hypothesis and the Forecastability and Persistence of Inflation', *Journal of Monetary Economics*, 19, 3–24.

Bernanke, B. and Mishkin, F. (1997) 'Inflation Targeting: A New Framework for Monetary Policy?', *Journal of Economic Perspectives*, 11 (2), 97–116.

Bohn, H (1998) 'The Behavior of U.S. Public Debt and Deficits', *Quarterly Journal of Economics*, 113 (3), 949–63.

Buiter, W. (1985) 'Guide to Public Sector Debt and Deficits', *Economic Policy: A European Forum*, 1 (November), 13–79.

Fischer, S. and Easterly, W. (1990) 'The Economics of the Government Budget Constraint', *The World Bank Research Observer*, 5 (3), 127–42.

Fisher, I. (1930) *The Theory of Interest*, Macmillan, New York.

Frederiksen, N. (2001) 'Fiscal Sustainability in the OECD: A Simple Method and Some Preliminary Results', *OECD Working Paper No. 3/2001*, Finansministeriet, Copenhagen.

Giavazzi, F. and Pagano, M. (1990) 'Can Severe Fiscal Contractions Be Expansionary: Tales from Two Small European Economies', in O. Blanchard and S. Fischer (eds) *NBER Macroeconomics Annual*, NBER, Chicago.

Giavazzi, F., Japelli, T. and Pagano, M. (2000) 'Searching for Non-linear Effects of Fiscal Policy: Evidence from Industrial and Developing Countries', *European Economic Review*, 44, 1259–89.

Gupta, S., Clements, B., Baldacci, E. and Mulas-Grenados, C. (2005) 'Fiscal Policy, Expenditure Composition, and Growth in Low-Income Countries', *Journal of International Money and Finance*, 24 (3), 441–63.

Makin, A. (1998) 'When Contractionary Fiscal Policy is Expansionary', *Agenda*, 5 (4), 419–26.

Makin, A. (2003) 'Inflation Expectations, Interest Rates and Arbitrary Income Transfers', *Australian Economic Review*, 36 (3), 283–90.

Mishkin, F. (1992) 'Is the Fisher Effect for Real? A Re-examination of the Relationship between Inflation and Interest Rates', *Journal of Monetary Economics*, 30 (2), 195–215.

Epilogue

Introduction

A major theme of this book has been the macroeconomic causes and consequences of global imbalances, capital flows and exchange rate movements, phenomena that remain at the forefront of international economic policy discussion. With greater international integration of goods, services and assets markets, the average size of current account imbalances in emerging and advanced economies has increased markedly over recent decades, which has concerned domestic and international financial markets and policymakers. Specifically, policymakers worry that sizeable external deficits and debt levels overexpose economies to sudden shifts in investor sentiment that may precipitate currency and financial crises and recession.

In external borrower countries, including the US whose external deficit regularly exceeded 5 per cent of GDP in the 2000s, it has also provided a rationale for advocating protectionist measures to restrict imports, subsidize exports and tighten fiscal policy. To minimize the risk of inappropriate market reactions and welfare-reducing policy responses of this kind, it is obviously important that the macroeconomic significance of external account imbalances, capital flows and exchange rates be clearly understood. Equally important is the need to understand how fiscal and monetary policies operate and how effective they are in stabilizing economies in a financially globalized context.

Are global imbalances a concern?

Contrary to policy perceptions, modern capital-theoretic approaches to external account determination do not imply that external imbalances *per se* are problematic. For instance, the intertemporal approach to the external accounts, based on saving-investment behaviour, well-founded expectations and the implicit assumption of flexible exchange rates and private capital mobility, suggests that current account imbalances essentially arise through the equalization of discrepant expected rates of return on capital across borders.

Gains from international trade in saving

As shown in Chapters 4 and 5 of this book, external imbalances can be growth and welfare enhancing to the extent that they permit higher levels of national income and household consumption than otherwise. Capital inflow equal to the CAD also allows productive investment to be higher than otherwise.

Similarly, a focus on the rise in external liabilities stemming from greater capital market integration with the rest of the world can enable higher national wealth because it allows the nation's capital stock to grow larger. Focusing on the CAD alone can be misleading if it ignores the benefits stemming from the matching capital account balance. External imbalances should therefore not be considered worrisome, in and of themselves, provided there is sufficient private capital mobility, exchange rates are flexible and banking systems are sound and appropriately regulated.

On the contrary, since capital inflow or foreign saving complements domestic savings, it can play an important role in the process of domestic capital accumulation enabling faster economic growth under these conditions. Meanwhile, the national income of creditor countries can also rise to the extent that international lenders earn higher returns on their saving than possible in their own economies.

Capital account surpluses measure the extent to which foreigners fund additional investment beyond domestic saving. To the extent that the productivity of the extra physical capital acquired through foreign borrowing exceeds the servicing costs on those foreign borrowings, then national income can grow faster than otherwise. If this was not true, then enterprises reliant on foreign saving would on average be sustaining losses.

External deficits that originate from changes in private saving and investment behaviour endure if foreign investors deem that the excess national expenditure over production that is funded by their excess saving will prove sufficiently productive. Economies such as Australia, New Zealand and a host of other borrower countries, including many fast-growing emerging economies, would be on a considerably lower level of economic development had they not attracted capital inflow from abroad on this basis in the past.

Provided exchange rates are not misaligned, from a flow-of-funds perspective the criterion which should be used to judge whether an external deficit is 'good' or 'bad' is simply whether the debt is being used productively. Alternatively, does the output gain arising from the capital inflow exceed the cost of acquiring the additional real capital? If so, both creditor and debtor nations gain through international trade in saving.

At the microeconomic level, when foreign funds are willingly provided to finance investment it should generally be assumed that individual enterprises, especially privately owned ones, correctly assess that if they borrow offshore, the return on the activity funded by their overseas loan-raising is greater than the servicing costs of the debt, including provision for repayment.

In other words, we can expect that firms borrow offshore when the marginal efficiency of capital exceeds the cost of the external finance, after allowing for exchange and foreign interest rate risk. Meanwhile, on the other side of the borrower–lender relationship, foreigners are unlikely to finance the additional investment if they do not anticipate sufficient return.

Foreign investors favour investing in financial instruments issued in countries whose economic policies enable higher economic growth for this implies higher returns on their investments. Foreign investors will remain wary of economies whose policies are inimical to sustained domestic output growth and hence avoid investing in countries characterized by political instability, wasteful government spending, unnecessarily high tax burdens and inflexible labour markets, all of which impede domestic productivity gains.

Hence the claim that increased integration with international capital markets has eroded the independence of domestic policymakers in the end only applies to imprudent policymaking since growth-enhancing policies that appeal to foreign investors generally benefit the domestic economy in any case.

Foreign investment by sovereign wealth funds should not be discouraged by host economies, though it should be recognized that its lineage is quite different to capital inflow from more traditional sources. If capital inflow from sovereign wealth funds raises domestic asset values and induces more domestic investment, it should in principle be welcomed. However, if economies with growing sovereign wealth funds due to accumulating foreign reserves revalued their exchange rates, this would be less politically sensitive in host economies, and possibly as beneficial, if this boosted the host economy's exports.

Addressing some fallacies

Many analysts deem external imbalances are unsustainable above a 5 per cent of GDP limit. Yet as argued in Chapter 4, this has not been justified analytically and seems arbitrary in light of the scope for much larger differences between the domestic saving and investment rates of advanced and emerging economies.

It is frequently asserted that external deficits are a sign that nations experiencing them are 'living beyond their means' because the trade deficit component is by definition equivalent to the difference between national output and national expenditure. Households which continue to consume more than they earn quickly have credit access denied.

However, this analogy is not applicable for an economy whose external borrowing reflects private sector decision-making because, as an entity, an economy is best considered as an aggregate production unit, rather than a large household. After all, GDP is primarily a measure of the value of the final output of production units operating in the economy.

A fundamental reason for the persistence of external deficits that arise due to the optimizing behaviour of private households and firms is that domestic private savings fall short of investment opportunities, as perceived by residents and non-residents alike. While this may suggest public policy initiatives of a microeconomic nature to encourage greater domestic saving, attempts to change saving behaviour permanently may well be frustrated since consuming less out of disposable income would immediately lower living standards for households.

Permitting international capital to flow liberally improves economic welfare for it frees borrower economies from the constraint of their own saving levels. Looked at another way, the CAD also measures the volume of consumption that domestic residents would have to forego in order to attain the same real increase in their capital stock.

It is sometimes argued that external deficits suggest domestic saving is 'too low' and that the external imbalance should be targeted by increasing saving relative to domestic investment via reduced private and public consumption. Scope may exist to raise overall domestic saving through fiscal measures that reduce public consumption. However, targeting the external deficit could prove elusive if it continues to result from international economic factors beyond domestic policymakers' control.

Any economy's external balance can change whenever its domestic saving or investment pattern changes, or whenever saving or investment patterns change abroad. For instance, as proposed in the international borrowing and lending framework of Chapter 6, it is conceivable that if saving and investment prospects of the economy stayed exactly the same, but saving increased relatively faster abroad than domestic investment opportunities increased abroad, then the economy's external account balance would widen commensurately as the additional foreign saving was invested there.

The larger external imbalance would be a sign of foreign investor confidence in the economy. Under such circumstances, an enlarged external imbalance would result from factors beyond the control of the domestic authorities. With a larger capital stock, courtesy of increased foreign capital inflow, domestic production, employment and income levels would all improve. This obviously should be welcomed.

However, the large body of theoretical literature that presents a strong case for free international trade in saving has to recognize that the macroeconomic gains that global finance can bestow can only be sustained, if exchange rates are not misaligned and a sound institutional framework exists for channelling foreign saving to ultimate borrowers.

In sum, global imbalances under floating rates are also regional saving-investment imbalances, meaning that growing external liabilities for one economy or region are matched by additional capital accumulation in that region provided domestic saving, net of capital consumption remains positive.

Hence, external deficits provide evidence of the extent to which borrower countries rely on foreign saving to finance growth of their capital stocks. At the same time, creditor nations also benefit in terms of higher national income provided their excess saving earns a higher return abroad than at home.

Crisis risk factors

This book suggests that CADs should not, of themselves, be of concern, provided banking and financial sectors are sturdy and resilient and exchange rates are appropriately valued. Yet at the same time there is justification for international investors and policymakers worrying about economies that borrow heavily through highly fragile banking and financial sectors beset by dangerous information asymmetries.

Economies that experience large external deficits and escalating foreign debt are more vulnerable to sudden capital flow reversals than economies with mature banking and financial systems since they are more vulnerable to sudden shifts in investor sentiment that may precipitate currency and financial crises. This especially applies to emerging economies that liberalize their capital accounts yet retain relatively fragile domestic banking and financial system.

International capital reversals experienced by East Asian economies in 1997–8 imposed short-term economic, social and political costs through large exchange rate depreciations, financial distress, higher domestic interest rates, lost output, increased unemployment and higher inflation. For this reason, external imbalances and debt levels feature prominently in empirical studies of the primary causes of currency crises, although to date no consensus exists on their explanatory power.

Underlying problems contributing to financial crises, from which models in this book abstract, are adverse selection, where too many bad credit risks acquire bank-intermediated foreign funds, and moral hazard, where domestic borrowers use foreign funds to engage in imprudent or excessively risky activities.

Expectations about the likely profitability of new investment projects also at times prove too optimistic, and international monetary conditions unexpectedly change, with adverse implications for national income in borrower countries. Incorporating such factors into theoretical international macroeconomic models remains a challenge for future research.

Moreover, the large US CAD entails additional risks because capital inflow to the US has been artificially distorted by huge inflows of central bank and sovereign wealth fund flows rather than private funds buying US government bonds issued to fund the large US budget deficit.

Excessive public debt

The previous chapter outlined fundamental principles for analysing the sustainability of public debt in emerging economies. Examining public debt ratios is important because high levels increase the risk of financial crisis, either through outright default, or through capital flight in response to a rising probability of default. High public debt levels also crowd out domestic spending as the interest risk premium rises and create monetization pressures which have inflationary consequences. Domestic and foreign investors need only rightly or wrongly anticipate future debt monetization or default for immediate capital flight to spark a financial crisis.

To lower public debt levels to more prudent levels, economies require larger primary budget surpluses. These can be achieved either through expenditure restraint or improved revenue-raising. Of these, raising tax receipts through new tax policies and administrative reforms is sometimes preferable for emerging economies, since there is often limited scope for fiscal adjustment on the public expenditure side of national budgets. This is because these budgets include a large non-discretionary element for essential services and relatively small capital expenditure outlays dedicated to growth-enhancing infrastructure development.

Restraining public expenditure in emerging economies that is already relatively low is likely to limit output and growth, especially if vital capital, rather than more politically difficult current expenditures, is cut. Meanwhile, tax revenues as a proportion of GDP tend to be less than those of advanced economies. This suggests considerable scope exists for widening the revenue base and raising direct and indirect income tax rates on households and firms, as well as through improved tax administration.

Exchange rate risk

International investment in financial assets is especially sensitive to changes in investors' expectations, including expected exchange rate devaluations that can spark massive capital outflows. Indeed, in financial crises, changes in investors' exchange rate expectations become self-fulfilling.

Investors expecting a future currency collapse will rush to sell financial instruments denominated in that currency to avoid capital losses. Accordingly, the severe contraction in demand for the currency can put official exchange rates under intolerable pressure, depleting foreign exchange reserves of central banks and perhaps pushing up short-term interest rates in the process.

In the Asian crisis case, foreign investors had initially misjudged the extent of exchange rate risk by effectively presuming that many Asian central banks were bearing the foreign exchange rate risk by maintaining pegged exchange rates. For instance, in the decades preceding the Asian crisis, the central banks of Korea, Malaysia, Thailand, Indonesia and the Philippines had provided domestic borrowers and foreign lenders alike a measure of exchange rate certainty as these economies had adhered to fixed exchange rates, or had strictly limited exchange rate flexibility. As a result, capital flows responded strongly to interest rate differentials, and foreign borrowings remained unhedged against the possibility of large currency depreciations.

Reimposing exchange controls, such as those of the Bretton Woods era is an inappropriate response to capital flow reversals and could prove costly to long-term development as suggested in Chapter 5. What makes many emerging economies more prone to macroeconomically debilitating financial crises is not excessively mobile international funds, but relatively poorly developed domestic banking and financial systems and excessive public debt.

Inflexible exchange rates and the global financial crisis 2007–9

Chapter 3 advanced a conceptual framework for interpreting the effect of exchange rates policy on global trade imbalances with specific reference to links between national expenditure, output and the accumulation of foreign exchange reserves via central bank intervention. This approach also has applicability to the US and global financial crisis of 2007–9.

Persistently large trade and CASs combined with capital inflow in the form of FDI and speculative inflows have enabled central banks to accumulate foreign exchange reserves at unprecedented levels. In the past these funds were routinely invested in US and other government bonds that helped keep world interest rates low. However, with the establishment of sovereign wealth funds, investment of the proceeds of foreign exchange market intervention by external surplus economies has become more diversified.

Once toxic US mortgage-related securities found their way into foreign government sponsored portfolios, the US dollars that central banks were taking from America stopped coming back in. This aversion on the part of sovereign wealth funds to invest in US securities has undoubtedly played a key role in drying up US liquidity. Therefore, as long as foreigners remain unwilling to act as 'banker of last resort' to the US, the international credit crunch continued.

Another way of thinking about this issue is that American national expenditure in excess of its national output became unsustainable and that foreigners decided not to fund it any longer. In other words, excess spending on housing and by the federal government, including on defence, had proved insufficiently productive.

Normally, unproductive expenditure in excess of national output leads to major exchange rate depreciation, but East Asian and Middle Eastern central banks refused to allow this, fearful of the impact of US dollar depreciation on competitiveness and their own balance sheets. Either way, credit crunches of this kind impact more heavily on US national expenditure relative to national output, thereby closing the US CAD.

Just as domestic expenditure increases in the past spill over into US imports with little impact on domestic employment (so called jobless recoveries), the reverse would imply that employment losses may be less severe as US expenditure contracts.

Therefore, with a large CAD, spending contraction is more likely to fall upon imports, not on goods and services produced in the US. Of course, this then rebounds on China, other East Asian economies and the oil exporters, as US spending on their exports falls. Under these circumstances foreign entities awash with US dollar holdings, including the sovereign wealth funds, should realize it is in their interests to purchase US financial and real assets during times of falling asset prices and liquidity shortage, instead of remaining highly liquid on the sidelines.

China's persistently sturdy economic growth and huge stock of reserves suggests scope for greater exchange rate flexibility. A more flexibile exchange rate would strengthen the overall effectiveness of China's macroeconomic management by allowing greater independence for monetary policy.

In addition, a more flexible exchange rate would better insulate China's economy from external shocks, such as further sharp rises in oil and other commodity import prices. It would also dampen protectionist pressures that have been building in its trading partners.

Yet a gradual approach to adopting a fully flexible or free-floating exchange rate would be advisable in view of the vulnerability of the banking sector and the underdeveloped nature of the foreign exchange market and instruments for managing currency risk. The next step towards a more flexible regime would be the announcement by the PBC of a wider band in which the daily value of the yuan could be set.

A new nominal anchor for monetary policy could eventually replace the nominal exchange rate. Money supply and credit growth targets may serve this purpose at the outset with progression to an inflation-targeting regime of the kind adopted in many other countries in East Asia that have experienced exchange rate regime change in the past decade, including Indonesia, the Philippines and Thailand.

It has been argued by the Chinese authorities that an undervalued exchange rate is not primarily responsible for the huge trade surplus of recent years. Rather, China's external surplus has been mainly due to the economy's openness to FDI and production by multinational companies for export, utilizing cheap and abundant labour. Yet, as the framework of Chapter 3 showed, while the significant presence of export-oriented multinationals in China may indeed be boosting its trade surplus, this is consistent with the exchange rate being misaligned.

It may also be argued that if the yuan was floated and exchange controls were simultaneously liberalized, then private capital outflows would replace current public capital outflows with little impact on the value of China's exchange rate. However, this is unlikely as capital account liberalization could not, and should not, occur before substantial reform of China's banking and financial system. Such reform would most likely lead to greater household consumption in China and better quality investment, reducing the excess of China's domestic saving over domestic investment that has flooded abroad as foreign investment.

Lessons for stabilization policy

Methodologically, the approaches of this book have departed markedly from the currently popular *modus operandi* of explaining macroeconomic behaviour with reference to utility functions, representative optimizing agents, price rigidities and imperfect competition. Micro-founded models lead to policy ambiguities because of the different assumptions that are made about the nature of the utility functions motivating agents and the source of price rigidities, but about which no consensus exists.

While demand-oriented, micro-founded, models yield useful insights, they neglect to explain the behaviour of important aggregates, such as the capital stock, GDP and the current account, with reference to links between monetary aggregates, interest rates and exchange rates over the short term to medium term. In contrast, the frameworks of this book derive clear results of contemporary relevance to the conduct of fiscal and monetary policy in financially globalized economies.

Intertemporal models provide an alternative to the MF approach by linking consumption, saving, investment and national income to international borrowing and lending. Models developed within this paradigm are usually characterized by explicit microfoundations, nominal rigidities and imperfect competition and mostly use a two-country global economy set-up.

Unfortunately, model results are highly dependent on microfounded assumptions about utility functions and price level behaviour. Moreover, many intertemporal models, like the MF approach before it, neglect the role of capital in output generation and have mainly been used to analyse the effects of monetary policy on consumer welfare, as opposed to improving policymakers' understanding of how fiscal and monetary policy may work as income stabilization instruments under alternative exchange rate assumptions.

Accordingly, the prevailing paradigm fails to comprehensively illustrate the effectiveness of changes in the stance of monetary and fiscal policies on real national income under polar exchange rate regimes, the *sine qua non* of the MF model. In response, to analyse the international macroeconomics of monetary and fiscal policy under fixed and floating exchange rate regimes this book has derived alternative open-economy approaches that combine aggregate demand, output and basic precepts from international finance to model monetary and fiscal shocks.

By uniquely introducing the domestic capital stock and capital productivity on the production side of the economy, frameworks in this book yield new results about the efficacy of macroeconomic policy under both fixed and floating exchange rate regimes that contrast with those derived from standard aggregate demand oriented models.

A key point of difference is the perspective on short to medium run national income determination. Whereas most extant short-run models simply assume national output is demand determined in the textbook Keynesian manner, models in this book emphasize the production side of the economy as the starting point for analysis, consistent with the spirit of orthodox growth theory.

In these models, domestically produced goods and services are made available for sale along with imported foreign goods and services and, in use, are treated as either consumption or investment items. Hence, the sequencing of macroeconomic activity is at the outset perceived as running from aggregate supply to aggregate demand, rather than the other way around, although production by firms is always obviously undertaken with prospects of aggregate demand in mind.

This alters standard results about the effectiveness of macroeconomic stabilization policy. Importantly, it suggests that on the fiscal front increased public consumption spending worsens an economy's external position and limits national income growth, although capital spending by governments can positively influence national income, provided it is productive. Hence, fiscal 'expansion' in the form of higher government consumption is an ineffective way of stabilizing national income in response to financial crises and economic downturns, contrary to standard new Keynesian-oriented approaches.

Index